THE BEST OF
MIRIAM LORD

Published by: The Irish Times Limited (Irish Times Books)
Design & Layout: Dearbhla Kelly (The Irish Times)
Edited by: Frances O'Rourke and Joe Joyce
Printed in Ireland by SPRINT-print Ltd.

© The Irish Times Ltd 2014

ISBN: 9780907011415

FOREWORD

So somebody had the idea of putting some of my columns into a collection. I'd forgotten most of them: things happen, you move on.

These pieces span the eight years or so since I joined the Irish Times in 2006.

Most of them are to do with politics, which is a fascinating business to observe. Sometimes, people can become so absorbed by the political world that they forget the real one outside.

This isn't a good place for journalists to be, but it's a sure-fire way to trouble for politicians.

They end up speaking to and at each other, instead of addressing the public they are supposed to serve.

By and large, I like politicians. The level of bile and vitriol they have to face these days is unwarranted. You mightn't want a politician to be your best mate, or you mightn't agree with their politics, but they aren't the incarnation of evil either.

I like them, but they drive me to distraction.

They begin with the best of intentions. For example, I always want a new Taoiseach to do well. I believe them when, starting out, they make heartfelt pledges about how they will be different and better and a new type of leader.

Hasn't really happened yet.

But they ask us and we give them our trust.

People like me keep an eye on what they're doing with it.

The columns included here are my thoughts on the major political events over most of the last decade, beginning with the death of former Taoiseach and Fianna Fail leader, Charlie Haughey. They aren't analysis pieces. I don't want to be a pundit.

It's just my take on what happened. You know when you're watching the news and some pompous TD pops up and starts defending the indefensible? And you roar "do you think we're all f****** eejits?" at the television? I feel that way a lot, listening to them.

And when government ministers pull strokes, then try to

pretend nothing happened, that makes most of us angry too.

It made by blood boil to see the way senior politicians ignored and waffled their way around the outrageous evidence of Bertie Ahern at the Mahon Tribunal, for example. But then, I was so proud of the man when he spoke in the British Houses of Parliament.

Nothing is black and white.

Best to just laugh, sometimes. It would be remiss to overlook the occasionally infuriating, occasionally daft, outpourings of our elected representatives (particularly the ones with a great welcome for themselves)

There are times you'd wonder how some of the ornaments we have in Leinster House manage to put on their drawers the right way around, never mind get elected to a seat.

Yet there they are. Put there by us, to uphold our democracy, so its only right to keep a proprietorial eye.

Thankfully, escape is possible. Hence the inclusion of such wonders as the saga of Bono's little trousers and the day Our Lady was supposed to appear at 3pm on the dot in Knock but failed to turn up.

Had I known that, some day, this stuff would be collected and put into a book, might I have written with a nod to posterity, as opposed to an eye on knocking-off time?

Not really.

These columns were done and dusted on the day, which is the way it should be.

Or at least the way it's always been for me - watching on.

Miriam Lord, Dublin, October 2014

6

Table of Contents

LEADERS

Charles Haughey, former Taoiseach and the most controversial politican of his generation, died aged 80 in June 2006

CHARLIE'S BEGUILING MOVES DISGUISED FEET OF CLAY, BUT I WAS MAD ABOUT HIM

Dammit, he's dead. Saw it coming, but it's still hard to take. And with a heavy heart, I have to write something about Charlie.

Some say he was mad, some say he was bad, but he was wonderful to know.

The canonisation has already begun. And yet, when CJH is finally laid to rest, they'll need maple-sprung turf on his grave to cope with the frenzy of dancing. My dancing is long done. We danced - the scary statesman with the mischievous twinkle and the northside young wan with the cheeky pen - the set-piece routines of reporter and quarry. Neither of us in any danger: he didn't mind being sent up and I loved doing it. Probably, because we were both winning on the deal; maybe, because we liked each other. Then he waltzed into a tribunal chamber and I stepped out in disgust. As if I never knew Charlie's beguiling moves disguised feet of clay.

It's easy to love and just as easy to loathe, the bit in between is where it gets complicated. Today, a lot of people will be lining out happily on both sides. One suspects an awful lot more will be wrestling with the contradiction that was Charles J.

Count me among them. I'll always have a soft spot for Charles J Haughey.

He'll be lying in State in Donnycarney church. Stand by for a monumental collision of top brass and old biddies in Charlie country.

As for the lying in State part, he was no stranger to lying and he did the State some service.

This final scenario is so, so Charlie Haughey. He bags the big funeral, the due recognition and the grand exit, but not in the Pro-Cathedral, where ordinary leaders might choose their final send off. It had to be Donnycarney.

"I love being among my people," he was fond of saying. He'll be among his people right enough in Donnycarney. Only problem is, who'll provide the guard of honour?

A phalanx of pensioners, forever grateful for the Christmas turkey when times were hard, lining up and forming an arch of outstretched bus passes? Or a K-Clubhouse of millionaires, fashioning a discreet tunnel from large cheques before suffering inexplicable memory loss? It'll have to be a job for the Army.

Until recently, I lived down the road from Donnycarney church. My neighbour, Mrs Byrne - she's dead now - chided me once for writing bad things about "our Charlie".

She reared a large family in a small house and had known the bad times as well as the good. My protests that Charlie, maybe, had feathered his own nest at her expense fell on deaf ears.

She recalled his Ma, "a great seamstress", cutting down and redoing a pair of his father's old trousers so Charlie had something decent to wear when he started university. She knew how hard young Haughey had it and didn't begrudge him a thing.

That story came to mind recently when listening on radio to former taoiseach Garret FitzGerald, on the occasion of his 80th birthday.

As he spoke of the south Co Dublin social whirl, and of setting the world to rights at Saturday lunches in Dún Laoghaire yacht club, I couldn't get that image of Charlie Haughey and the hand-me-down trousers out of my mind.

It excuses nothing, but it explains a lot.

There were many sides to Haughey. He could be nasty and breathtakingly rude - I never experienced that. He cultivated sycophantic friends. He was a politician on the take. He cheated on his wife. He was also charming and generous and very funny.

Hugely gifted and a man whose enduring legacy will, in the shake-out, be about a lot more than Charvet shirts, Le Coq Hardi and generous "gifts" from rich well-wishers.

Charlie was at the height of his power, well settled into his Napoleon complex, when I wandered into his orbit wielding a notebook and a youthful ignorance of his fearsome reputation.

It didn't take long to see the effect he had on people. His entourage twittered and trembled around him in a state of nervous obeisance. They spoke of him in hushed tones. Most of his Fianna

Fáil backbenchers did the same. Those who despised him stashed vengeance in the long grass.

The frantic scenes before he arrived at an official function verged on the comical. As Taoiseach, he would sweep in, bang on time, schmoozing the welcoming committee lined up to greet him.

He worked a room like a pro, moving steadily through the crowd, shaking hands, leaning in slightly, making vital eye contact. People were charmed (except those who felt his much-vaunted charisma was more reptilian than rakish).

Haughey was secure then, after his years in the wilderness and the years fighting to get to the top. The 80s were a time for consolidation, for building up his statesman image and leaving the proper sort of impression behind for posterity.

His vanity, like his appetite for handouts, knew no bounds. Journalists who asked hard questions were dismissed with a cutting remark or simply ignored.

How did he get away with it? Probably because a lot of reporters saw it as a badge of honour to be given a rocket by Charlie Haughey and the story of how it happened always got richer in the telling. I can't remember the first time I met CJH, but I know I poked fun at him the following day. In the following years, he was always available for a few lines.

For me, the famous malevolent glare was more an avuncular glint.

Sometimes, I wondered if, deep down, he couldn't believe his own luck. He was mad to show off his wealth. In Kerry, invitations to join the party on the Celtic Mist were always extended and the best of wine flowed.

There was the obligatory tour, not to mention the obligatory leer, for visiting female hacks when the cabin housing his enormous bed was displayed. He was such an old charmer, such a desperate old goat, it was impossible to take offence.

When I won my first media award, a letter arrived at the office. The address was clumsily typed by an inexperienced hand; the printed "Abbeville" on the back of the envelope betraying the typist.

"Miriam, A hundred thousand congratulations," it began. "What with the All-Ireland and now the National Media Award, our cup overflows. As I feel very much part of it all, I would suggest that a quiet celebratory luncheon a deux might be appropriate?" It was signed "Charles J." and followed on by a bottle of champagne and a huge bouquet of flowers.

I never took him up on the offer.

Occasional notes charting the progress of my career followed. By now he was "Charlie." Not having a car, he often offered me a lift home if he was on his way back to Kinsealy.

On a long journey from Listowel, we stopped at Matt the Threshers for a mid-morning snack. He ordered champagne and revelled in the mini-commotion this caused in the bar. Ostentatiously pouring, Charlie purred: "I love being among my people." What affectation. Except, as was so often the case during our exchanges, it was said with a self-deprecatory glint.

That look that seemed to say "Isn't this gas, but look, they're all swallowing it."

As we neared my house in Dublin, we passed Donnycarney church. "My mother built that church," he declared, with typical modesty. Mère Haughey, it appeared, had been as adept with a trowel as she was with the sewing needle.

Then the tribunal and the day when he appeared in the box and asked people to take him for a fool. Nobody did. To an accompaniment of snorts and sniggers, he protested he didn't have "a lavish lifestyle."

Yacht, offshore island, north Dublin mansion notwithstanding, my mind went back to a sunny Sunday afternoon a few years earlier in Abbeville, when he invited me in to join his friends.

First, the obligatory tour, which just happened to go through a cold, round room in the basement. "We're restoring the dairy," he declared loftily. Then, seeing my eyes fall on the numerous boxes of empty champagne bottles, he murmured with no small amount of pride, "we had a little party last night".

His risible response to the Moriarty tribunal is best summed up in this magnificent answer: "Well, I think it all goes back to the fact I know nothing . . . and I am sure I am right in my recollection that I know nothing."

Dingle Pier a few years ago, and Charlie is too frail now to start the annual regatta by firing a shotgun from a launch out at sea. His presence still causes a stir among the adults. Haughey walks with his head held high, looking around the crowd with the air of a man who knows he is somebody. And he is, but to a dwindling audience.

"He used to be the Taoiseach" a mother explains to her child.

That he was, and I was mad about him. I'll be in Donnycarney to say goodbye.

June 14th, 2006

Bertie Ahern became the first Taoiseach to address the Houses of Parliament in London as the first Northern Ireland Executive was established between the Democratic Unionist Party and Sinn Fein – and in the midst of a difficult general election at home for Fianna Fáil as questions about his personal finances as Minister for Finance in 1993 refused to go away

Thanks, Bertie, you did us proud

Yes, Bertie Ahern from Drumcondra.

That was you.

Guest of honour in the Palace of Westminster, like statesmen Yeltsin and Mitterrand and Clinton before you, feted by the Commons and the Lords and thoroughly deserving of your place in history.

No one man or woman brought about this wonderful new era for the Republic of Ireland, Britain and Northern Ireland. But you've more than done your bit.

This day, Bertie, was for you.

There was something about him yesterday, sitting pensively in the gilded surrounds of the Royal Gallery as the illustrious assembly stood and applauded him. Him, Bertie, the boy from the northside.

He had just notched up another historic milestone as the first Taoiseach to address the joint houses of parliament. Tony Blair, not half an hour earlier, had paid him the most glowing, heartfelt of tributes. His words went far beyond the normal call of commendation.

The guest list was an impressive roll call of British and Irish politicians past and present. The warmth of their welcome for Bertie was generous and genuine. Yet, for a few moments, it was as if the man they had come to honour was a bit taken aback by it all. He remained in his chair, as the speaker of the House of Commons, applauding, moved in from one side and Tony Blair, leading the ovation, moved in from the other.

Both men appeared to be signalling the same thing: "Get up!" Eventually, almost reluctantly, Bertie Ahern got to his feet. No big smiles, although he must have been delighted. He must have been the proudest man in the room.

Yesterday evening, he was back in his Dublin North Central constituency, knocking on doors, looking after business. People on the Navan Road, who had been watching the Taoiseach on the six o'clock news in the houses of parliament, opened their doors to find Bertie on the step.

People who claim to know him would say that cementing his place among his own has always been what drives him. Even now, as one of the biggest vote getters in the country, he obsessively pounds the pavements on his own patch. Even now, when the mother of parliaments has gone out of its way to recognise him as a political great, he still worries.

While Mr Blair spoke of his "formidable" role in the Northern peace process and the development of his country's economy, the Taoiseach's fingertips fidgeted.

What was he thinking? Not far away, sitting in the front row to his left, was Fine Gael leader Enda Kenny. He looked good. Afterwards, when the two prime ministers left, deputy Kenny was surrounded by well wishers. Former Conservative prime minister John Major shook his hand. "Go for it, man! Go for it!" said John.

What was Enda thinking? They know how to lay on a good ceremony in Westminster. Staff looking like they've stepped off the set of a BBC costume drama, resplendent in black tails and white tie. Bertie arrived with Tony at the Sovereign's Entrance, just like the Queen does at the opening of parliament. A fab'lus hall - as Albert Reynolds might have put it - providing a magnificent setting.

It was clear that Tony, who has run his race and will step down next month, wanted to do well by his "personal friend", who is still very much in the political running and in the thick of a tough general election battle. "There is no side to Bertie," he said, recalling negotiations on the North. "He would absorb the harsh, occasionally insulting words." At this point, the Taoiseach looked up with a rueful smile. One suspected his mind was more on current travails.

"I often say to people I have met many big political leaders over my 10 years in office but I have never met a bigger one than Bertie Ahern." Tony and Bertie. A great double act. Tony, bowing out, doing his best for his old pal.

The Taoiseach spoke of a shared history and a new partnership between the two nations. It was a wonderfully well crafted speech and he delivered it well.

There was a sense of two men rounding off a decade of fine achievement, recognising that their unique political relationship is coming to an end. "Tony Blair has been a true friend to me, and a true friend to Ireland." You could feel the emotion in Bertie's tone. As he concluded, he quoted John F Kennedy when he addressed the Dáil. Ireland, he said then, "is an isle of destiny. . . when our hour has come we will have something to give to the world." There was a quiver, a slight catch in his voice as he invoked the iconic spirit of JFK.

"Ireland's hour has come," said the Taoiseach. "A time of peace, of prosperity, of old values and new beginnings. This is the great lesson and the great gift of Irish history. This is what Ireland can give to the world." The crowd rose to him - northern secretaries, past and present. Gordon Brown - PM in waiting. John Hume, Peter Sutherland, John Major, Neil Kinnock, Ken Clark. Lords and ladies, honourable members, ambassadors.

Writer Edna O'Brien, motor racing mogul Eddie Jordan, rugby great Keith Wood, fashion designer Paul Costelloe, actor Fiona Shaw. Bertie's friend Des Richardson was there with his wife Fran, along with property developer Seán Dunne and his wife Gayle.

This was a great occasion. Bertie's occasion. And yet . . . other matters rumble on at home.

Enda Kenny gave an interview on the lawn outside. "I wanted to be here, as an Irishman and the leader of my party," he said. "It was a fine speech, well delivered." The Taoiseach, his rival, was entitled "to real public credit, and it's richly due." Deputy Kenny was speaking "as one who looks to be Taoiseach". Here, perhaps, was one reason for why Bertie looked so pensive. With one part of the double act going, and Bertie having achieved the pinnacle of political achievement, there was a sense yesterday of things coming to a natural conclusion.

He will not want that view to go abroad.

But maybe, that air of modesty about the Taoiseach had more to do with the man who is still not quite sure of his place. History is sorted, without a doubt, but is Bertie? Hence yet another Dublin Central canvas last night, crazy as that might seem.

Let's be parochial for a moment. From this particular Northsider: Thanks, Bertie, you did us proud.

May 16th, 2007

Michael McDowell, Justice Minister in the Fianna Fáil-Progressive
Democrats coalition, was elected leader of the PDs to replace Mary Harney

Cuddly PD king reverts to type, attack-dog style

Michael McDowell was so very happy there was every possibility he might explode. The new PD leader floated up the steps of the Westin Hotel and was bounced into a side room by handlers, who tethered him to a heavy table until the preliminaries were done.

"We've a minute to go, lads," he squealed excitedly.

High-ranking underlings, Tom Parlon and Liz O'Donnell, moved into position, firmly anchoring themselves on either side of the gently levitating lawyer. Then, once everyone was satisfied that Michael would not drift out the window, the two set about signing his nomination papers.

Tom appended his signature first, followed by Liz. She sat and signed with the sort of elegantly authoritative flourish that wouldn't look out of place in Áras an Uachtaráin. People fell to thinking .

Finally. After all the years of working and waiting, barking and biting, Michael McDowell's moment was upon him. Hand poised, his pen hovered over the paper. Such excitement. We thought of Dr Jekyll raising that foaming test-tube to his lips for the first time. Anything could happen.

"I hereby accept the position of party leader of the Progressive Democrats."

How those words must have thrilled him. Nevertheless, Mr McDowell's legal training kicked in. He scanned the document first, looked at the date and checked his watch to make sure it was correct. Then, to a round of applause, he signed.

Immediately, the euphorically red-faced leader of the soon-to-be Aggressive Democrats was whisked into another room to be fitted with rubber teeth. Just a temporary precaution until he settles.

While this was going on, Mary Harney's husband, Brian Geoghegan, arrived to witness McDowell's installation, which would take place in the impressively opulent surroundings of the hotel's Banking Hall. Brian hasn't stopped grinning since his wife decided to throw in the Tánaiste's towel during a moment of clarity in Tuscany.

The Banking Hall, with its enormous crystal chandeliers, marble pillars and gilded columns, provided a fitting backdrop to Mr McDowell's accession. Presumably, given the enormous welcome the self-important PDs have for themselves, Dublin Castle's Throne Room was unavailable for their small but perfectly formed celebration.

To underline the sense of unity the party wants to portray following Michael's relatively smooth path to the leadership, PD icon Des O'Malley slipped in through a side door and gave his blessing to the new regime. He was mobbed, in the nicest way, by admiring lawyers and PD ladies with impressive Monday morning hair.

Not long after midday, guests were told to take their seats. When the double doors at the back opened, everyone turned to look at a radiant Michael McDowell as he glided up the aisle, almost on the arm of a smiling Mary Harney.

No wonder she looked pleased. She was giving him away.

Following behind, the two lovely bridesmaids: new deputy leader, Liz, and new party president, Tom. There should have been some music. Wagner, perhaps.

It was a very short ceremony. The party chairman formally declared Mr McDowell elected to the position of party leader. There was more applause. Mary Harney looked happy enough to cry.

And so, a new era dawned for the Aggressive Democrats. Michael ambled across to the microphone, script in hand.

To the delight of his handlers and sinking hearts of the hacks, he stuck to it, word for word.

He remembered his manners and thanked everyone who helped him get to where he is today. He thanked Tom Parlon and Liz O'Donnell for their "generous and selfless agreement" to nominate him for the job, and for agreeing to join him at the head of the party. Liz studied the chandeliers with interest.

True to form, Mr McDowell couldn't resist indulging in a bit of Latin. The lawyers present swooned, particularly as it was the

Gonzaga School motto that he quoted. "Fortuna favet fortibus," he boomed.

This will have come as welcome news to his right-hand man, Senator Tommy Morrissey, who has long been arguing for more buses. Forty is a good start. Truth to tell, all this cuddly, Dimples McDowell act was becoming tiresome. Not before time, the Minister for Justice began to revert to type.

"While my primary focus today is on the business and the future of the Progressive Democrats, I think it is only right to point out some fundamental realities . . ." Whereupon he embarked on the first of many swipes at the Fine Gael/Labour coalition.

"The entire political enterprise, in reality, amounts to a recipe for a Slump Coalition," he announced, repeating this "Slump Coalition" jibe at every opportunity. As killer slogans go, it's nowhere near, but Michael is determined to stick with it, which means he thought it up all by himself.

In this dawning age of the Aggressive Democrat, politics will be restored as a noble pursuit, engaged in setting out "a vision to bring Ireland forward to new heights". Michael McDowell wants people to know that he and his new very best friend, Bertie Ahern, "share the value that politics is not about survival, but achievement".

While exploring this touching revelation, the leaders of the Opposition came to Michael's mind.

He took out the rubber teeth, all the better to blow his own trumpet on the subject of his great achievements in Justice.

"I look at Enda and Pat, who have 48 years of Dáil experience between them. I won't say anything negative here today, but I will say this: an outstanding achievement doesn't immediately leap to mind in respect of either of them."

He just couldn't help himself. You can teach an attack dog new tricks. But the old ones never leave him, thank God.

"Will you be cutting down on the red meat?" a fearful journalist asked. "I will not disappoint the media," dripped McDowell, drawing the most pathetically heartfelt applause of the day.

And with that, the parliamentary party went off to lunch. Michael, we understand, played safe and had the fish.

September 12th, 2006

BERTIE MANAGES GRAND ENTRANCE BUT FINAL EXIT STILL HIT HIM LIKE A TRAIN

Head high, shoulders back and arms swinging, a smiling Bertie Ahern led in his troops.

The public gallery was heaving. The press gallery packed. The Dáil chamber filling up. Everyone waiting for Bertie.

It was a quarter to four in the afternoon. Wednesday, April 2nd, 2008. It was the end of the Ahern era.

Eleven years as Taoiseach. Fourteen years as Fianna Fáil leader. All over now for Bertie. His backbenchers looked stunned. His Ministers looked pensive.

The Taoiseach's smile remained fixed, his chin set at a confident tilt, as he strode purposefully around the chamber railings towards his seat.

When he reached the top of the steps, his deputies, arrayed in descending rows to his right, rose to their feet and applauded. (They had received a text from the whips office earlier in the afternoon, demanding "full attendance" for Leaders' Questions.) The Opposition stayed put, and silent.

Still smiling, the Taoiseach bustled to his place. The applause subsided. The deputies subsided. And Bertie - well, Bertie subsided. He had managed the grand entrance. But now, he looked shattered, gazing listlessly across at the Fine Gael leader.

It was a difficult situation for Enda Kenny. Until yesterday morning's shock announcement, he had been preparing a major attack on the Taoiseach's suitability for office and his ability to govern in the teeth of the growing scandal over his finances.

Enda was generous, if somewhat measured, in his tributes to the Taoiseach, who will leave office on May 6th. (Although in true Bertie fashion, it appears that he won't officially go until May 7th, because the Dáil is closed the day before.) "This day had to come," said Enda. There was genuine regret in his voice.

It's always the same in Dáil Éireann, when a big star finally falls from the political sky. It may seem strange to hear politicians, who have spent years lacerating somebody from across the floor, suddenly standing up and expressing regret when the outcome they demanded so vociferously, for so long, has finally been realised.

But there is a strange solidarity among the breed. When one of their number is taken down, there is a genuine sense of sadness. There but for the grace of God go us, and all that.

Enda asked about the date for the Lisbon referendum. He could have been reading his favourite passages from Finnegans Wake for all the attention people were paying.

Bertie appeared to be listening, but his head was down. He bit his lips, the picture of desolation. Was he that shocked? Had his decision been so sudden? Was it really an overnight thing, as some were saying? What prompted him to make his announcement in such a rushed manner? Is there more to come from the tribunal? But yesterday was not the day for such speculation.

The drama began just before half nine yesterday morning, when journalists were told to be at Government Buildings by 10am for an announcement by the Taoiseach. No further details were given.

A large crowd galloped to Merrion Street as rumour spread that Ahern was going to announce he was stepping down as Taoiseach and leader of Fianna Fáil. Journalists, photographers and television camera crews squeezed into the small space at the foot of the main staircase.

A plain wooden lectern was placed on a landing many steps above the journalists. Meanwhile, RTÉ television went live, with newsreader Bryan Dobson plucked from a radio discussion on Irish Protestants to anchor the broadcast, and a dishevelled looking Charlie Bird blinking excitedly into the studio camera.

The Taoiseach had yet to announce his intentions, as former Labour leader Pat Rabbitte was intoning on radio: "he has done the State some service". Back at Government Buildings, the media waited. Earlier, in scenes reminiscent of the Oklahoma land grab, they swarmed at great speed from the holding security hut at the gates to the main building. Once inside, their simmering sense of excitement verged on the hysterical as the Taoiseach kept everyone waiting.

Finally, at 10.48, Bertie Ahern appeared at the top of the stairs. He stopped and stared into the distance, above and beyond the crowd and out into the wider world.

Was he a man facing his destiny, or had his eyes been drawn to the large red banner that a number of his constituency workers had unfurled across the road in front of the gate? "Ballybough Loves Bertie." Then, having struck a statesmanlike pose, the Taoiseach began to walk down the stairs, a large group of Ministers behind him. It was an impressive show of strength. This was not a man about to hand in his resignation and scuttle away.

He reached the lectern. He looked down, paused, and looked up again.

For a second, just a split second, there was total silence. The chatter stopped. The sound of the camera shutters stopped.

Then Bertie spoke.

His hand trembled a little as he held his script. He sounded nervous and his voice wavered a little.

Above his head, his staff looked down from the marble balcony two floors up. From top advisers to the cleaners, they came out to listen to Bertie. Some started to cry.

The Ministers clustered around their leader, Brian Cowen at his shoulder, looking grave. The two Marys - Coughlan and Hanafin - seemed close to tears. This was emotional stuff.

Bertie delivered the most difficult speech of his life with dignity and determination. Once or twice, his voice thickened. Unlike in his interview with Bryan Dobson, there was no doubting the Taoiseach's pain.

His statement can be dissected at another time.

"I know in my heart of hearts that I have done no wrong, and wronged no one," he said.

But Bertie's problem is that too many people, in their heart of hearts, do not believe him now when he says he has done no wrong.

His fingers played nervously with the end of his jacket as he spoke. Cyprian Brady, his constituency colleague and loyal supporter, stood to one side, like a boxing trainer watching his man going down, in slow motion. Seán Haughey, who witnessed his own father's fall from grace, looked on.

Statement over, Bertie Ahern turned and went back up the stairs, his Ministers applauding and the applause of his staff ringing around the lofty marbled hall.

An hour later, Enda Kenny was on the plinth calling for a general election. (Marvellous move there by the Fine Gael leader, looking to go to the country when the nation is riding a wave of sympathy for poor Bertie.) Various Ministers were talking down their chances of going for the leadership. Brian Lenihan, meanwhile, was ruling himself out. Tánaiste Lenihan? Where did we hear that before? The action moved back to the Dáil in the afternoon, when Bertie took Leaders' Questions.

He looked awful. He looked sad and rather shocked. His backbenchers sat quietly, particularly the new intake, getting their education in the cruel nature of politics very early in their careers.

Labour's Eamon Gilmore welcomed the Taoiseach's decision to resign. He appreciated how difficult this was for him to do. And Eamon said what opposition leaders have been saying ever since the dawn of parliament: he had done his duty as he saw it, but he did it "on a political basis, not on a personal basis".

Bertie, head down, slumped sideways in his seat, nodded.

Above anyone else, Bertie, the most successful politician of his generation, should know the score. But yet again, his demeanour showed that no matter how much a politician knows the end is coming, it still hits them like a train when it does.

The atmosphere in the chamber was flat. Perhaps Bertie's news had come as a shock, but not a surprise.

The Taoiseach made a second statement. It echoed the one he made in Government Buildings. His party applauded him again when he finished. So, too, did the Labour benches. But not all on the Fine Gael side afforded the Taoiseach this courtesy, Enda Kenny included.

Then the Ceann Comhairle acknowledged Ahern's enormous contribution to the nation and the "countless generations of yet unborn Irish men and women".

We're still scratching our head over that one. One time, when in one of his put-upon modes, Bertie complained that if the cat had kittens, he'd be blamed for it. We fell to wondering if there was another reason for his hasty exit.

25

He stayed a long time in the chamber. When a vote was called, party members came over to wish him well. Conor Lenihan seemed particularly distraught.

Meanwhile, Brian Cowen and Willie O'Dea shared a joke, laughing uproariously while Brian Lenihan looked on. Biffo took off his glasses and wiped his eyes.

Finally, Bertie's business in the house was finished for the day. But he sat with Minister for Foreign Affairs Dermot Ahern and the rest of his party as he spoke on the Lisbon Treaty Bill. But Bertie didn't seem to be listening. He was gazing into space, a faraway look in his eyes . . .

How could this have happened?

April 3rd, 2008

Mr Liu's walk-out puts extra spring in Gormley's step

Grey and sleek, John Gormley padded into the Great Hall of the Greens, smiling from ear to ear. Tail up, double cream dripping from his whiskers.

He should really have come in on all fours. The Minister - yes, it's really true, guys! - purred through his speech.

Oh! Such a contented Gormley.

Oh! Such a happy leader.

Oh! He could eat himself without pepper and salt.

Could it get any better? Yes, it could.

God bless Mr Liu for giving John an extra spring roll for dinner on Saturday night.

Courtesy of the Chinese ambassador, Minister Gormley ended up enjoying the best of both worlds in the aftermath of his keynote address: a radical alley cat with his paws on the plump cushions of government.

Until Liu Biwei got into an oriental huff, the Green Party convention had been very run of the mill. Jolly and self-satisfied (in a save-the-world sort of way), delegates were understandably upbeat at being in Government for the first time.

The mood in the Fairways Hotel in Dundalk was good-humoured and relaxed, with no real prospect of dissent from the platform or the floor.

A few weeks ago, it could have been much different. The party leadership was genuinely worried that the ghost of an embarrassing relative, with a history of financial amnesia, might turn up and cause havoc at their family get-together.

However, once Bertie Ahern announced his resignation plans, John Gormley and his Government colleagues were freed from the mortifying task of trying to convince their comrades that they were not ethically compromised by choosing to turn a blind eye to the

Taoiseach's Mahon tribunal evidence.

Bertie's decision to step down couldn't have come at a better time.

And so, it was business as usual, but this time with two State cars and better suits.

At the weekend, Trevor Sargent, in charge the last time they all met, became to the Greens what Des O'Malley is to the PDs. No PD conference is complete without reverential nods, standing ovations and mentions from the platform for Des, their former leader and founding father.

Now Trevor, the former leader who steered the Greens to the promised land, is similarly revered. Every time he appeared on the platform, he was lauded for his role in steering the party to greatness and his services to root vegetables.

He was in nostalgic mood, remembering the time he first met John Gormley. It was in the 1980s on O'Connell Bridge. John was wearing a gas mask and protesting against smog, recalled Trevor. He went on to wax fondly about how, back then, he used to spend a lot of time digging compost toilets.

Which moved some of us to wonder if John had been telling Trevor the full truth about why he was wearing that gas mask.

There was a beehive with real bees in the display area. You could buy little bags of seeds from Irish Seed Savers for €2.50 or purchase an eco T-shirt for €7.50 and a jute bag for €7.

Deputy Ciarán Cuffe held a workshop on Saturday afternoon, advising people how to minimise their carbon footprint. He was a mine of information on such diverse topics as how to boil potatoes, do your washing, dispose of doggy poo and keep rats off your compost heap.

Things flagged a little as the day wore on, particularly as some people like Senator Dan Boyle had been up very late on Friday night singing medleys of Beatles songs.

Then Deputy Eamon Ryan threatened to take his shirt off on the podium and caused quite a frisson among the ladies. But he was only speaking metaphorically.

Ah, but it's great to be in Government. A very glamourous looking Mary White did the warm-up for John Gormley, and she packed her well delivered speech with an assortment of one-liners.

Some, it has to be said, were better than others.

She had her own version of Brian Cowen's famous "If in doubt, leave them out!" line.

"Leave us out, and you're up the spout!" chorused Mary.

Doesn't that mean pregnant? Maybe she meant "up the sprout".

Finally, John Gormley had his moment in the sun, which is just the perfect place for the cat who has just got the cream.

His speech purred along nicely, if in a non-controversial, self-congratulatory way. Then he came to the bit on China, and human rights abuses in Tibet.

The Chinese ambassador had been told that Minister Gormley would be addressing the subject, so he was fully prepared to be insulted.

Mr Liu Biwei, accompanied by Wang Xiusheng and Du Lei, sat next to the door. So when the time came for them to take the hump, they hadn't far to go.

John Gormley got a rousing round of applause as they left, and the atmosphere lifted. The young Greens were particularly impressed. Short of handcuffing himself to the railings of the nearest Chinese restaurant, the Minister couldn't have impressed them more.

Even the anti-Lisbon [Treaty referendum] people were delighted. A smiling Mr Liu was interviewed outside before he left. Delegates hit the bars and dancing went on until all hours.

April 14th, 2008

A YEAR IN THE LIFE OF BRIAN

Predictions are the bane of a political correspondent's life. Some of us take great pleasure in reminding these media sages of their sweeping statements when nothing of the sort comes to pass.

There was one political correspondent who would never shirk his duty when asked to make a call. If his predictions turned out to be wide of the mark, it didn't bother him in the least.

"Well, I was right at the time," he would say.

Which brings us to what was written and spoken about Brian Cowen when he became Taoiseach a year ago this Thursday.

The prints glowed and the airwaves sparkled. There was a sense that Cowen was the right man for what was going to be a difficult job. He had the qualities to lead the country through the post-Bertie years - tough but fair, straight-talking, no frills, politically astute, witty, bright, popular with colleagues and liked by the media, passionate about his country and in tune with the ordinary man and woman in the street.

He walked into the job without having to fight for it. There were no contenders. Most political observers, from all sides, were rooting for him.

He had the best of starts.

Twelve months later, and I pull out the pieces I wrote on those first days. They're a bit embarrassing now, to be honest.

I cringe and tell myself I was right at the time.

"Leadership seems to suit him . . . What a blessed change from the bland . . . Brian Cowen is a natural . . . Captivated his audiences . . . He hasn't advisers plotting his every move . . . Doesn't need the comfort blanket of a prepared script."

The celebrations in his native Offaly were wonderful. Looking back now, maybe we got a little carried away:

"And there it was at last: proof that he has those qualities of leadership that so many in his party have talked about for years.

Here was the reason his Dáil colleagues seek out his company. Here was why he is so highly regarded and loved in his hometown of Clara."

I was right at the time. I was right at the time . . .

The first sign there might not be a fairytale ending came before he was confirmed in office. It was during Dáil tributes to Bertie Ahern. Cowen's contribution was eagerly awaited. He was free to cut loose and be himself, no longer the loyal lieutenant.

The speech was a big disappointment. He made a lot of noise, but delivered what sounded more like a rallying cry to the Fianna Fáil troops than a tribute to Bertie Ahern. He failed to capture the mood.

No matter. The new man was full of fire and hope and a touching humility. "I am excited by the challenge and daunted by the responsibility," he said, when becoming taoiseach designate. He spoke of patriotism, invoking the name of Seán Lemass. As we were to find out, he talks about patriotism a lot.

Back then it was refreshing and it fuelled a sense of optimism. Now, when he talks of patriotism, people get annoyed.

On May 7th, 2008, half of Offaly seemed to descend on Leinster House. The Offaly Rover must have been sung a hundred times, as Cowen's countrymen and women celebrated his elevation.

Cowen was elected Taoiseach. He accepted the honour "with a genuine sense of humility". He spoke of his family, voice breaking when he remembered his father and grandfather.

His script trembled in his hand. We willed him through that speech. His supporters had a huge party. The AA issued a traffic alert for Tullamore and Clara in advance of the homecoming. T-shirts featuring Cowen, Che Guevara style, with flowing locks and a shamrock on his beret, were sold on the streets.

Locals called his return "the Cowenation".

Crowds lined the streets. He stood in the back of a jeep - the Biffomobile - and was driven through the streets. A pipe band led the way. There was bunting and there were speeches on the back of a lorry in O'Connor Square.

There were two powerful speeches on that Saturday. Mesmerising performances, old-style rhetoric, rich in emotion and love of place. The Taoiseach spoke of a better Ireland, of the way things used to be, when the values of community and patriotism and pride in your place were important. When people looked out for each other.

"It's not about what's in your pocket, it's as much about what's in your heart," he said. You could see he was making a connection. Ireland, the Ireland of Bertie's bling, was already beginning to change.

He could say that then. After his Government's performance, he'd be wise not to repeat the statement.

Cowen sang. My Way was one of the songs. And boy, did he mean it. In Clara he spoke of his father. He sang "Ber Cowen he is a TD, me boys, Ber Cowen, he is a TD. He got Clara a swimming pool, because it isn't by the sea!"

Some people complained about his performance in Offaly. They sniffed prissily that this was not the way for a Taoiseach to behave. Why not? It wasn't like he was standing at the podium in the UN. Good on ya, Cowen, don't let the handlers snuff out that spirit.

Biffogate struck in the middle of May. The Taoiseach had to apologise for conduct unbecoming when the Dáil microphones picked up his use of an expletive. "Bring in those f***ers," he said to his Tánaiste, Mary Coughlan, in an apparent reference to the National Consumer Agency.

It was much ado about nothing, except for one thing - it highlighted Cowen's irritation at Opposition questioning.

A couple of days later he announced that Fianna Fáil would not be continuing with its annual fund-raiser at the Galway Races and the Galway Tint.

"I was never really that arsed about it anyway," remarked EU Commissioner Charlie McCreevy when he heard the news.

McCreevy was canvassing with the Taoiseach in advance of the Lisbon Treaty referendum. Very late in the day, Cowen and the rest of the political establishment realised that they might lose it. An uneasy alliance ensued.

But the Taoiseach upset the delicate balance when he commented that the Opposition, and Fine Gael in particular, were not working as hard as Fianna Fáil. If the treaty was to be delivered, they would have to pull up their socks.

Fine Gael leader Enda Kenny was seething. "I think there are occasions, in the country's interest, where the Taoiseach will have to resist the temptation of giving the Opposition parties a kick every time he sees us," commented Labour leader Eamon Gilmore.

Cowen has never heeded that advice.

Early on, the promise of Tullamore and Clara began to evaporate. In the Dáil, Bellicose Biffo was easy to rile. After years of frustration opposite the unflappable Bertie Ahern, Opposition deputies were delighted with their volatile Taoiseach.

Then Lisbon was lost. Cowen seemed to be heading that way too.

By the end of June, he couldn't duck the recession. He stressed that the situation was not as bad as it was two decades earlier. People who were comparing Ireland in the 1980s were suffering from "delusions".

The new leader relied heavily on jargon when talking about the economy. His opponents began to ask where the straight-talking Cowen had gone. (To the Department of Finance, four years earlier.) In July, the economic outlook worsened. On the last day before the summer recess, Cowen was still refusing to mention the word "cuts".

"We must work within the spending limits we have set ourselves to underline confidence in ourselves going forward and to devise a strategy next year that will be sufficient to be sustainable going forward. That is the position," he told the House.

Summer was a merciful release for all concerned. But back in Leinster House at the end of September, the pressure was piled on.

Then came the midnight meeting in Government Buildings, and the deal with the banks. Fine Gael backed the plan; Labour didn't.

It was a question of liquidity, insisted Cowen. What about capitalisation? What about insolvency? The Taoiseach wasn't very forthcoming. People began to worry.

On whose advice did he act? "On the advice of those from whom we should take advice."

Day in, day out, as concerns grew about the country's financial situation, Cowen continued to spew the usual economic jargon.

the budget was brought forward to October. It made a start on pegging back some of the deficit faced by the State. But it turned into a fiasco. Worried people protested vociferously over the plan to remove medical cards from some elderly people. There was pandemonium, but the Government was slow to act.

Eventually, without notice, the Taoiseach appeared on RTÉ's Nine News in an attempt to mollify the pensioners. "Not everyone, perhaps, has internalised the situation," he told the furious pensioners, who replied by marching in their thousands on Leinster House.

The economic situation worsened. The Opposition demanded a plan. Cowen countered by asking what they ever did when they were in power. (All of 11 years before.) Increasingly, the Taoiseach's much vaunted leadership abilities were questioned. There were calls for a state-of-the-nation address.

Back in Government Buildings, nobody seemed to know what to do. "I keep hearing all this s**te about leadership. What's he supposed to do? The global economy is collapsing. Just look at London and New York - nobody can cope. What's the man supposed to do?" said a Cowen supporter.

There were long talks with the social partners and emergency Cabinet meetings. The Opposition got more angry. The public, more and more worried.

In January, Cowen let fly in the Dáil.

"As long as I am running this Government, I will run the Government as I see fit, as I believe it, based on my philosophy. I will run this country on the basis as I see it."

That image of him, angry, shouting, stabbing the air with his finger, will be hard to shift.

In February came a spate of quasi-state-of-the-nation addresses. There was one in the Dáil - a lacklustre performance with little spark, followed by a live TV address. "Today, we start the fightback ... There's a whole lot of initiatives we can take, and a whole lot of things we can do."

A nation shrugged. Well, do it so.

He went to a Chamber of Commerce dinner and delivered his third state-of-the-nation speech in so many days. He brought the crowd to its feet with his fighting talk.

"A new dawn!" we trumpeted, still hoping. In hindsight, the

reaction to this one speech was a measure of how confidence in the Taoiseach had declined. "It wasn't the Gettysburg address," snorted Enda Kenny.

The figures got worse. Cowen said there no point in telling the Opposition anything, as they would just "rubbish" it. "I can't rubbish anything I haven't seen?" asked Eamon Gilmore.

No. There would be no mini-budget. Well, there might. No, I won't name the date. Well, I might. Eventually he did. He would not be reducing the number of junior ministers. Eventually he did. The trouble with the banks escalated. Cowen and his Government appeared all at sea.

Portraitgate livened up March, when a couple of very unflattering caricatures of the Taoiseach were sneaked into and hung in two galleries. RTÉ carried an item. Feathers were ruffled in Government Buildings. The Government press secretary conveyed his displeasure.

A minor event was blown out of all proportion. Cowen's stock fell further. The opinion polls have been horrendous. He's already lost one deputy, and a former junior, John McGuinness, is in open revolt following his recent demotion. With the local elections looming, his troops are jittery. Some of the grassroots are complaining he doesn't come to see them the way Bertie used to.

At the moment, Cowen looks isolated. When he has time to unwind, he takes a drink in the Dáil members' bar with a small group of friends, some of them former deputies. Doubtless, they tell him what he wants to hear.

But what of the man who thrilled the crowds in Offaly a year ago? Is he gone? Some of us like to hope he's not.

Everybody knows he had a terrible job to do. Everybody knows he can't come up with a plan to make everything better.

It's just that the other side of the song doesn't have to be so out of tune.

Just do it. Then you can always say: I was right at the time.
May 2nd, 2009

AND THE WINNER IS . . .
MARTIN BY A SMILE, THANKS TO A
BRILLIANTLY INOFFENSIVE OFFENSIVE

Micheál Martin won by a mile, thanks to a brilliantly inoffensive offensive.

That's his style. Relentlessly nice, as he edges relentlessly towards the crown.

He has long been Fianna Fáil's cool, clean hero.

Yesterday, newly installed as the party's eighth leader, he became its cool, contrite hero.

It's unusual for the leader of a political party to set out his stall with a series of apologies, but that's exactly what Martin did.

He knew exactly what he was at.

By distancing himself from his most recent predecessors - one too proud to apologise for the mistakes of the past and the other too deluded to admit they ever happened - he immediately put the public on notice that he is not the same as them.

But he was ever so nice in the way he did it.

Even his reluctant challenge to Brian Cowen's leadership was done by way of a polite cough to signal his intent, followed by the offer of his resignation.

Yesterday's well-crafted victory statement and assured handling of the subsequent press conference also told us that he had been thinking about this moment for a very long time.

There was nothing thrown together or last minute about it. The deputy for Cork South Central had been working towards the leadership for a very long time.

How many times had he rehearsed the scene in his head? Had he hoped the opportunity would come years earlier, when the leadership was last up for consideration?

He never got the chance to challenge then, though, because Bertie Ahern anointed Brian Cowen and Micheál's race was over before it started.

The parliamentary party took just an hour to deliver its result. The news was announced at 3pm: "Born Leinster House, January 26th, 2011, a healthy new leader, Micheál. Successor to Jack. Cork delighted."

The accession was choreographed from the very beginning. A small number of supporters arrived on the plinth, jubilant and itching for a party. They stood around in quiet celebration, wondering when their man was going to stride out and accept their adulation.

It didn't happen. For these are difficult times and Fianna Fáil is in the doghouse. It's not so long ago since Enda Kenny won his leadership contest and the "Up Mayo" parochialism that greeted him on the plinth grated with the public.

Under no circumstances would there be any buck-lepping and roars of "Up De Rebels!" to add a touch of Leeside high spirits to Micheál's big day.

He would speak to the media at the Royal Hibernian Academy down the road from Government Buildings in Ely Place - a few doors down from the Labour Party headquarters.

The word was not put about. As a result, very few party cronies turned up to sully the carefully contrived atmosphere of confidence and contrition.

The new leader's arrival was met with a smattering of applause. The Fianna Fáil backdrop behind his podium looked a bit battered, like it had been given a few kicks. But still standing, just like the party Micheál pledges to rebuild and reintroduce to its core values.

The event was scheduled to start at half past four, but had to be delayed because a vote was called for the same time in the day. Two of the defeated contenders, Mary Hanafin and Éamon Ó Cuív, had already arrived at the RHA and were giving interviews outside when deputy Chief Whip John Cregan rushed up and told them to get back to the Dáil for a vote.

Mary clattered at speed in her high heels back to a waiting car and dived inside. Éamon, spellbound by the cameras, continued to talk.

He reluctantly returned to the car before he was lassoed by Cregan.

Low key was the order of the day for Micheál. There was notable absence of jargon when he spoke. Hanafin and Ó Cuív galloped back to the RHA to hear the end of it, quickly followed by Brian Lenihan.

One bank of photographers concentrated on the vanquished trio; the other on the victorious leader. Between them all, surely one of them would capture a tear? They didn't.

Everyone was calm, with handshakes all round and lots of forced banter and uproarious laughter for the photographers. Micheál shook journalists' hands and looked happy.

He's already trying to smoke his Opposition rivals. He challenged Enda Kenny and Eamon Gilmore to not one, but two live television debates, along with a third one to be conducted in Irish.

Soon the air was thick with flying gauntlets as the offers were accepted with bullish counter offers.

Meanwhile, the joke doing the round is that Sky News will be offered the debate to be held as Gaeilge.

Yesterday morning, it looked like the passage of the Finance Bill would overshadow the election of Fianna Fáil's eighth leader. But the mavericks who had threatened to vote against the Government, thus precipitating an immediate election, climbed on board having extracted a last few baubles from Biffo.

Nobody really cared. Like, do you remember where you were the moment Mattie abstained? As for this critically important debate, shortened after fierce arguing between the various parties, it turned into a forum for retiring deputies to make their valedictory speeches.

Both Bertie Ahern and Brian Cowen looked weary and pensive as the energetic Micheál Martin barrelled in a businesslike fashion into the chamber after his win.

Everyone wanted to shake the new leader's hand.

The other two drifted away to leave him to his moment.

As for Micheál, there'll be plenty of time for a few bars of De Banks when the fuss dies down.

January 27th, 2011

HIGH-FLYING ENDA
BRINGS IT ALL BACK HOME

The helicopter lifted into the night sky from Dublin's docklands. Enda Kenny looked out the window, watching the lights of the capital city spread out below him - a breathtaking sight.

He was lost in thought, a pensive finger pressed to his lips. Who'd have thought it? Taoiseach-elect. Returning home in a chopper (paid for out of party funds) for the declaration that Mayo had returned an unprecedented four Fine Gael deputies. He had to be there.

The noise of the rotors. That smell of aviation fuel. The twinkling tapestry unfolding below. High-octane stuff.

After all the years.

"Well, Enda. I think this is it. Finally." And we look at the view, me and IndaKinny.

"Yeah." He fell silent again.

Minutes earlier, Enda had been addressing a simmering rally of successful candidates, party workers and supporters. He entered the Burlington Hotel into a maelstrom of jostling photographers and cheering faithful. People falling over in the scrum of flying elbows and camera flashes. The cheers building from down the corridor in the banqueting hall.

Kerryman Mark Kennelly, his chef de cabinet, steered him through the madness.

"Ladies and gentlemen, Taoiseach-designate, Enda Kenny!" Kenny hopped onto the platform and reached for his inner JFK. As he spoke, some of his more hard-bitten enforcers choked back the tears. An elderly man in a voluminous pin-striped suit fished a large handkerchief from a bulging pocket, wiped his eyes and blew his nose.

A young woman toppled from the chair she was standing on, still waving her little flag and hardly spilling a drop of drink - caught by a delighted young blueshirt.

He talked of duty and responsibility and "above all, in the midst of what is for many a national heartbreak, let us be mindful of each other".

He had taken a phone call from former taoiseach Liam Cosgrave. The crowd applauded at the mention of the name. Cosgrave told him: "I am an old man, but you've made me proud." The man in the suit blubbered like a baby.

It was a brief but galvanising appearance. As soon as the Taoiseach-designate finished speaking, he was whisked out a back door and into a fast car. Security men whipped barriers across. The gateman saluted.

Changed times.

Enda sank back in the passenger seat. He had started his day in Castlebar and would finish it there. "I couldn't see a thing going into the Burlington. It was a total blur. I just saw a wall of light," he said, shaking his head.

It had been a hell of a day, but there was more to come. He didn't leave the count centre until five in the morning.

The action began in the afternoon with the arrival of the candidates. The auditorium in The Traveller's Friend theatre was stuffed with supporters. Michael Ring made a spectacular entrance on the shoulders of two supporters. To roars of "C'mon Ringo!" the unsteady trio, picking up speed, lurched dangerously down the hill to the front door. The wishbone of a chicken came to mind as one bearer headed one way with a Ringo leg and the other veered in the opposite direction with the other.

Undaunted, Ring conducted a radio interview from his lofty perch, one trouser hem above his knee and the corresponding foot hitting a woman on the chin.

His two bearers staggered inside, almost decapitating the Ringer on the lintel.

After the chaos caused by the Ringer - God bless his gusset seams - it was decided to sneak Enda into the building. He waited with his wife Fionnuala in a side room until it was time to enter the tumult. The future Taoiseach swigged a bottle of water and made small talk. Fionnuala handed him her mobile phone and he read the message. "It's from a doorman in a hotel in New York, wishing me all the best." The candidates arrived. "Howarya, Mickey Ring, me aul' segotia!" said Enda. The four waited. The noise of the crowd grew louder.

Finally, the double doors were opened and the four faced into a terrifying crush of photographers, reporters and television crews.

Fionnuala hung back. "Did you ever think you would see the day Enda would become taoiseach?"

"I could have told people that 20 years ago, if only they had asked me."

She knows her politics. She was Charlie Haughey's press officer during the turbulent years. She's a good cornerwoman - lets himself out to do the business, comes in with the towel when needed.

Eventually, the media moved back and Enda moved into the auditorium. The reaction was visceral. The crowd rose and cheered. They stamped on the wooden floors and the balconies above. The whole building seemed to shake. Count staff rushed to the barriers to offer congratulations.

The Taoiseach-elect moved slowly down the hall, accepting the good wishes of his countymen and women. At the far end, his sons Ferdia and Naoise waited, along with his brother Henry and sister Maria.

"I climbed Kilimanjaro with him," said Paddy McGuinness, weeping copiously. "I'm a Monaghan man, living in Mayo since 1960. I can hardly talk, sorry, I'm so emotional. He's going to prove the intelligentsia in the media completely wrong. He's the new Jack Lynch. A fair, decent and honest man."

Enda lapped up the adulation. "It's not about me," he kept saying. "You can feel the pride in these people. It's hard to describe the feeling of it, really. I can see it in their faces. We're going to make a new start."

All the same, there has to be a personal aspect. A sense of vindication, at the very least? "I do see this as a vindication of my self belief and conviction. It's not been easy, in many ways."

As the day goes into night, we can't help thinking that Enda is struggling to hold it all together. When he meets Kathleen Coady, the wife of the late Liam, his driver for many years, the two embrace. Time and again, the tears well in Enda's eyes.

On the trip to Dublin, we listen to the radio. Seán O'Rourke welcomes Brian Cowen, who is on the line from Offaly. Brian is just getting into his stride when O'Rourke cuts him off: "Taoiseach, we have to go to Mayo where the first count is about to be declared."

Then onto the madness of the Burlington. MEP Mairead McGuinness has left her mother's 88th birthday to be there. "Mammy didn't mind. She's 88 but we are all up to 90."

The clock is ticking towards midnight as Enda gets back to the helicopter.

We wonder how his father Henry, whose untimely death led to young Enda becoming a TD at the age of 24, would feel about his son's achievement. Enda doesn't answer. Again, his eyes brim and he looks out the window. "That's Longford down there." His mother Eithne was 93 recently. "I visited her last night. She had a Fine Gael sticker on her dressing gown. Her mind is sharp, she'll probably say she wants to go to the Dáil with me. I'll have to hire another helicopter." Again, he's struggling with his composure.

Suddenly, it's midnight over Mayo. He hasn't thought much about his new office in Government Buildings, or what personal touches he might bring. "Maybe the picture of Davitt, and I suppose we'll have to have Mick as well."

The pilot, Tom O'Connor, comes through on his mic. "Mr Kenny, ATC and the staff at Knock airport pass on their congratulations."

They are waiting on the tarmac. Some have brought their children. More photographs. On the drive into Castlebar, he points out landmarks. "Enda, back in Mayo now as Taoiseach-elect. That must be some feeling," we venture.

"That's Swinford up ahead of you."

Taoiseach? Elect? There's a pause. And a sigh. "Yeah."

He rings Fionnuala to make sure the two boys and Aoibhean, his daughter, will be at the count centre. Will he have a lie in on Sunday morning? "Sure I don't sleep at all, for feck's sake. I'm awake at five o'clock. It takes three weeks for an election to soak out of you."

Enda goes home for an hour before returning to the theatre. The place is hopping. A publican from Kiltimagh tells us it's a great moment. "I'm Fianna Fáil, but it doesn't matter a s****. He may be a Taoiseach for Ireland, but he's a Taoiseach for Mayo."

The results are announced at four in the morning. "Dara! Dara!" chant the supporters of Fianna Fáil's Dara Calleary. "Four-one! Four-one!" comes back the good-natured chant.

The three successful FG candidates are tossed around in the air. "Enda doesn't like to be lifted," we're told. So he isn't.

Two armed detectives materialise. Locals swarm the stage, the queue stretches down the steps. The Taoiseach-elect poses for photographs until everyone is satisfied. He heads for home at five in the morning.

We want the best for Enda. He faces a torrid time. We remember Bertie and Biffo. Wanted the best for them too. Hoped for it. It ended in tears. Twice bitten (won't even think about CJ Haughey) should counsel us to be three times shy.

We wish the best for Enda, pensive as he sits in the helicopter, looking down on the lights. And we apologise in advance to Fionnuala. He's going to have a bloody awful job. But he's not the only one.

February 28th, 2011

GILMORE DEPARTS AFTER
A VERY CIVILISED COUP

The Gilmore generation: he brought them in and they brought him down. But it was a well-mannered mutiny: a civilised coup.

They owed him that much. Eamon Gilmore could have hung on as Labour leader for a good while longer. He could have followed the party rulebook and delayed the inevitable. But his time was up. The Tánaiste – he remains in office until a successor is chosen – said he reached his decision over the last few days. "Agonising" over what to do in the wake of overwhelming rejection at the polls, while robustly declaring in public he was staying put.

"You go through a weekend and you think, you know, should I fend off all comers or should I, you know, pass on the baton. . ."

By yesterday morning that wasn't a difficult choice. He could either pass on the baton or get beaten over the head with it. So Gilmore did something he should have done a lot more times during his tenure as party leader: he moved quickly and he made a decision.

He announced his resignation in the rarefied confines of Iveagh House, headquarters of the Department of Foreign Affairs. A fitting location for a man who promised so much upon getting into government, before disappearing down the back of an antique sofa in the ministerial mansion. The scene in the downstairs reception room spoke volumes yesterday. Gilmore, dignified and measured, taking full responsibility for his party's collapse and facing up to that responsibility by standing down after seven years in charge. Senior colleagues clustering protectively around him – all the "heavyweights" with their years of Cabinet and Dáil experience. They were never going to be the ones to call a halt.

Set in their ways. Some set for retirement. Two of them past leaders, with Gilmore soon to join them.

A trio of youthful Ministers of State only served to point up the age profile of the ubiquitous others. There they stood, looking crushed and forlorn, amid the plush drapery of the Minister's anteroom with its ornate mahogany fireplace, floor-to-ceiling windows, crystal chandelier and oriental urns.

Earlier in the day, much earlier, a different group of Labour politicians assembled in Deputy Ciara Conway's flat in the Coombe. None had ever held high office. None has been around long enough to accumulate a nice pension. First-timers all, brought into politics by Gilmore, stirred by all he stood for when the party was in full opposition cry. They backed him to the hilt when older heads lost faith and abandoned the parliamentary fold. They were his strongest supporters. Even when they felt he should be more assertive in Government they gave loyal support.

It must have rankled hugely when critics sneered at their lack of backbone. Newbies afraid of their own shadows. Reports came back of stormy parliamentary party meetings. The first-timers brought their complaints to the old hands. The heartland was hurting, people were losing patience. As committed Labour representatives they were reduced to defending the indefensible. They pleaded with Gilmore to leave Iveagh House. They wanted more than just occasional visiting rights to their erstwhile mentor, that's when he was in the country. Last weekend the Gilmore Generation finally had enough. At that meeting in the Coombe, after much soul searching, they realised they had to cut the ties to their Tánaiste.

Those patrician elder statesmen and women weren't up to the task. To his credit, Gilmore realised it was time to go before they forced him. But that won't be enough for the new intake. Yesterday, over the airwaves, they made it clear they want new blood at the top, not a reshuffle of the same old names.

Things moved quickly. But not, perhaps, as quickly as the Tánaiste and his people would have us believe. There was talk of some last-minute attempts to persuade the group to back down. They refused. Gilmore said he had no knowledge of their deliberations. Which is strange, when the Taoiseach, beyond in Castlebar, told reporters he had heard the rumblings and had tried to contact his Tánaiste by telephone. Gilmore didn't answer his calls. Which isn't surprising, in a chaotic Government where ignoring telephone calls seems to be the order of the day. The Attorney General wouldn't talk to the Taoiseach on the phone either, while Enda didn't care to call Eamon when the Shatter crisis was at its height. In the end, the new generation cast Labour's Cabinet heavyweights aside and asserted its authority.

Gilmore, a decent man, left with dignity and spared his party the ordeal of a public unseating. In their quest to pull the country from the brink of disaster, he said the Coalition had to make tough decisions.

"A course that carried a high political risk and Labour has paid the price for that."

He sounded sad, struggling to smile through his personal upset, trying to remain upbeat. "I asked the party to take on the responsibility of government. I still believe that that was the right decision," he said. And in a sideswipe at Sinn Féin – now celebrating as Labour mourns – he declared "real politics is about finding real solutions". But the public's resounding verdict could not be ignored. "We've got the message. We've heard it," he said. It's time for Labour to "recover, regroup and renew".

Who will take over? There will be elections now for a new leader and deputy leader. Outgoing second-in-command Joan Burton will have to put up or shut up now after long months of shadow-boxing around Gilmore's job. Joan has to lay her cards on the table now.

But it may be too late for her. The Gilmore Generation wants a regime change. Of the old guard, it seems Brendan Howlin is the only one they have any time for.

"The renewal of the party needs a new voice at the microphone," said the departing Gilmore.

Meanwhile, Enda Kenny waits. He's not the only one doing that in Fine Gael. They have a new generation too. And they ain't happy either.

Gerry Adams and Mary Lou, on the other hand, are laughing.
May 27th, 2014

DEFINING MOMENTS

The Moriarty Tribunal's report on Charles Haughey put the final cap on his reputation six months after Haughey's death and state funeral at which one of his successors as Taoiseach and Fianna Fail leader Bertie Ahern had given the eulogy

Judge casts a cold eye on Haughey's life

In death, as in life, Judgment Day arrived on the double for Charlie Haughey.

That would be him all right. Always demanding at least twice as much as everyone else.

In life, he bade farewell to a turbulent political career and settled into comfortable retirement. He held open days for charities at his lovely home. The dark memories faded. There was talk of the presidency. The future looked good for the former taoiseach.

Then the past came calling and ripped gilded posterity from his grasp. The nation reassessed. Second time around, judgment was less kind.

In death, the pattern is repeated. Twice this year, the career of Charles Haughey has been assessed, with very different outcomes.

The first assessment was delivered on a Friday in June, from the side of a hill in a chilly north Dublin graveyard. The second was distributed on a Tuesday in December, from a suite of cosy offices in Dublin Castle. (Yesterday, to be precise.) The first, spoken by Taoiseach Bertie Ahern at Charlie's graveside, was heavy with admiration and emotion. There was a note of defiance in his voice as he recalled with pride, and a catch in his throat, the man he called "Boss".

Nobody expected Bertie's words at the funeral of his old friend and mentor to be anything other than generous and kind. But the manner of his eulogy, conveyed in a pitch verging on the aggressive, raised eyebrows. The only thing the Taoiseach didn't do was organise a national whip-around to get a statue of Charlie erected in the GPO next to the dying Cúchulain.

The second, written by Mr Justice Michael Moriarty, is not

constrained by the bonds of lifelong friendship or political loyalty. While Bertie Ahern drew on a Fianna Fáil lifetime to compile his report, Mr Justice Moriarty had a mere nine years in a tribunal chamber to concentrate on his. He has looked at the "Haughey Years" – times when Bertie was busy forging his career and picking up tips from a populist master – with a dispassionate eye. When not examined through the green-tinged lens of the Soldiers of Destiny, the Charles Haughey that Michael Moriarty sees is far less heroic than the figure Bertie Ahern wants us to remember.

That is not to say these two very powerful men – Taoiseach and High Court judge – disagree on everything. They don't. They are in hearty agreement on one point: Charles J was a very hard and diligent worker. (It's when it comes to the nature of some of that work, and the beneficiaries, that these distinguished gentlemen part company.) Of the two assessments, the report Michael Moriarty produced after nine years is a more unforgiving exploration of "The Squire's" interesting life, or "extraordinary journey", as the awestruck Bertie put it last June. In mitigation, the Taoiseach only had 15 minutes to deliver his conclusions on CJ. The judge had the luxury of 700 pages.

"He was a legend, and a man." – Ahern.

"Devalued the quality of a modern democracy." – Moriarty.

It's very difficult to reconcile the two Charlies.

There's Bertie's "Boss" – the hero. "Charlie had a steadfast love for this country," trembled the Taoiseach at the graveside. "This love was a central element of his political life. He was patriotic to the core. He had a great respect for every aspect of the life of this country – our noble heritage, our rich culture, our ancient tongue – and a special interest in historical and literary matters."

(Bertie forgot to mention how CJH also had a great devotion to amassing large amounts of money, spending it lavishly, then forgetting he ever got it.)

There's Michael's witness – the liar. The judge doesn't feel any need to wax lyrical about him. Just straight facts will do.

He categorises Haughey's reign as "a dismal period in the interface between politics and business in recent history".

The facts back him up. In his report, Mr Justice Moriarty charts the years of "clandestine donations." He reckons, conservatively, that

Haughey amassed over £9 million above his normal entitlements between 1979 and 1996.

And how much would that be worth in today's money, judge? Again, no hyperbole or tales of old Ireland from Michael. That, he concludes, would be in the region of €45 million. The money was sloshing into the Taoiseach's coffers as fast as he could spend it. Sadly, as the report notes, Charles Haughey wasn't fussy about where that money came from.

"If the definition of a patriot is someone who devotes all their energy to the betterment of their countrymen, Charles Haughey was a patriot to his fingertips." – Bertie.

"Unbelievable – Bizarre – Unprecedented." – Mr Justice Moriarty. (He nearly got the full house in the course of his report, but he just couldn't manage to slip a "grotesque" in there too.)

June, 2006, and it's Bertie again. "Today, I recall his singular combination of love for great literature and great politics." Yesterday, Michael recalled his singular pursuit of cash, his improper interference with the Revenue service at a time when the country was on its uppers and his regrettable attempts to "saddle others" with responsibility for some of his financial affairs.

"Have no doubt that the ultimate judgment of history will be positive. He was one of the most consequential of Irishmen. And when the shadows have faded, the light of his achievements will remain." That's Bertie, ever the optimist.

And the achievements will, deservedly, remain. But after the Moriarty report, the shadows are there forever too. They include the "elements of fear and domination engendered by him in individuals in both the public and private sector." And the tribunal's finding that he failed to co-operate at all stages.

Still. We're all human. The Taoiseach could have been talking about any man, not just Charlie, when noting "he could err, but he was always valiant". CJ's errors are well documented, but where is the valour in pocketing substantial subscriptions left over from a fund to pay for a best friend's liver transplant? Michael Moriarty can't find it.

In fairness, sentiment and loyalty allow Bertie to say what he likes at his friend's graveside.

But, after the publication of yesterday's report, one suspects not many will agree with the Taoiseach's assertion that "he was one of us". Raking in 171-times his actual wages? Bullying a major bank? Telling the little people to tighten their belts? Brazenly denying the obvious in a witness box? Profiting from a friend's misfortune? One of us? Back to Michael, before the apologists start. "It would be quite unwarranted to conclude that 'everyone was at it'." Unless, perhaps, you were connected enough to be "one of us".

December 20th, 2006

The first meeting between the Taoiseach Bertie Ahern and the Northern First Minister-designate Ian Paisley in Dublin was a hugely symbolic event that many witnesses could scarely believe was happening

Ahern and Paisley's handshake melts away decades of suspicion

They said it could never be done.

After decades of bigotry and hatred and suspicion, the shattered lives, the heartbreak and the hurt; the fear, the cynicism, the false dawns; the oceans of empty talk and the acres of newsprint, the godawful spirit-sapping sameness of it all.

Was this it? Could this really be it? Yes. Pinch yourself. Remember the date: Easter Week, April 4th, 2007. A momentous day in Irish history and joy it was to be there.

It took an epic journey to prove it, but politics truly is the art of the possible. For years, as the tortured progress of the Northern Ireland peace process stuttered along, politicians and pundits talked of choreography. Positive developments seemed less important than the race to spot which party put a foot wrong.

There was no such talk at Farmleigh House yesterday, where the choreography was purely celestial. The grounds, bathed in glorious spring sunshine, carpets of daffodils and blue wood anemones provided a fitting backdrop for the extraordinary events to come.

Three minutes to 11 and word came through: "They're at the gate." Two cars rolled up the gravelled driveway. Taoiseach Bertie Ahern emerged from the old mansion, patting down his jacket as he waited to welcome his guest.

No big ceremony was laid on for Ian Paisley. His presence supplied the fanfare. Bertie bustled over, a wide smile on his face. Dr Paisley, the old warhorse, sprang from the car and met him halfway.

"Good morning!" boomed the leader of the Democratic Unionist Party. "I have to shake this man's hand! Give him a grip!"

With arm outstretched, he made an enthusiastic lunge for the Taoiseach. They shook hands. Bertie grasped the top of Big Ian's arm. Big Ian gave Bertie a manly wallop on the shoulder. They were like two auld farmers at a mart, striking a deal over a bullock.

The media looked on, dumbstruck. Ian Paisley of the Free Presbyterian Church, the Dr No of hardline Northern unionism, in Dublin and doing business with the leader of the Irish Republic in a building built on the proceeds of beer.

And that was it, the moment in Ireland's history we thought we would never see. Seismic, earth-shattering and over in a minute – but the symbolic importance of that handshake cannot be underestimated.

Countless lives and lifetimes to get to here. But at last, when Bertie met Ian, courage and hope finally got the chance to shine.

The meeting took place in the Library room. They sat opposite each other at a small square table. They ate egg and cress sandwiches and drank pots of tea. The mood was friendly and very relaxed, like they had been having these little tete-a-tetes for years.

The two men discussed practical issues, such as investment projects and tourism initiatives. Dr Paisley, who had previously only visited the Pope's heathen South to protest, marvelled at the growth of Dublin.

The atmosphere was friendly. There were no awkward moments.

Next month, Ian Paisley takes office as Northern Ireland's first minister, sharing power with Sinn Féin. The soon-to-be legislator and his vastly experienced Dublin counterpart swapped ideas.

They talked about the Battle of the Boyne site in Co Louth. Bertie invited Ian to visit it with him. Ian accepted and said he might even drop in for a preliminary look on his way home.

Their meeting went on longer than intended. Afterwards, they walked together into the sunlight. The media scrutinised their body language. It was good.

Taoiseach Ahern was beaming. Dr Paisley looked very relaxed. Bertie spoke first.

"At this important time in our history, we must do our best to put behind us the terrible wounds of our past and work together to build a new relationship between our two traditions." Big Ian nodded in agreement. "The future for this island has never been brighter. I believe that this is a future of peace, reconciliation and rising prosperity for all."

Then it was the Doc's turn. We remembered the man who spat fire and venom at politicians from the South. We remembered the man who marched to Carson's statue and swore "No Surrender!"

We remembered the man who was jostled and jeered when the Belfast Agreement was endorsed by the people of the North and we remembered the survivor who used that unswerving opposition to revive his political fortunes.

The voice is not as strong as it once was, but the preacher can still impart a message. "Some say hedges make the best neighbours, but that is not the case. I don't believe we should plant a hedge between our two countries," he began.

Journalists who have been writing about Ian Paisley for 30 years looked on in wonder. Was this really happening? As he spoke of being a proud Ulster man, it was hard not to feel moved. Spellbound, we waited for the "but" to arrive. It didn't.

"We both look forward to visiting the battle site at the Boyne, but not to refight it," said Dr Paisley with a chuckle. This was incredible stuff. "I look forward to future meetings and trust that old suspicions and discords can be buried forever under the prospect of mutual and respectful co-operation." Truly incredible.

When he finished, there was silence. The journalists looked at each other in disbelief. Nobody even attempted to ask a question.

What they really wanted to do was applaud. Afterwards, old hands wandered about, shaking their heads. "Is this a dream? Am I dreaming?" asked UTV's Ken Reid.

We weren't dreaming. Bertie gave Ian a book about Farmleigh. Ian gave Bertie a book written by his wife Eileen called Take a Break. Four hours later, the Government published its report on the Dublin/ Monaghan bombings that killed 33 people in 1974. Ian Paisley's meeting with Bertie Ahern will forever stand as a magnificent milestone in this island's troubled history. It was a privilege to be there.

April 5th, 2007

The appearance at the Mahon Tribunal of Bertie Ahern's former secretary was for many of his peers the final straw in his attempts to persuade them that there was nothing underhand in the monies he received while Minister for Finance

PROUD DAY FOR BERTIE AS FORMER SECRETARY BREAKS DOWN IN THE WITNESS BOX

Bertie Ahern must be a very proud man today.

His Ministers must be so proud of him too.

It's such a pity none of them could make it to Dublin Castle to watch Gráinne Carruth give her evidence.

They would have seen a woman, alone and trembling in the witness box, battling back the tears as she whispered in tones so anguished they were barely audible: "I just want to go home." It was so pitiful, it's just a pity Bertie wasn't there to see it.

He might have stood up and shouted like a man: "Let the girl go. It's me you want!" But that only happens in the movies.

The Taoiseach was unavailable to the media yesterday.

If he had been in Dublin Castle, he would have witnessed the distress of his former secretary, loyal servant to the last, struggling to maintain her composure in the face of strong but fair questions about his finances.

His finances.

If Bertie had been there, he would have witnessed her obvious discomfort as she continued to insist she cannot remember three occasions in 1994 when he gave her big wads of British currency and told her to tip across to the bank and change them into Irish punts.

Gráinne Carruth, who earned £66 a week back then, would have gone into the bank on each occasion and handed the teller bundles of money that were far in excess of her annual salary.

Six thousand, five and a half thousand, four thousand. In sterling. In cash.

But she just can't remember. She can't remember the foreign exchange element of the transaction. She can't remember splitting up the resultant punts and lodging separate amounts into Bertie Ahern's account, and into accounts in the names of his two daughters.

All she can recall is that she used to cash her boss's pay cheques and lodge a few bob from them, upon his request, into his daughters' accounts. "I always remember just the girls."

These were the days when people had passbooks, and transactions were recorded as they occurred.

Bertie would hand Carruth the girls' building society books before sending her over to the Irish Permanent.

But of the amounts she banked on those three trips, by far the largest ones went into her boss's account. Carruth, to this day, still can't remember he had one.

"So you would have had three passbooks then, would that be correct?" asked Judge Keys.

"I only remember the two," replied Carruth in a faltering voice.

A few people laughed in the public gallery. But for the most part during her evidence, the audience just watched and listened in amazement.

To the even most casual observer, Carruth's obvious agitation would have been apparent.

She was forced to accept, in the face of the documentary evidence, that she had converted sterling and lodged some of it in Bertie Ahern's account. All she could say, the only thing she could say, was that she couldn't remember.

Truly, the Taoiseach, had he been at the Mahon tribunal yesterday, would have been proud of what he heard.

For he has told the tribunal, Dáil Éireann and the Irish people that he never had any dealings with foreign currency. (Apart from that one unsolicited whip-round in Manchester.) And Carruth, the woman who once worked in his office, was able to repeat what she has told the inquiry all along: as far as she remembers, she only ever cashed his pay cheques for him. She never saw or handled sterling.

The tribunal proved that this is not true.

"I can't dispute it. It's here in black and white in front of me. I don't recall it, but it is here in black and white in front of me," was

56

the best she could manage.

"I don't believe I ever told an untruth," she said forlornly.

However, Carruth, echoing a phrase already used a couple of times by her solicitor, accepted that she changed sterling for Bertie Ahern "as a matter of probability". But this mother of three young children, who gave up her job as the Taoiseach's constituency secretary in 1999, is not in the same league as Bertie's cohort of amnesiac businessmen; that swaggering stream of pin-striped amigos who have blustered in and out of the witness box, brazenly vague and forgetful, and not in the least bit bothered that nobody is buying their tall tales.

(For those of you looking for something to do on Good Friday, here's a suggestion: Google "Mahon tribunal". On the left-hand side, click on "transcripts" and look up April 3rd, 2006. Marvel at the evidence from Tim Collins, Bertie's close associate who gave entertaining evidence last week.)

Carruth isn't like Celia Larkin either, who couldn't remember much when she appeared, but clothed her memory lapses with a certain style, addressing the tribunal's lawyer on first name terms and airily dismissing his rising incredulity with icy disdain.

No, unlike the others, Carruth was not able to hide the fact that she didn't want to be in the witness box. She radiated unease and apprehension. She only spent an hour and a half on the stand, but it will rate as one of the most uncomfortable tribunal sessions that observers have had to sit through.

At one point, she was asked why she changed her solicitor. At the outset, she had the same solicitor as Bertie Ahern. She met this solicitor to discuss what she knew before she went to talk to the tribunal in private session two years ago.

Carruth told Des O'Neill, who managed to be both solicitous and incisive yesterday, she "was upset and this was coming on a daily basis to my door and I just wanted it out of my house and my husband, my husband found Mr Millar".

A change of solicitor so, for Carruth, as any citizen is entitled to. Her husband, as he is entitled to do, found Hugh Millar, who took on her case.

Millar also represents Celia Larkin and businessman John Kennedy, who attended Bertie's famous whip-round dinner in

Manchester.

One wonders if the highly regarded Millar had a Humphrey Bogart moment when he heard the identity of his new client: "Of all the legal joints, in all the towns, in all the world, Gráinne Carruth's husband walks into mine."

Perhaps the most telling moment of the morning came when O'Neill asked Carruth why she hadn't contacted Ahern when she finally saw the documents linking her to the sterling transactions. After all, she couldn't remember a thing.

She said she didn't contact Bertie because her children are her main priority.

O'Neill, gently, pressed the issue. Did she not want to clarify matters "of crucial importance" to her and her family? Why didn't she call Bertie? Carruth's voice began to crack.

"Because I'm hurt."

"Because why?"

"I'm hurt."

"You're hurt?"

Bertie Ahern's former office secretary began to cry.

"And I'm upset."

"Yes," soothed Des. "And what is upsetting you about your evidence before the tribunal today?"

"Because it's taking me from my family, and that's why I'm upset," sobbed Carruth.

"Is there any other reason, Ms Carruth?" asked Des, softly.

There was a tortured pause.

"I just want to go home."

A proud day for Bertie. A proud day for his Ministers, and the rest of his parliamentary party inbertiebrates.

Brian Cowen is in Vietnam.

March 21st, 2008

The financial crisis was littered with meetings of banks' small shareholders who, unlike depositors and bondholders, lost almost everything in the bust

CAN'T MAKE EGM WITHOUT BREAKING SOME EGGS

It took just a few cracking moments and a strong throwing arm to bring about the most puntastic scramble in the history of Irish banking.

Apologies in advance. But in these dark times, we must keep the sunny side up. Splat! Splosh! A brace of eggs whizzed past the ears of startled bankers and hit the backdrop beyond. One clipped a microphone mid-flight, spattering an eggy reprimand down the chairman's sleeve.

Gary Keogh resorted to a hen's egg yesterday for one simple reason – thanks to the AIB, he doesn't have a nest-egg to throw. So if one must lob comestibles at the top table during the egm of the bank which has gambled away your rainy day reserves, eggs would seem an appropriate choice. Egm? Yes missus, that would be an Eggstraordinary General Meeting.

In this case, the bank in question was AIB, but most of our big financial institutions are in the firing line for their profligacy and hubris over the last few years. Egg and blue chips anyone?

Puns are not much consolation to those people who worked hard down through the years, putting money by for the future. They were the smart ones, the thrifty ones, and yes, the lucky ones. Why shouldn't they have invested their money? There's no safer bet than the banks, they were told by the experts.

But share prices collapsed like a soufflé. The results have been devastating for many small investors.

Even the strutting roosters of high finance have suffered. There is no doubting their regret – there was a lot of sincere regret from the top table yesterday – at what has happened. They have had to endure ruffled feathers, what with their reputations in shreds and the cuts to their massive salaries which have now left them with marginally less massive salaries.

"We drank too deeply from the national cup, I suppose, of confidence," sighed Dermot Gleeson. It's just as well that Mr Keogh and his little brown paper bag had been removed from the hall by then, otherwise Dermot might have found himself drinking deeply from an egg-in-a-cup of comeuppance.

The stories are sadly familiar now. They were retold at the recent egm of the Bank of Ireland, and again yesterday. Provision put aside for nursing homes, gone. Funding for care, gone. Income in old age, gone. Dividends depended upon, gone. Hard earned money, gone.

Shareholder Susan Kelly summed up the mood of despair: "Have you any understanding or comprehension, as a board, of the pain you've caused? The pain I can tell you is real; it's unbelievable, it's breathtaking and life-taking in some circumstances. I hope you, the board, will carry the burden of this pain, for the rest of your life, that you have inflicted on . . . us."

Mind you, she wasn't addressing all the directors. It's amazing how, when things are going well, a company board has to stretch the full width of a room to accommodate the suits. There were only five on the platform yesterday, including the formidable Gleeson, who knows how to handle a crowd.

Michael Riordan demanded to know the whereabouts of the rest of the directors. Can they not sit at the top table? They might end up getting hit by an egg, sniffed Dermot, looking at his jacket.

So where were they? In the front row, top right, sat a quiet line of men in suits. What stood out were the gleaming white shirts, the cufflinks and the shoes. It was the shoes that really gave them away, a long dark gleam of leather.

In the afternoon, these other directors had to stand up and identify themselves. Some shareholders shouted that they should parade down the centre of the hall.

A few speakers rambled on, determined to have their say. There was a lot of talk about letting off steam. Gleeson was charm itself, at pains to be fair, ignoring the insults and glacial tones. Most of the speakers were calm and commendably measured, given the depth of their anger.

But the reality yesterday was that words are all they have.

Ordinary shareholders may have come in search of answers and some hope of restitution, but the best they could do was take out their frustration on the banking bosses. And in the case of Gary Keogh, a recently retired grandfather of five from Blackrock, that frustration and anger led him to fire a couple of eggs at the platform. He said afterwards he'd never done anything like that before, but "there's always a first time".

When he heard the chairman tell an angry shareholder to sit down, he says he saw red and let fly. To his disappointment, he narrowly missed Eugene Sheehy, but scored an indirect hit on the chairman who should have brought a frying pan along with his script.

The same Mr Sheehy was looking very tanned and fit, despite having protested he would "rather die" than raise equity. Outside in the atrium, we peered up to the offices of the top brass to see if the balcony railing had been set higher following the chief executive's rather dramatic promise. It was still at chest height. Eugene must have changed his mind about ending it all when that first tranche of government money came in.

Sixty-six-year-old Mr Keogh was some distance from the platform when he struck with his long range eggs. A medical officer monitored proceedings from the back of the hall. The AIB might have been better sending in a chef. The nasty marks on the backdrop were removed during the lunch break. Time to clean up and move on.

If only it were so easy for the small shareholders. Nest-eggs are far messier to clean up when they hit the floor.

May 14th, 2009

In the days before agreeing to an IMF/EU bailout, the Government continued to deny that it was seeking one

Biffo tells gasping Dáil there's no such thing as a bailout

The EMU has landed.

It's all about the euro, stupid. It's why the Men in Suits are arriving here today to run the rule over our books.

Not a bailout, so?

No such thing, bristles Biffo. That's what he told a gasping Dáil and two senior officials from the British embassy in the distinguished visitors' gallery who were taking notes with alarming speed.

Nor are there any negotiations going on with the Bailout Boys.

It's just "technical" stuff, insisted the Taoiseach, as his own backbenchers scrunched up their faces in despair.

Anyway, it's the fault of "the markets" for creating this difficult situation for the euro, and unfortunate that when a big economic squeeze is imminent the markets go in search of the choicest lemons.

No wonder our leaders looked so haunted yesterday.

They are now contriving to feel very hard done by. Throughout the day, in Leinster House and on the airwaves, our governing lemons, from the Taoiseach down, put out the message that their handling of the economy had been nothing short of impeccable since they banjaxed it.

If Brian Cowen's performance in the Dáil was jaw-dropping for its bloody-minded insistence that the Bailout Boys are merely dropping by for some "engagement" and to conduct a routine check-up, Frank Fahey delivered a tour de force on radio.

The Taoiseach's loyal lieutenant was in such an upbeat state of sunny denial we feared he might be removed to hospital to have the party line surgically removed from his toes.

Speaking on Newstalk's Breakfast Show, Frank began: "Well. I think we're in a pretty good position . . . the Government have handled this situation well in that we now have the various players coming to Ireland tomorrow to look at the structure of our banking situation . . ."

When the Government asks, the "players" jump.

Fahey stressed that Ireland would play its part "in ensuring the continuing strength of the euro . . . This is a euro issue."

Or a ransom note.

Fianna Fáil's Frank couldn't speak highly enough of the lemons. "For the last 2½ years Brian Cowen and Brian Lenihan have taken all the right actions . . . We've done all the right things."

Off microphone, a guest seemed to be hyperventilating. Fine Gael's Brian Hayes. Mad as hell. "It's a pile of shit, Frank," he snorted, "and you don't believe it." All over the country, people drew closer to their radios and cheered.

The Greens went missing. Dan Boyle issued a plaintive tweet about trust and uncertainty. Nobody paid much attention.

Back in the Dáil, Biffo was getting very frustrated with the Opposition and their questioning of his non-bailout/non-negotiating mantra.

And we harked back to happier days when we had no such thing as a recession either. It took months and months for the Taoiseach to utter the R word. He's at it now with the B word.

Cabinet members drifted away – Hanafin, Martin among them – until the faithful four remained: Cowen, Coughlan, Dempsey and Ahern. Éamon Ó Cuív departed, in deep negotiations with Jackie Healy-Rae.

Pat Rabbitte exited the chamber in disgust. "This is calamitous. I can't listen anymore. The banks are going to cannibalise the country."

Have faith (even if some Fianna Fáil backbenchers, privately, have lost it). For if all goes to plan, those Europeans in denial will take their courage in both hands and allow plucky Ireland rescue their single currency.

Whether or not Gunther and Gaston like it, we will force Brussels to bow to our demands for "financial assistance". They may resist, but the money is there and by God we will force them to make us take it. We will emerge as heroes when Europe capitulates.

Brian has a cunning plan. Mess with the big boys at your peril, eurocrats. The Taoiseach played minor hurling for Offaly.

Meanwhile, the Minister for Finance was in Brussels seeking to spare his Government's blushes at this difficult time. It was encouraging to hear him concentrating on the good news (and buttering up the Brits, who are keen to give us a dig-out).

"The engagement now takes place," declared Lenihan.

Yes indeed, wonderful news from Buckingham Palace. All the best to William and Kate in their forthcoming nuptials. They were so right to delay their marriage plans: housing is much more affordable for young couples now.

The Government plans to give them Louth as a wedding present. Just to spite Gerry Adams. And it'll please the IMF too.
November 18th, 2010

The Dail approved the Government's plan to save Irish banks in a late night session – even though Minister for Finance Brian Lenihan revealed that Anglo-Irish Bank might require €10 billion more of taxpayers' money on top of €8.3 billion committed as part of a €21.8 billion bank recapitalisation package

DÁIL ROLLS UP FOR BIFFO'S TRIPLE BILL OF SCALPINGS, SHOCK AND AWE

Toxic Tuesday – we saw it coming, but that doesn't make it any easier.

Destitution Day – when Biffo's Government went over the top and landed us in hock for the foreseeable future.

Broke Bank's Mountain (of debts) – a gritty story of financial cowboys who fall in love with themselves and drag a nation to the brink of ruin.

We had the political equivalent of fright night in the Dáil yesterday. It was the horror triple bill nobody wanted to see, but there was no choice.

Richard Bruton frightened the life out of us with his predictions of the consequences. So did Joan Burton. We'll be in the workhouse by Christmas.

Then we had to endure The Head with Two Brians – not for the faint hearted. The sight of Cowen and Lenihan reassuring a nervous public that they will lead them on the path to financial salvation is not a good one.

"We need an Irish banking system fit for purpose . . . this is the way forward," says BrianC.

"We are now in a position to stabilise the deficit and we are on a firm path to economic security," soothes BrianL.

But they have a dark past – their previous promises haven't worked out. Why believe them now? That's what Richard Bruton wanted to know, when he said the latest phase in the Government's attempt to save the banking system would lead to a doubling of the national debt and the mortgaging of our futures.

An air of the crypt hung over Leinster House. It was cold and quiet. People drifted about, saying little. The flabbergasting figures about Anglo Irish bank and the news about high-flying Quinn Insurance worsened the mood.

The proceedings had been well flagged in advance. Up for dissection: the restructuring of our main banks and building societies. "I think that today is the day that's going to be remembered for a very long time in this country," predicted Labour leader Eamon Gilmore. "This is the day the Irish taxpayer gets the invoice for the bailout of the banks."

What was to come had been labelled "Super Tuesday." But there was nothing super about what was to come. We have been banjaxed by the banks, confirmed the two Brians. Minister Lenihan then confirmed that full extent of the nightmare.

Joan Burton didn't hold back. "The figures are truly awesome," said Labour's finance spokeswoman. She hunted around for a suitable catastrophe that might illustrate the gravity of the situation. She plumped for the military doctrine employed by the Americans during the bombing of Baghdad. "These figures are about shock and awe. And I am shocked and I am awed."

So what are the figures? Far too much for most of us to comprehend. The language of Nama is impenetrable to most of us, which makes what went on in the Dáil all the more frightening.

The Government had predicted the financial institutions would take a "30 per cent haircut" when they were taken over by Nama.

But no. They were scalped. "The weighted average haircut across these institutions is 47 per cent," Brian Lenihan told the chamber. Richard Bruton and Joan Burton looked scandalised, and started scribbling notes for their replies. Some of us just couldn't get our heads around the whole idea of financial haircuts. However, it seems, if the word of Biffo is to be followed, it is wise to have a good trim in order to make your head fit for purpose.

Or something like that.

"Fit for Purpose" is the Taoiseach's new favourite phrase. (It's also the phrase on the minds of many of his backbenchers, who have formed the opinion that their boss isn't fit for purpose any more.) The figures for Toxic Tuesday were worse than most imagined. The banks had tried to talk themselves out of their problems, and the Government, for too long, was well disposed towards listening to them. That's all changed. "At every hand's turn, our worst fears have been surpassed," said Lenihan, who at least had the good grace not to sound surprised.

He talked calmly of the tens of billions to keep our banks and building societies in business. More than €20 billion alone to keep the rotten institution that was Anglo Irish Bank under Seán FitzPatrick in business.

It's our money that's keeping them afloat, which means we all own a few banks now. It can't be long now before the bumper stickers and T-shirts appear with the slogan: "My Other Bank is a Building Society."

Brian Lenihan did his best to sound optimistic. He didn't look it – nor did the rest of the Fianna Fáil front bench. But at least we are keeping up with the Joneses. He says the neighbours are very impressed. There was "widespread international confidence engendered by last December's budget", said the Minister. "The citizens of this country have shown grit and determination in facing up to our severe budgetary difficulties and it has paid off."

Where, exactly, he didn't say. Perhaps he meant the Greens, who are doing handsomely out of this Government.

Brian urged the public to look on the bright side. "Others believe in us. We must begin to believe in ourselves!" he exhorted.

"Not today," snorted Fine Gael's Paul Kehoe.

Richard Bruton and Joan Burton blew Lenihan out of the water. They focused on the disgusting amounts of taxpayers' money needed to keep the developers' piggy bank – Anglo Irish – from going under. "It is simply wrong for Ministers to come in here and pretend that taxpayers have an obligation to pay off all that money," said Bruton. "It's wrong . . . it's monopoly money. It's no such thing. It's hard cash that our grandchildren will have to pay." The Opposition was in no doubt that the decision by the Government to commit, for years to come, so many billions of taxpayers' money to the banks will have disastrous consequences for the country. By the look on the faces of many across the floor, they aren't so sure about it either. The shocking figures about Anglo Irish Bank hit them hard. Fit for purpose? The banks or Biffo's Government?

March 31st, 2010

Finance Minister Brian Lenihan introduced the last Fianna Fail Budget shortly after his government negotiated a bailout from the IMF and EU

SCENE-STEALING NOONAN TUGS ON HEARTSTRINGS AT LAME PUPPET SHOW

There is every reason to be "confident".

This is a "new start".

We are taking our "first step".

Chin up! chivvies Brian as he unveils Ireland's first puppet Budget.

Fair play to the Minister for Finance. He was on his feet for three-quarters of an hour and you could hardly see the wires.

The same goes for Brian Cowen: very lifelike, even though the IMF has one hand stuck up his Government's fundament while the long digits of the EU dance overhead, pulling the strings.

Oh but "there are clear signs of hope".

Outsiders running the country with the help of a Taoiseach and his highly paid Cabinet of clerical assistants.

Crowd-control barriers surround Leinster House, keeping protesters out and politicians in. As night falls, the Kildare Street gates are locked and the Garda dog unit moves in closer to the angry crowd.

It's freezing cold. Dirty snow is banked up along treacherous footpaths. Dublin's water supply is cut off by the council.

What look like election posters have gone up on the lampposts along Merrion Street. They are adverts for a chain of bookmakers, offering odds on who will become the next leader of Fianna Fáil and who will become next Taoiseach.

Reasons to be cheerful? Not many in Leinster House yesterday.

But "every reason to be confident", Brian Lenihan told a sullen Dáil, even if he looked anything but.

"Today's Budget is our first step."

As opposed to "The Next Steps" – which was Fianna Fáil's election slogan. Their next steps tipped the economy headlong into a black hole.

The jig is up, but never mind. We just have to learn some

new moves. Going forward. That's important, because they went backwards in 2007.

This, despite what some begrudgers might say, is not because our political leaders lost the run of themselves and became what Michael Noonan yesterday called "the braggarts of Europe".

It was because they wanted "to spread the benefits of the boom across every section of the population".

Brian Lenihan said this with an admirably straight face.

But back to taking our first step. The Minister for Finance feels we are up to it now.

He wasn't so sure just before he arrived in the chamber to present the puppet Budget.

"Be careful walking out – it's very slippery today," he cautioned photographers at Government Buildings during the traditional Budget-day photocall.

"Minister, stay out of it!" roared a handler when he looked like he might step into a hillock of slush.

Things are bad enough.

He held the document like an open book, each side in an upturned palm. Like Moses bringing down the tablets of stone – Lenihan can't erase or rewrite them. That's the preserve of the IMF-EU puppeteers.

The distinguished visitors gallery was packed for the occasion. Even the British ambassador sat through all the speeches. This Budget was of huge international interest.

Former Taoiseach Garret FitzGerald sat in the front row, a splash biscuit beige among all the dark navy suits.

Outside, news crews from TV networks around the world looked for eccentrics to interview. No shortage there.

The two Brians wore similar shirts – blue and white stripes, but Biffo's garment was a darker shade of blue.

The Minister's speech was short on specifics and long on buzzwords. Welfare cuts became "social protection adjustments" while jobs were "activation places" while Lenihan had high hopes for "a new national performance indicator to allow a variety of quality of life measurements to be assessed and reported on a regular basis".

He said he wouldn't be reducing the old-age pension. The

terrible twins of the 30th Dáil – Jackie Healy-Rae and Michael Lowry – looked pleased.

There were smirks in the direction of Michael D Higgins when it was announced the President's salary would be capped at €250,000 and wry smiles from the Opposition when it was announced that the use of State cars would be pared down.

(Afterwards, Fine Gael's Simon Coveney claimed that the changes wouldn't affect Ministers.)

Then Brian said he would be introducing changes in relation to the property market. Had they been in place years ago, the bubble wouldn't have been so bad. Pity they didn't introduce the measures back then, so.

The speech was met with restrained applause from the Government benches.

There was a sense of power passing. Everyone was waiting to hear what Michael Noonan would say for Fine Gael.

He didn't disappoint. "This Budget is the Budget of a puppet Government . . ." he began, before comparing Fianna Fáil to the Bourbons. He was very impressive. "I came in early and wrote the start and the ending and then just winged it in the middle. Once I got going, it kinda flowed . . . I'm good with sums," Mr Noonan explained afterwards.

Dr FitzGerald was very impressed.

"Absolutely excellent speech," he told us as he was leaving. "So little time to absorb so much. I couldn't do it."

Then he left with his copy of the Budget. "They asked me to go on television tonight, but I said no. Too much reading to do," he said, tapping the document happily.

Labour's Joan Burton described the Budget as "Unislim for the rest of us while Drumm and Dunne party on in Connecticut."

It was a lame sort of day. Too much given away in advance.

Even the bar was quiet – for a Budget day.

Without a doubt, Noonan stole the show. And just in case the Government didn't sense the passing of power, he finished with a quote from Michael Collins: "Give us the future, we have had enough of the past. Give us back our country to live in, to grow in, to love."

December 8th, 2010

REBUKE OF VATICAN MORE HARD-HITTING THAN A BELT OF THE CROZIER

There was never anything subtle about a belt of the crozier.

That would have defeated the purpose.

It was the ecclesiastical equivalent of a kick in the shins, and politicians feared it. The mere thought of a belt from a bishop was enough to make the most powerful legislators bend the knee.

It didn't do to upset the church, whose princes were all too ready to remind the lawmakers of this.

But yesterday in the Dáil, Enda Kenny, with steely eloquence, ended decades of government obeisance to Rome. What was most striking about this watershed moment was that nobody batted an eyelid. He said what he said, and it was generally accepted.

Down through the years, when clerical interventions came, they were accompanied by controversy and breast-beating. The Taoiseach's political intervention was accomplished with quiet determination and a declaration of who has the right to run this country.

It had been a slow afternoon in Leinster House: the Dáil winding down ahead of the summer recess, deputies heading to lunch or busy in their offices, crocodiles of constituents wending their way through the corridors on guided tours. The House was debating an all-party motion deploring the Vatican's role in the investigation into child abuse in the diocese of Cloyne. Not so long ago in the Irish parliament, such a motion would have been unheard of.

The Taoiseach was first to speak. His contribution wasn't flagged.

Just a handful of TDs were in the chamber to hear him. Some daytrippers looked down from the public gallery. Few journalists sat in for the speech.

"This is not Rome. This is the Republic of Ireland 2011, a republic of laws," said the Taoiseach, in the course of a searing rebuke of the Vatican.

As he read from a prepared script, reporters monitoring the debate in their offices, pricked up their ears. This was no safe speech, throwing out the usual condemnations and hoping for better things to come.

Enda Kenny spoke in a controlled manner, his voice tinged with anger and regret. He didn't raise his voice. There was no attempt at grandstanding. The words were enough.

Within hours, his speech was making news around the world – the leader of Catholic Ireland denouncing the Vatican in the strongest possible terms.

"Dysfunction". "Disconnection". "Elitism". "Narcissism". Was this really a Taoiseach saying this on the floor of Dáil Éireann? In a country where Taoiseach John A Costello once declared: "I, as a Catholic, obey my church authorities and will continue to do so in spite of The Irish Times or anything else, in spite of the fact that they may take votes from me and my party." When Noel Browne, having resigned from Costello's cabinet in the 1950s after the rejection of his Mother and Child Scheme, publicly said "I, as a Catholic, accept unequivocally and unreservedly the views of the hierarchy on this matter."

And the late Brendan Corish, former leader of the Labour Party, once famously said: "I am, of course, a Catholic first, an Irishman second." Bring it forward a few decades to 2001, when Bertie Ahern was Taoiseach. He hosted a State reception for Cardinal Connell, who had just returned from Rome with the red hat.

The invitations came from the Taoiseach – who was separated from his wife – and his then partner, Celia Larkin. A controversy ensued, and on the big night in Dublin Castle, it was the Taoiseach alone who joined the receiving line to be greeted by the cardinal. Celia Larkin remained at the back of the hall.

As clerical scandal built on clerical scandal, there always seemed to be reluctance at government level to stand up to the rule of Rome. By the time the Cloyne report was issued, the Vatican stood accused of subverting the Irish bishops in their desire to bring the abuse cases into the open.

Into this situation stepped Enda Kenny yesterday. If one were ever to predict who might be the person who would, finally, lay down the law, his name would not have been the most likely to emerge.

Taoiseach Kenny – family man, father of the Dáil, cut from the cloth of old Fine Gael. No. One might have expected one of the younger breed to make the call. That it was Enda issuing the challenge made it all the more compelling. His speech was well crafted and took little more than 15 minutes to deliver.

He spoke of the downplaying of "the rape and torture of children" in favour of upholding the primacy of an institution, its power, standing and reputation.

"Far from listening to evidence of humiliation and betrayal with St Benedict's "ear of the heart" . . . the Vatican's reaction was to parse and analyse it with the gimlet eye of a canon lawyer."

It was astonishing stuff. All the more so because the Taoiseach said he was speaking "as a practising Catholic". Earlier, he had been jousting in the Dáil with Opposition leaders during a lively Leaders' Questions and Questions to the Taoiseach. He had today's crucial summit in Brussels to consider.

In the middle of it all, when the House had gone quiet and was almost empty, he rose to make the speech which will be remembered as a highlight of his time in office.

When he concluded, there was silence. Then the Fianna Fáil leader rose to echo his sentiments, followed by a raft of speakers who spoke in favour of the motion.

Enda had done what needed to be done – and no amount of swinging croziers can undo it now.

July 21st, 2011

Pensioners descended on Leinster House in protest when Finance Minister Brian Lenihan tried to remove the entitlement of all over 70s to medical cards in his first Budget after the bust

SIGHT OF PILLARS OF COMMUNITY LAYING SIEGE TO DÁIL WAS TRULY UNPRECEDENTED

They scuttled in when the division bells rang and did what they were told.

Fianna Fáil's backbenchers, conspicuous by their absence from the debate, pulled together last night and voted not to restore the over-70s medical card scheme. They had to do it – that's the price of party membership.

But the effort may cost them dearly in the long run. Over in China, Brian Cowen's ears must have been burning.

Bertie Ahern of the broken foot arrived on crutches, providing an added touch of drama at the end of an incredible day. A chair was procured for him, and he sat, like a favourite gouty uncle, with his bad leg outstretched and colleagues beating each other out of the way to talk to him.

He was all smiles. But then, he will have heard the pensioners out on the street earlier in the day, saying poor Bertie would never have put them in this horrendous situation and poor Charlie Haughey was up there in heaven, looking down on them, appalled.

Chinese papers, please copy.

There was always only going to be one result. Transported by the heady grip of people power, the pensioners believed they could influence the vote. If they couldn't shame Fianna Fáil, they could make a show of the Greens.

But the Greens have nailed their colours to the Fianna Fáil mast. Some, like a distressed Ciarán Cuffe, were clearly distraught by the policy, but he held the line.

"This Judas response . . . will be your epitaph," Fine Gael leader Enda Kenny told the Government.

The first vote was called at 8.34pm. The public gallery was packed. The quiet man at the centre of the storm, former Fianna

Fáil deputy Joe Behan, voted with the Opposition.

But the numbers are still with the Government. Wearily, Cowen's tortured deputies did their duty. Their heads were with the party, but their hearts were with the pensioners.

Because the OAPs were brilliant yesterday. Unlikely militants, they took their anger to the national parliament and raged outside the gates. Thousands upon thousands of pensioners. They travelled from all parts, filling two city streets with the sound of protest.

They were like a force of nature. With an hour to go, only a couple of hundred people were assembled outside Leinster House, and Government deputies dared to hope that Cowen's climbdown on Tuesday had achieved the desired effect.

Then the floodgates opened and a seething deluge of OAPs poured in. By God, but they were livid.

Inside Leinster House, those Fianna Fáil and Green backbenchers who were not hiding in their offices stood around in anxious little huddles, whispering. Word was relayed from the front.

Five thousand.

Ten thousand.

Fifteen thousand.

More, maybe.

The scene outside was truly extraordinary. The sight of so many elderly people, pillars of their community, committed voters, decent law-abiding men and women, out on the streets laying siege to the Dáil, was unprecedented.

The gardaí on duty were afraid to move anyone on, even though the crowd was only supposed to be in Molesworth Street, instead of spilling right down Dawson Street as well.

So they minded them instead.

And the deputies listened to the dispatches and blanched. A slight air of hysteria took root in the House. The deputies shook their heads and abandoned any pretence that the situation was anything but an unmitigated disaster. Worse still, they admitted that they had brought it all on themselves.

Out on the streets, the pensioners were building up a head of steam. It was a brave Government deputy who would risk going out to meet them.

Brave, or foolhardy.

Which brings us to Fianna Fáil's Michael Kennedy, deputy for Dublin North, who went outside and tried to plamás the protesters. He was savaged.

Yes, the crowd was packed with the infirm and the lame. Yes, there were elastic stockings, bad hips, sticks and furry hats. The walking, heartrending clichés were out in force, but so too were the healthy, the glamorous and the strong.

"I was minding my own business when suddenly people started slapping me on the back and shouting 'Well done, Joe!' 'Well done, Joe!'" They had mixed him up with the hero of the hour, Joe Behan, who resigned last Friday in protest at the removal of the universal medical card for over-70s.

Joe, for his part, watched the astonishing scene from the security hut inside the gates. People kept telling him to go out and take a bow. But he wouldn't.

"That's not my sort of thing," he said.

The view from the platform, which stretched across the top of Molesworth Street, was unbelievable. So many people, senior citizens, for heaven's sake, venting their fury at the Government.

For the Government, the view from Leinster House was terrifying.

Walking sticks, Zimmer frames, wheelchairs. One man taped his message to a crutch and waved it in the air.

A group of women tried to get a chant going. "All de Marys out! All de Marys out!" At the main gate, a woman in a wheelchair watched proceedings, a placard resting on the tartan rug over her lap. She was a lovely sweet lady, and said she was 82 years of age and had come up from Cork.

At this stage, an ashen-faced Ciarán Cuffe of the Greens was at the microphone and battling a chorus of derision. "On yer bike!" sneered the crowd. "I am here to apologise," said Ciarán.

Whereupon the lady in the wheelchair, thoroughly incensed, took leave of her senses entirely.

"You are in your f***!" she roared.

"Oh, God forgive me."

They sent deputy Cuffe off with a flea in his ear.

The crowd could have stayed all day. But they had to make way for the students, who were also protesting.

Over at Leinster House, old student radicals were dreamily reliving their youth. What a day. There's life in the aul dogs yet! Thirty years ago, they said the seventies would be socialist. Now, the socialists are 70.

October 23rd, 2008

Martin and Fianna Fáil
can spare us the act,
we don't want to hear it now

Spare us your indignation, Micheál Martin.

Button your disgust, Fianna Fáil.

We don't want to hear it.

You had your chance and you chose to do nothing.

So don't pretend to be shocked now. Just do us that much.

We won't buy it.

If the tribunal were to take another 15 years to deliver its findings, you'd still be sitting on your hands.

I sat through all of Bertie Ahern's evidence. It was appalling.

Hilarious? Frequently. Pathetic? Often. Infuriating? Utterly. Embarrassing? Completely.

I didn't believe it then and I don't believe it now.

And, unlike the clever people entrusted by us to run the country at the time, I didn't have to wait years for a tribunal of inquiry to tell me.

But did it matter? Well yes, it did, because this man, grinning in the witness box, was our Taoiseach.

He wasn't a corner-cutting property developer. He wasn't a millionaire builder, doing what you have to do to close a deal. He wasn't an amoral middle-man or a small-time councillor on the make.

Bertie Ahern was the prime minister of our country, holder of the highest office in the land.

That's supposed to mean something.

And he was lying through his teeth. Anybody with half an ounce of wit could see it.

Reporters detailed his ridiculous explanations for the huge amounts of money washing through his myriad accounts, and resting in his office safes. The most cursory of examinations of the daily transcripts would have shown up his risible stories for the twaddle that they were.

But throughout, his government and party turned a blind eye; squirmed and twisted and gave every manner of excuse to avoid the blindingly obvious taking place in full public view in a State-established inquiry.

He was lying.

"Due process," they spluttered, when not muttering about being too busy to read his lengthy testimony. "It's not an issue on the doorsteps," they parroted, as if that made all the difference.

Of course, they couldn't prejudge the report either. We can't interfere: let the tribunal take its course, they chorused.

Rubbish.

They commented when it suited them, taking selective quotes from the transcript to bolster their arguments, like when ministers mobilised to insist the tribunal had cleared Ahern of allegations of non-compliance.

It wasn't true.

The tribunal merely stated it wasn't addressing these allegations, one way or the other.

Bertie Ahern was not in front of the courts. His evidence was not sub judice. Ministers, backbenchers and cheerleaders could comment, and act, as they saw fit.

But they turned a blind eye to the lies of their leader and instead, attacked the tribunal for daring to ask him legitimate, hard questions. Party, and political expediency was more important than political integrity and public trust in our democracy.

It was spurned for one more twirl on the political gravy train.

If Bertie Ahern was making a mockery of us inside that tribunal chamber, his colleagues were every bit as bad outside of it.

Worse, even. For Bertie was fighting tooth and nail to save his reputation – at least he had a reason.

No surprise then, to see that when the Mahon tribunal chickens finally came home to roost yesterday, Fianna Fáil pushed the young people forward into the line of fire.

Par for the course.

Micheál Martin surfaced on the evening news. Talking to Dobbo – looking almost as sad as Bertie Ahern on that famous evening in

September when he poured out his heart to the RTÉ anchorman –
Deputy Martin said he accepted the findings of the report and took
them very seriously.

Back in 2008, when his leader had them rolling in the aisles
with his far-fetched yarns of wads of cash turning up in his office
and a "sinking fund" of money to stop that same office from sliding
into the river Tolka, Micheál robustly declared that he believed
Bertie's evidence and accused the opposition of using the tribunal
process to undermine Ahern's political leadership.

He wasn't alone in taking up the cudgels for his beleaguered
boss.

But Mahon nailed the spineless and cynical response of those
senior ministers to the cross-examination of their leader, their
election winner who had to be protected at all costs.

There were "unseemly and partisan attacks" on the tribunal
with a "sustained and virulent attack" on their work from "senior
government ministers." It didn't bother those political paragons in
2007/2008, as they trotted out on to the Leinster House plinth and
fanned across the national airwaves to defend the indefensible.

Those of us who were enduring Ahern's farcical evidence
couldn't help but feel angered and demoralised by the closing of
ranks in the cabinet.

Bertie's colleagues eventually took him out because even they
could not stomach the mounting shame caused by his tawdry
excuses for all the money he amassed when Minister for Finance.

Money which was far in excess of his earnings and for which he
couldn't plausibly account.

When a low-paid office secretary, through her tears, was forced
to endure two harrowing days in the witness box as part of his
faltering efforts to keep up his cover story, they could take no more.

But as a consolation prize, they let Bertie off on a lap of honour
around the world and lauded him as the finest politician of his
generation.

The former Taoiseach was lying even before the tribunal began.
After The Irish Times published that first story of very large sums of
money flowing into his coffers, Bertie met it head on.

"Off the wall!" he declared, when presented with a figure of
between fifty and a hundred thousand pounds.

He was right, in a way. That figure was far larger.

Punts. Sterling. Dollars. It didn't matter to Bertie. Once it was hard cash. He always dealt in cash, we were repeatedly told.

The saga of the two digouts will go down in song and story. The explanation, told in tearful tones to Bryan Dobson, was that he was hard up for money after his marital separation and his pals rallied around to give him the deposit for a house.

That was another fairytale. His mates, smirking and swaggering, corroborated it. Nobody believed a word of it, not least because the tribunal had already established that Bertie was awash with cash.

Then there was Micheal Wall, the North of England businessman, who attended the Manchester whip-around night but "didn't eat the dinner."

He bought a house for Bertie and provided the money to build a conservatory while tens of thousands more were lodged in the bank by Celia Larkin to do up this mini-Versailles in Drumcondra.

She had the receipts. About the only documentary evidence surviving. The tribunal dismissed the entire caper.

Tall story piled upon tall story, until the former Taoiseach had to fall back on the time-tested "won-it-on-the-horses" defence to account for some of the cash.

The timing of the hearings was lucky for Bertie. The sums of money involved would have been huge, back in the early 1990s. But he took the stand during the building boom, when the most of the figures under examination could be compared to the deposit on a shoe-box apartment on the outskirts of town.

People, shelling out hundreds of thousands for badly built starter homes, shrugged. Small beer, or so they thought.

Today, deep in negative equity, they think differently. The actions of people who subverted the planning process had a consequence, one they are now living.

But, as Bertie Ahern's supporters were quick to point out yesterday, he subverted nothing. The tribunal found no proof of corruption.

Just all this money, for which they found he had no credible explanation. In fact, in the circumspect way of judges, they essentially said he lied about where he got that money.

Look. Bertie doesn't matter anymore. Nor does the buffoonish

Pee Flynn or those grasping councillors. Most of Ahern's cabinet have departed the political scene.

"I believe political loyalty is a virtue and that loyalty will be maintained by the government for the Taoiseach on the basis of his achievements" said Brian Cowen, his eventual successor.

But Bertie Ahern was not just their Taoiseach.

He was our Taoiseach too.

And that's the tragedy.

He lied. I heard him.

We all saw it.

Our Taoiseach dishonoured the office with his tribunal performance. And by deliberately averting their gaze, so too did his colleagues and his party.

So spare us your indignation, Micheál Martin.

Button your disgust, Fianna Fáil.

We don't want to hear it now.

March 23rd, 2012

Queen honours those who died in the fight for Irish freedom

This was the moment many thought they would never see.

The Queen of England, standing in the Garden of Remembrance, head bowed in a mark of respect for the men and women who fought and died for Irish freedom.

Here, in this revered shrine to republicanism, the strains of God Save the Queen swelled in the quiet of a Dublin afternoon, played with the full blessing of the President of Ireland and the political establishment.

These electrifying minutes signalled the end of a long and very difficult journey, when two neighbouring heads of state finally stood together as equals in a display of friendship and reconciliation.

There was a communal catch in the throat when Queen Elizabeth and President Mary McAleese laid wreaths beneath Oisín Kelly's evocative sculpture of The Children of Lir. Then a spine-tingling minute's silence, before buglers played the last post and the Tricolour fluttered to full mast.

Suddenly, as the band broke into a proud rendition of Amhrán na bhFiann, even the cynics confessed to being a little moist of eye.

For it was an extraordinary day.

A day when the power of music and memory and mythology fused and sparked and swept us up in its dignified embrace.

This was a different class of pomp, for a whole set of very complex reasons.

May 17th, 2011. One hundred years on from the last time a British monarch visited our capital city and an age in terms of political history.

Back then, King George V came to Dublin to visit his subjects across the water. Queen Elizabeth II was invited to come.

Not so long ago, such a trip would have been unimaginable, but yesterday, the Republic of Ireland hung out her brightest colours for the Queen of England – a guest of the nation.

The green carpet was rolled out in style, with an Irish welcome on the mat for Her Majesty.

Her jet – flying the royal standard – touched down at Baldonnel just before noon. Tánaiste Éamon Gilmore greeted the distinguished guest as officials from both sides of the Irish Sea munched on their indigestion pills and crossed their fingers.

The Queen scored top marks for her choice of outfit. Her wearing of the green was met with a chorus of approval.

At Áras an Uachtaráin, President Mary McAleese, resplendent in magenta, waited to receive her royal guest. The Union Jack flew above the entrance gates alongside the Tricolour, the EU flag and the presidential colours.

The Queen's armour-plated Range Rover sped through the deserted city streets to the Áras. Her Majesty, escorted by the President, signed the visitor's book in front of the Bossi fireplace, which was decorated with a spray of red roses, white lisianthus and blue hydrangea.

She removed one black glove and made confidently for the middle of the page, writing "Elizabeth R" with a flourish and underlining it for good measure.

She gestured to her husband, who fished a pen from his top pocket and wrote "Philip" underneath.

Afterwards, Her Majesty and Her Excellency repaired to the courtyard, where the Army paid its compliments to "Banríon Eilís a Dó". Then the monarch, as her great-great grandmother Victoria did before her, planted an "upright Irish oak" in the garden. We're not sure if this was a reference to the species or sobriety of the tree.

Taoiseach Enda Kenny and the luncheon guests pootled across the gravel to join the VIP party.

Enda got stuck into conversation with one of the ladies-in-waiting – Diana, Lady Farnham.

British foreign secretary William Hague was in flying form as he chatted to Éamon Gilmore.

The Queen was all smiles.

The two women and their consorts returned inside for lunch, dining on smoked chicken and boxty, followed by a nice piece of roast turbot.

It was a lovely morning, perhaps best summed up by the plaster centrepiece on the ceiling of the reception room depicting "Time Rescuing Trust from the Assaults of Discord and Envy." And then, after quick changes of outfits for the President and the Queen, the scene switched to the Garden of Remembrance and that ceremony suffused with symbolism.

Heavy security kept the public away from the action, lending a sterile feel to the proceedings. This was the one discordant note of the day, and it was a pity.

People want to see the Queen and show her a céad míle fáilte.

There was some interaction at Trinity College Dublin, where she was cheered by a crowd in the quadrangle.

GK Chesterton said of the Irish that "all their wars are merry and all their songs are sad." Not yesterday. All mood music was merry.

May 18th, 2011

Sinn Fein's Gerry Adams extended his sympathy to the family of Det Garda Adrian Donohoe, killed in a raid on a Louth credit union, and for the first time, apologized for the republican killing of Det Garda Jerry McCabe in Limerick in 1996

APOLOGY GREETED BY ICY SILENCE IN CHAMBER

That's that, so.

It took nearly two decades for him to do it, but Gerry Adams has finally apologised for the shooting dead by republicans of Det Garda Jerry McCabe in Limerick in 1996.

Another box ticked on the road, going forward.

The Sinn Féin leader won't have been expecting any thanks for this unexpected declaration in the Dáil yesterday afternoon, welcome as it might be.

Which is just as well, as his words were greeted by icy silence in the chamber.

The House had been hearing expressions of sympathy on the murder last Friday in Dundalk of Det Garda Adrian Donohoe. He died in similar circumstances to Jerry McCabe: one man gunned down by criminals robbing a post office, the other by thugs raiding a credit union branch.

The Dáil benches quickly filled as deputies came to the chamber to express their solidarity in the face of this heinous crime. The depth of their revulsion was almost palpable.

The party leaders were first to speak. The Taoiseach, then the Tánaiste, then the Fianna Fáil leader, eloquent in their expressions of anger and condemnation as they echoed the thoughts of a nation sickened by the murder of a serving garda and family man.

"Today I know I speak for everybody in this country and in this House, because today our nation speaks as one," said Enda Kenny.

He pledged that everything possible will be done to hunt down the perpetrators and bring them to justice. "We cannot and will not rest until we have done so."

There was a brittle tension in the air as he spoke, a raw edge to the proceedings. Like people were holding their breath, waiting. "An attack on a member of the Garda Síochána is an attack on all of us," said Eamon Gilmore, speaking of "a man who lived for the ideals of public service and service to the community".

Micheál Martin spoke of the nation's deep shock at the news of "the cold-blooded slaying" of Det Garda Donohoe. "The State has suffered a direct attack. There is something truly harrowing about young children being robbed of their father at such a fragile age."

Many of the politicians had experienced this situation before. Some were experiencing that communal feeling of shock and sorrow for the first time as public representatives.

And yet, there was something deeper about what was taking place in the Dáil chamber. You could feel it.

It was because of the presence of Sinn Féin, and in particular, its leader Gerry Adams and, sitting behind him, the TD for Kerry South, Martin Ferris.

Down through the years, through a miasma of double-speak and refusals to condemn, Adams had refused to apologise outright for the IRA's murder of Det Garda McCabe in Adare. And when his killers were released from Castlereagh jail in 2009, a smiling Ferris was waiting at the gates to drive them away.

These things are not easily forgotten, even if the same men helped bring about the peace process and have embraced democracy.

When the other leaders recalled the murder of Jerry McCabe, accusing eyes burned across at the Sinn Féin benches.

The Leas Cheann Comhairle called next on Gerry Adams. He seemed nervous as he waited his turn to speak, studying his script; Martin Ferris seemed uncomfortable as he shifted in his seat.

The Sinn Féin leader took a drink of water and got to his feet.

You could have cut the air with a knife. Across the floor, through Fine Gael to the Labour Party and over to the Technical Group, an awkward silence prevailed.

Nobody, not even the dyed-in-the-wool hecklers, made a sound.

"I want to extend my deepest sympathies to the family, friends and colleagues of Detective Garda Adrian Donohoe," began Adams. "On my own behalf and on behalf of Sinn Féin I want to express especially our solidarity and sincerest condolences to Adrian's wife

Caroline and his children, Amy and Niall."

The closed body language of the deputies opposite said it all. Most chose not to look at him. Arms folded, jaws clenched.

The Sinn Féin deputy for Louth spoke of how Det Garda Donohoe "was a valued member of our local community" and told of how his killing had shocked the community in the Cooley area.

When he said the death of Adrian Donohoe has "also provoked memories of the killing of Garda Jerry McCabe and the wounding of Garda Ben O'Sullivan in June 1996", the chamber took a sharp intake of breath.

"I want to apologise to Mrs McCabe and the McCabe family, and to Garda Ben O'Sullivan and to the families of other members of the State forces who were killed by republicans in the course of the conflict. I am very sorry for the pain and loss inflicted on those families. No words of mine can remove that hurt. Dreadful deeds cannot be undone."

Deputy Adams finished with an appeal to people who might have any information to come forward to the Garda or the PSNI.

He said his thoughts and prayers are now with the Donohoe family.

And that was it.

There wasn't a word from anyone, including the grave-faced Sinn Féin TDs. He sat down. The sullen, cold silence remained.

Afterwards, Government deputies shrugged and wondered why a man who insists he was never a member of the IRA would apologise on behalf of comrades he never had. And others wondered what "conflict" had been taking place in the quiet Limerick town of Adare when Jerry McCabe was callously gunned down.

Then they shook their heads and said the apology had to be welcomed.

It's the only way. They know it. But you could see it stuck in the craw nonetheless.

January 30th, 2013

Deputies get a little out of hand on day of Historic Handshake

On a slow news day in Leinster House, Gerry Adams drew quite a crowd to the plinth for his official reaction to the Historic Handshake.

Perhaps he was going to award marks out of 10.

Technical merit? 8.5 (excellent grasp). Artistic impression? 9.5 (genuine warmth conveyed). Overall score? Full marks. ("A real gesture beyond the rhetoric" – Adams).

This marked a great improvement on Sinn Féin's personal best last year when the party refused to meet the queen of England in Dublin and organised a protest against her visit.

While Gerry very much welcomed the development up North, he felt it couldn't be compared with what happened last year in the Republic.

"The visit here was different to today's visit, not least because what happened here – and it was a good thing – was a normalisation of relationships between this State and the British monarchy. In the North it's a different matter entirely; the island is still partitioned. What we were doing was trying to reach across partition..."

Gerry understood the subtleties, if few around him on the plinth did. Last year, as part of the "normalisation" process, Sinn Féin chose to reach across the partition of crash barriers and riot police and loudly boo.

He rejected a charge that these very different reactions to the British monarch's presence smacked of hypocrisy.

"We have moved to a different plane," Gerry explained.

At this point some commentators thought he was referring to his party's ongoing difficulties with the Oireachtas expenses regime and was indicating a move to budget airlines for members travelling abroad to fundraisers.

Yet while the huge significance of the handshake between

Martin McGuinness and Queen Elizabeth was not lost on people in Leinster House yesterday, it wasn't a major talking point. The economy, Europe and the banks took precedence.

Events in the other jurisdiction merited just one mention, and that was only so Enda Kenny could deliver a vicious one-liner to a flat-footed Adams.

On the eve of the Brussels summit, he heaped scorn on the what he saw as the Taoiseach's lack of negotiating ability, and accused him of supporting a federal Europe.

After a lengthy reply from Enda, Gerry dropped his guard and declared the Taoiseach was engaging in "extreme revisionism". Howls of derision greeted that unintentional clanger.

"You'd know all about that!" snorted Minister Reilly. "Never in the IRA!" roared Minister Howlin.

Still on the subject of revisionism, Labour's Alex White asked, "Are YOU shaking the queen's hand?"

Which reminded Fine Gael's Patrick O'Donovan of the man who danced with a girl who danced with the Prince of Wales.

"Shake the hand that shook the hand..," he carolled across the Chamber.

Gerry was not amused.

Then Enda struck.

You mentioned the phrase "extreme revisionism", he began. "Well, this is a day of particular significance in the country and, for you, extreme revisionism is something that you could be open about now, because while we differ here on all of these political issues, there is one thing that I have in common with you..."

Gerry sat forward. "Only one?" he smirked. "Only one?"

And Enda continued: "And that is, in the context of extreme revisionism, neither you nor I were ever members of the IRA or the IRA army council."

The chamber erupted.

Jerry Buttimer burst into applause. Pat Rabbitte, he of the polished quips, looked across at the Taoiseach, mightily impressed. Perhaps even jealous.

There was no coming back from that for Gerry. All he could manage was a wan smile.

For all the goodwill breaking out in Belfast, there was precious little of it in the Dáil.

The same Deputy Buttimer, clearly still smarting from last week's redrawing of the constituencies, could hardly listen to his Cork South Central colleague during Leaders' Questions.

As Micheál Martin attempted to embarrass the Taoiseach over the previous day's shambolic press conference to launch the Personal Insolvency Bill, Buttimer repeatedly drowned him out.

"Don't be getting shirty about it," cried Micheál, as his constituency rival led the hecklers' chorus.

"You're only a con artist," roared Jerry. "You should be ashamed of yourself. You're a fraud!"

He made a terrible racket. Mary Mitchell O'Connor, a primary school principal, was transported back to her days before the general election. She put up her hands and covered her ears. "Stop it. Stop it, please," she mouthed, to no avail, as the Buttimer contagion spread.

So she turned around and had a few quiet words with her colleague. He shut up sharpish.

In Belfast's Lyric Theatre one may have felt the hand of history on one's glove. In Leinster House Buttimer was lucky he didn't feel the hand of Mary Mitchell O'Connor on his throat. That's the dividend of normalisation.

June 28th, 2012

The Magdalene women accepted a long-awaited apology with grace and dignity

'I, AS TAOISEACH, ON BEHALF OF THE STATE, THE GOVERNMENT AND OUR CITIZENS, DEEPLY REGRET AND APOLOGISE UNRESERVEDLY TO ALL THOSE WOMEN FOR THE HURT THAT WAS DONE TO THEM'

The Dáil was charged with strong emotion as Kenny made his apology.

It was dark when the Magdalene women left Leinster House. They joined hands and formed a line across the width of the granite plinth.

"Come into the light!" shouted the photographers.

And these elderly women began to walk, and as they walked towards that light they quickened their pace and some began to cheer. All smiling – but through tears, for some.

"See ya, ladies. Night, night. Safe home now," shouted a friendly young policeman.

This was the night the women of the Magdalene laundries thought they would never see, and a night that those who were present in the Dáil chamber will never forget.

It was an evening when our Taoiseach and national parliament did the right and decent thing by the wronged Magdalene women.

It was a powerful, compelling speech from the Taoiseach. It was riveting. And with it, he answered those people who questioned his sincerity and motives after that first, wishy-washy response to the McAleese report.

But it wasn't Enda Kenny who stole the show, rather it was the response of the women in the wake of his address.

Who would blame them if they were to show a hint of bitterness or anger? Of if they had shrugged their shoulders at a gesture which has come years too late? Yet they didn't.

They wanted that apology and that vindication and validation. When it came, they were the epitome of grace and dignity. "I thought it was wonderful. God bless him. Now I'm a proud woman today. God bless the Taoiseach," said Marina Gambold, echoing the gratitude expressed by her companions-in-arms for what Enda Kenny had done for them.

They arrived at Leinster House in the late afternoon, wondering what would happen.

A few arrived early. A handful of grey-haired women with careworn faces, they settled in the gallery to watch Leaders' Questions. On both sides of them sat groups of secondary schoolgirls, spruce in their uniforms, with their laughing faces and lovely teeth.

We wondered if they felt sad, looking at the girls, for the youthful fun they never had. But, as their reaction to the speech would later show, the Magdalene women aren't like that.

Seats were reserved in the gallery for the women. Soon, it was standing room only. Alan Shatter called up to talk to them before the debate began. A babble of female voices filled the Dáil. Then, on the stroke of half past six, the Taoiseach led in his Cabinet. He took his seat in total silence.

Joan Burton waved up to some of the women. Clare Daly, opposite, did the same.

Enda stood. He thanked Martin McAleese for his report and all those who assisted in its compilation. Then he quickly got down to business.

"The Government was adamant that these ageing and elderly women would get the compassion and the recognition for which they have fought for so long, deserved so deeply, and had, until now, been so abjectly denied. The reality is that for 90 years, Ireland subjected these women and their experience to a profound and studied indifference."

In the gallery, some of the women held hands. Some were crying. You could almost see the weight lifting from their shoulders. It was so quiet, we could hear the clock ticking.

At times, the Taoiseach's voice thickened and it seemed like he might falter.

He spoke of the Magdalene women having to bury and carry in

their hearts the dark secrets of "a cruel, pitiless Ireland" for all their lives. Innocents forced to carry an unjust stigma foisted on them by a pious and prim society.

The Taoiseach's voice was steady and clear: "From this moment on, you need carry it no more. Because today . . . we take it back." There were gasps in the gallery. Deputies blinked and welled up. Outside the round railing, Senator Marie Maloney wept. Clare Daly wrapped her arms tightly across her chest, her eyes brimming. Billy Kelleher fought back the tears.

In the public gallery, they didn't hold back. The Taoiseach listed some of the things that happened to these dignified older women when they were young girls – some told to him by them when they met last week.

It was a long, heart-wrenching list. Things like "I felt all alone, nobody wanted me . . . We had to sew at night, even when we were sick . . . I heard a radio sometimes in the distance . . . I broke a cup once and had to wear it hanging around my neck for three days. I felt always tired, always wet, always humiliated . . . I never saw my mam again – she died while I was in there . . ." Tissues were passed around. Noses blown, spectacles pushed up and eyes rubbed.

Fifteen minutes into the speech came the apology. The air crackled with emotion.

"I, as Taoiseach, on behalf of the State, the Government and our citizens, deeply regret and apologise unreservedly to all those women for the hurt that was done to them, and for any stigma they suffered, as a result of the time they spent in a Magdalene Laundry."

Enda hadn't let them down.

Hands were clapped across open mouths. Hankies appeared again. There were hugs and smiles, lots of smiles.

Arrangements would be put in place for compensation and a permanent memorial will be erected. Finally, the Taoiseach remembered one of his meetings with the Magdalenes. One woman sang him a song at the end of it – Whispering Hope – and quoted a line which stayed with him. "When the dark midnight is over, watch for the breaking of day." Enda paused. "Let me hope that this day and this debate . . ." and he stopped, fighting back the tears. "Excuse me" he murmured. He took a gulp of air and went on " . . . heralds . . ." and he cleared his throat and paused again "a new dawn for all those who feared that the dark midnight might never end." And it was over. Enda sat down, pale and drawn.

The women started to applaud. Louder and louder, some with their hands in the air. They stood and clapped the Taoiseach and they embraced and then they applauded themselves. It was such a happy, heartbreaking scene. And then the deputies began to applaud, rising too to their feet.

Even the Ceann Comhairle knew there are times when rules just have to be broken. He stood and applauded too. Ushers were in tears. Civil servants in tears. Journalists in tears.

Later the Taoiseach went into the gallery to met the women before they left, tired but walking taller, happy. A huge burden lifted.

There are times when the Dáil makes you want to bang your head off the wall in frustration. And there are times when our parliament can make us proud. Last night was one of those times. And Enda Kenny can feel proud too.

He made it a special night to remember for his, and our, special guests.

February 20th, 2014

Better to light a scented candle than curse the darkness of Leinster House

They lit candles in the abortion capital of Ireland and stood in silent protest. But it was a small gathering in London.

Dublin was different.

Saturday's "March for Savita" was a solemn occasion – tinged with sorrow at the death of a young woman and suffused with anger at the failure of successive Irish governments to legislate on abortion.

It's been 20 years since the Supreme Court handed down judgment in the X case, but politicians have dodged their responsibility to act on it.

And it's 30 years since a poisonous referendum campaign (on both sides) ended with a constitutional ban on abortion.

What has changed over those years? Nothing much.

The arguments grind on, the marchers march, the legislators ignore and the furtive trips by Irish women to English clinics continue.

But the candles are classier.

On Saturday, when winter darkness fell and the temperature dropped, an unmistakable scent of summer hung in the air around the Dáil.

Pleasing pockets of fragrance punctuated the long lines of people moving slowly towards Leinster House, hints of lavender and vanilla and rose wafting up from flickering candles cupped in cold hands.

That's women for ya, as a certain former taoiseach might say.

But this wasn't only a women's march, even if the floral nature of many flames added a feminine note to the candlelight vigil.

The crowd mustered in late afternoon. The turnout looked poor, made up of what seasoned protest observers might call "the usual suspects".

Some took the opportunity to hand out flyers for this weekend's austerity protest.

But after the appointed hour, people suddenly converged on Cavendish Row in great numbers, with homemade placards and candles, children and buggies and dogs in tow.

For older people preparing to march, there was a weary familiarity about this event – been there, done that, admired the slogans decades ago . . .

"Am I going to have to do this again when I'm 50?" was the question on one young woman's placard; "20 years later and we're still protesting" proclaimed another, held by a girl wearing a hat with furry ears on it and surrounded by her furry-hatted friends. They were barely out of their teens.

The march moved off in driving rain, the crowd swelling all the time.

Vickey Curtis from Dublin 7 was with 15 friends, all wearing headbands displaying a large letter X.

"I thought of Savita and what happened to her, and I thought about the X case. If it was any of us, we'd just be deemed another X too. We want to show unity and want to call for change."

A man in a bobble hat walked along, holding up a piece of cardboard. It read: "My mother is a woman." There was a quietness about onlookers along the route. Perhaps it was the sight of the large coloured banners. Made by NCAD students, they featured a stylised image of Savita Halappanavar's face.

Chris Murray waved a painted paper lantern on a stick. "My children, Jack and Ruby, made this on St Martin's Day last weekend – it's a German festival. I'm meeting them on Kildare Street and you'll see us all holding up our lanterns."

"Never again! Never again!" chanted the marchers.

Trinity College students Alison Connolly (Dublin), Tara Roche (Galway) and Clare Kealey (Dublin) were part of a 30-strong group.

"Woman Up and Legislate!" demanded Alison's placard. Tara carried a scented candle in a glass. "And I've brought my mom," said Clare.

The mom, Bernie, held a candle (pomegranate fragrance) in a little ceramic bowl. "My daughter Anna is in America and would love to be here. She sent me this candle and asked me to carry it for her today," she said. Kathleen Lynch, from UCD and "a proud Clare woman", marched with her daughter Nora (24), along with Kathleen's golden labradors, Poppy and Bonnie.

The light faded significantly by the time we got to Grafton Street and the candles came into their own.

When the head of the protest reached the gates of Leinster House, people were still rounding College Green. There were speeches from the back of a truck and the crowd cheered when a turnout of up to 20,000 was announced.

Gráinne Griffin (24) from the Choice Network ran out of candles. "I had about 500 in the bag and I thought I'd be ages giving them away. But they went in no time," she said.

"I'm here because I'm furious. I'm just so angry." It was dark and circles of white lights now framed the images of Savita on the banners.

Gráinne pointed towards them. "People haven't been listened to for 20 years and this is what it's led to." In her impassioned address, ULA deputy Clare Daly castigated Taoiseach Enda Kenny for saying he would not be rushed into a decision. "He sat in the Dáil for over 30 years while 150,000 Irish women were exported out of here. . . to maintain the hypocrisy that there are no Irish abortions."

When speakers made political points, it was abundantly clear that the crowd wasn't interested. Attempts to start a "Shame on Labour" chant went nowhere.

A minute's silence was observed in memory of Savita. The only sound was the rasping of flints as candles were lit.

The crowd dispersed and the flames were extinguished. A bright light glowed above the main entrance to Leinster House.

But the building was in darkness and the doors were closed. And it remains to be seen whether all those touchingly optimistic girls in their furry-eared hats will still be marching when they are 50 – assisting the cynical 80-year-olds to light their candles so they don't set fire to themselves in frustration.

November 19th, 2012

ELECTIONS

Showtime is more like a showdown as Bertie is Browned off

Standing amidst the wreckage of a disastrous first week, Bertie Ahern prepared to face the most difficult challenge of his leadership career.

Shell-shocked troops to the left of him. A hostile media to the right. His once-strutting officers arrayed on either side – like they were about to be shot at dawn.

The mood in the Mansion House was as upbeat as a dentist's waiting room. Party advisers, battalions of them, tip-toeing around the margins. The room was dark – it suited the tense, subdued atmosphere. Security men patrolled the aisles.

Happy days? Emphatically not.

When Fianna Fáil launched its manifesto in 2002, the happy spirit was summed up in one word by PJ Mara: "Showtime!" Yesterday felt more like a showdown.

As Bertie read his script, Cabinet colleagues looked glum. Nobody noticed when he came to the end.

"I'll now take questions, ladies and gentlemen," said the Taoiseach. It was only then that the huge number of supporters in the Round Room realised he had finished, and clapped.

In the meantime, PJ Mara had shimmered from the shadows and materialised before a microphone at the edge of the stage.

From the off, this was not an easy experience for Bertie. Questions over the party's U-turn on the stamp duty issue were raised. Recent comments by a party backbencher that Fianna Fáil was getting "hammered on the doorsteps" were brought up.

The Taoiseach handled them well. The supporters, outnumbering journalists at what was supposed to be a press launch, perked up.

It didn't last. A reporter questioned his credibility before the electorate in the light of the unanswered questions about his personal finances.

Ministers sank down further in their seats, while the supporters, seated in the main down one half of the room, glared over, shaking their heads at the impertinence.

Clearly uncomfortable, in apologetic tones, the Taoiseach admitted that in Fianna Fáil, "in the past, there were individuals" who might not have operated to the highest ethical standards.

The shade of Charles Haughey loomed large, while his former adviser PJ Mara stood by.

In this highly charged atmosphere, Bertie battled on. "I don't think there's any problems hanging over my head," he declared. "I have to deal with these issues as we go forward, and I will." Another question on stamp duty. It wasn't just his personal finances that were under attack.

Minister for Finance Brian Cowen, who had categorically stated there would be no big announcements from Fianna Fáil, remained expressionless as the Taoiseach tried to extricate his party from this policy promise.

"Can the minister tell us what it tastes like to eat his own words?" asked RTÉ's Bryan Dobson.

He got no answer.

This was damaging for Fianna Fáil. In normal circumstances, the stamp duty U-turn would be hugely embarrassing, but this wasn't normal circumstances. On the scale of calamities, it wasn't the worst.

It was a case of: ask all you want about stamp duty, just don't ask about the "stamp duty issue" that Bertie claimed swallowed up some of the £30,000stg in cash he got in relation to a rented house.

But the money quickly resurfaced. Why should voters wait until after an election to hear an explanation about his personal finances? Had any of his ministers asked him to clarify the situation? Said Ministers were looking like stunned mullets. Even Dick Roche's smirk vanished.

Then Vincent Browne got the microphone. What followed was an absolutely astonishing exchange between the journalist and the Taoiseach. It lasted 12 riveting minutes, punctuated by heckles and applause from the Fianna Fáil claque and a few ineffective bleats from PJ Mara as Browne got stuck in.

Why didn't he tell Bryan Dobson in that clear-the-air interview last year that Michael Wall called to his office in 1994 and gave him a briefcase containing £30,000stg in cash, three days before he expected to become Taoiseach? At the time, Mr Wall was renting a house to Bertie Ahern and his then partner Celia Larkin.

"That money was not money for me. It was money for his affairs, in his house. I hope that answers the questions." A party officer went to take the microphone, but Vincent had no intention of relinquishing it.

"No, it doesn't," replied Vincent. And he took it from there. Bertie repeated that this was Mr Wall's money. "It isn't credible," asserted Vincent, explaining why.

"It was Mr Wall's money administered by Celia Larkin," insisted the Taoiseach. Nothing at all to do with him.

Or as Bill Clinton might have put it: "I did not have financial relations with that woman." Bertie stood his ground. He thrust an arm out to silence the supporters when they started to heckle. Vincent went from the suitcase of cash to the Taoiseach's own money – that £50,000 he managed to save in a 12-month period when he says he was so strapped he had to rely on handouts from friends.

Last November, with stated reluctance, he tearfully said he had to think of his children's education.

Why had he put a portion of that figure into a house he didn't even own, that was only a few years old? "It ain't credible," repeated Browne.

But the Taoiseach stuck to his story. His fighting spirit went down well with the supporters. Brian Cowen shushed them. That money was his own money, bristled Bertie. He was entitled to spend it any way he liked.

When PJ tried to intervene, he was reminded how Charles Haughey had sought to silence the media when his finances were under question.

Finally, as journalists heaved their jaws off the floor, the duel ended. A measure of the disaster that was this manifesto launch was the look of relief on Fianna Fáil faces when talk turned to the nurses' strike.

Whatever the outcome of this election, this public interrogation of a Taoiseach over his financial affairs at his own party's manifesto launch will be seen as one of the defining moments of Irish politics.

Amazing stuff.

Bertie hits the country today to repair the damage. He has enough time to do it, if the country is of a mind to listen.

May 4th, 2007

Enda's pedometer signals distance FG has travelled

Diffidence and demoralisation signalled the undoing of Fine Gael in 2002.

Memories of that horrendous campaign still haunt the party. From the outset, all but the most blinkered of Blueshirts shared a sense of impending doom.

Defeat came as no surprise: it was the catastrophic scale of the collapse that was so devastating.

Watching Enda Kenny as he tore through country towns yesterday like a man possessed, it was hard not to conclude he is overcompensating for the abject failure of his predecessor to make any connection with the electorate the last time out.

It's as if he is fighting two elections — trying to atone for past failures, while striving to convince voters that he has what it takes to lead Fine Gael back to that distant land they once called government.

The faster he runs, the more distance he puts between his party and the embarrassment of the last election. The faster he runs, the quicker people will forget. The faster he runs, the less chance there will be for awkward questions.

And if he runs fast enough, he might even outpace Bertie.

Enda is wearing a pedometer on his waistband. If reporters ask he'll pull aside his jacket and let them marvel at the reading.

"Three thousand, eight hundred and forty nine?" repeats Enda. "It's going up! Fine Gael is going up!" In terms of putting a figurehead out front and pushing the man and his personality above all else, Fine Gael is fighting a presidential-style campaign. But there is nothing presidential in the shameless manner of Enda's pitch.

As his highly successful rival Bertie knows, dignity and reserve go out the window once you hit the hustings. When you can stride through the ladies' lingerie department and accost a woman with a bra in her hand; when you can gaze lovingly into the glassy eye of a turbot while the fishmonger beams beside you; when you can wrench a squalling infant from her pram and not get arrested, then you have what it takes.

It may be toe-curlingly embarrassing to disinterested observers, but it has to be done.

Enda is doing it, and his footsoldiers have fallen in behind him with an enthusiasm they can't quite believe themselves.

How is it playing with the public? The media cynics bussed around in his wake will stand back and sneer. Enda knows that. So does Bertie Ahern. But column inches in the nationals can't compare with those happy pictures in the local press of the day the election roadshow blew into town.

While the Taoiseach did his bit in Stormont, striding into the history books in front of the world's cameras, Enda was in Portlaoise delivering an old-style oration to his troops. As they cheered and fought over FG baseball caps, their leader told them to get out and fight for votes.

"G'wan Inda" they roared, bunching up in front of him, fizzing with excitement. "Make it look good for RTÉ," urged a man in a cap, "push up there for God's sake!" Local workers were anxious to point out their campaign trophy. "There's Tom Mulhall, the man who used to put up the big PD posters for Tom Parlon. He returned to us about three weeks ago." Enda's zeal for pressing the flesh borders on the manic. He runs into shops and banks, he accosts people taking money out of ATMs, he is incapable of passing a butcher's shop or a chemist.

The fixation with these last two establishments is puzzling. But then the answer comes to you: it's all to do with women. Enda is very good with the women. If they have children in tow, that's a bonus, and he pulls them in to get their photos taken and reminds them to put on a big smile for the camera.

He grabs mammy's hand, puts an arm around her shoulders and looks into her eyes. They blush and simper: "Hello, Inda!" And they'll remember the moment he connected, and tell their friends.

He's gone in seconds, already reaching for the next hand to grip or the next arm to pummel.

There's a slightly hysterical air to it all. "All right, all right, all right, all right," he repeats, clapping his hands together, racing out one door and spinning on his heels to go in another.

He's been to Tullamore, Portlaoise, Birr and now he's at the social services centre in Ballinasloe. A large elderly group are waiting, waving flags, already in high spirits thanks to the band. In no time at all, Enda is waltzing a lady around the room.

Local deputy Paul Connaughton is beside himself with delight, dancing on his own like a man demented, tongue lolling out. He doesn't have his leader's sense of rhythm, but he doesn't care. Only one leg seems to be in tune with the music, so he goes around in circles.

In Athenry, Enda climbs up on a dumper truck. "Like Boris Yeltsin on the tank," he exclaims, as party supporters fall around the place. Enda's one-liners are chronic, but they crack up his people every time.

He is always aware of the cameras. If one is held up, and he isn't holding a voter, he points to some non-existent face in the distance and smiles. He broke into song twice yesterday.

He left by helicopter, the last few hours of the night spent canvassing in Leixlip and Lucan in Dublin. He is successfully erasing the memory of 2002. When he meets people now, they automatically call him Enda.

"The people of Ireland are sick and tired of listening to the ins and outs of Bertie's house," he said yesterday. He's sticking to the bread and butter issues, and hoping for jam at the end of it all.
May 9th, 2007

The Battle of the Ranelagh Lampost was one of the more surreal episodes of the 2007 election campaign

McDOWELL'S INTENDED RETURN TO POLE POSITION ENDS IN SHAMBLES

Like a myopic mongrel recognising the scent of his favourite lavatory, Michael McDowell panted blissfully down Ranelagh Avenue towards the fourth telegraph pole on the left.

God, but the Tánaiste looked pleased with himself. Wreathed in smiles, he saw the microphones and the cameras and the reporters, and couldn't have been happier.

This telegraph pole was kind to him during the 2002 election, when he climbed it one Saturday afternoon near the end of the campaign and attached his famous "Single Party Government? No Thanks" poster. Not soon after, the PDs returned to the Dáil with double the amount of seats.

The received wisdom has it that McDowell's publicity grabbing stunt was the turning point in that election, depriving Fianna Fáil of their overall majority. One grinning man and his billboard changed the course of Irish political history, apparently.

Sometimes, you might fall to wondering if the nation really is that impressionable. But who are we to argue with our betters, the people who claim to understand these things? Michael McDowell certainly believes his own publicity, and that is all that matters.

And so yesterday at lunchtime, when journalists got a text message saying the PD leader intended to resume pole position within the next 90 minutes, they abandoned their grub and hot-footed it to Ranelagh.

This would be history in the making. At least that's what one PD handler said, proof that they've lost their marbles.

Of course, the whole thing was ridiculous. Televison camera crews, photographers and over 20 journalists from the daily and Sunday newspapers gathered in a cul-de-sac near the Tánaiste's constituency office.

Please don't write in. I know. We're worse for taking the bait.

The pole was still there. Outside a very nice house. Two children peeked out the downstairs window at the commotion. Sensibly, their parents kept them indoors: there was a lot of ribald talk outside about the wisdom of those PDs getting themselves up the pole again.

John Gormley, chairman of the Greens and the Tánaiste's constituency rival, ambled down the narrow street.

He had been dining in the Dáil canteen, when a throng of belching journalists rushed past his table. Through their last mouthfuls of lunch, they told him Michael McDowell was planning a spectacular at the Ranelagh triangle. A poster would be involved. He followed them out.

Oblivious of the pandemonium about to happen, a delighted Michael, with deputy leader Liz O'Donnell and Senator Tom Morrissey flanking him, rounded the corner and made for the telegraph pole. The billboard of history was about to be unveiled. The lovely Liz would do the honours this time.

"At least I have trousers on today," twittered deputy O'Donnell. Quite. "Oh, thank God," wheezed a jaded political correspondent.

With the Tánaiste gallantly holding the ladder, Liz and her high heels clacked gingerly up the first few rungs. Then she pulled a string and her party's "Don't Throw It All Away" poster fell to the ground, discarded in favour of the new one beneath.

The PD supporters cheered in an effort to imbue the occasion with a bit of drama. Slack-jawed journalists, realising that dog-lover McDowell had sold them a pup, stared at the uninspiring message.

"Left Wing Government? No Thanks." That rules out any continuing partnership with Fianna Fáil, given that Bertie is a socialist.

Everyone gathered around the Minister for Justice, parked contentedly at the base of his favourite telegraph pole and preparing to relieve himself of his magnificent script.

Deputy Gormley lurked.

Michael launched into his speech. It wasn't long before he got to the Greens. John started to roar. "It's a lie. It's a lie. It's an absolute lie." The Tánaiste looked over. "Is that Michael Foot or John Gormley?" he asked. "It's John Gormley," came the strangulated reply.

His blood was up and he would stand for no more "nonsense" from Michael McDowell. "Calm down, John. Calm down," urged the Minister.

Talk about a red rag to a compassionately reared organic bull. The media parted generously to, push, er, allow John to the front. He launched an unmerciful verbal onslaught at Michael. There was no calming the Green Party chairman, who demanded that the Tánaiste retract inaccurate claims made in a PD pamphlet about the Greens' taxation policy. "Michael, I'm sick and tired of this. Smear, negativity. That's all you do." PD supporters began to heckle. "We're sick of you! Bye Bye." The photographers were fighting over the ladder.

"You're losing it!" said Michael, gripping his script. "No, you're losing it!" said John, brandishing his pamphlet.

The Tánaiste asked to be allowed finish his speech. John assented, but reserved his right to interrupt.

"Your party is behaving like headless chickens." "Relax John. Relax"

"I AM RELAXED!"

Liz O'Donnell was highly amused. "It's like street theatre," she murmured.

Michael tried to plough on. A photographer emerged from a nearby house with a kitchen chair and stood on it. McDowell: "You're out of the picture, John." Gormley: "No, We're in the picture, we are very much in the picture." Then he got carried away and declared the next government would comprise "the Green Party, the Labour Party and Fine Gael." It was like a good night out at the Abbey for Liz. "That's a scary thought, scary, scary, given your performance today, John." Deputy Gormley's phone rang. "They're just ringing to say 'don't make a fool of yourself John'," sniggered the Tánaiste.

"You're the guy that's made a fool of himself in the last two weeks. You've gone completely gaga."

At this point, Cllr Lucinda Creighton of Fine Gael – a third candidate – raced into Ranelagh Avenue with a group of supporters and another ladder. Michael's spectacular was in a shambles by now.

Lucinda made for the telegraph pole opposite and shot up the ladder with a poster of her own, featuring half of the Tánaiste's face. "Don't want single party government? Well, thanks to him, it's a reality." She was jubilantly breathless. The journalists deserted Michael. A man at the corner asked what all the fuss was about. We told him about Michael McDowell's lamp post."Huh. If I was a dog, I wouldn't piss on it." Just as well. The Minister got there before him.

May 17th, 2007

After a shaky start Fianna Fail emerged victorius in the 2007 general election but its junior partner, the Progressive Democrats, were not so fortunate

BERTIE TUGS HEARTSTRINGS AND PURSE STRINGS

Love and money – an irresistible combination.

The heart and the head. It delivered this election for Fianna Fáil.

Bertie Ahern strengthened his hold on the nation's affections yesterday, sealing his place in the history books and cementing his reputation as a remarkable political phenomenon.

He's up there with Dev now.

Short of the nirvana of an overall majority, he's done it all.

Throughout the white-knuckle ride of an often bruising campaign, the Taoiseach held his nerve. The voters, he gambled, always come through.

And in the end, they rallied to him – the bloke they've always liked, who was there when they got the second car and plasma TV and who they now hope will steer them through the economic turbulence ahead.

Above all, when it came to making a critical choice between the man they know and newcomer Enda Kenny, the voters were unambiguous: it's still Bertie.

Fine Gael had a great election. Fianna Fáil's was better. The dream return with Enda died. As one observer put it: "Fianna Fáil and Fine Gael are like Bing Crosby and Frank Sinatra. Bing is a lovely man, but you can't help liking Frank more."

In the main Dublin count centre at the RDS yesterday, even the Soldiers of Destiny seemed shell-shocked by the extent of their leader's popularity. As the results came in from around the country, they grew in confidence.

If they were too excited for lunch, and their Opposition too despondent to eat, the pundits were already sprinkling on the salt and pepper and preparing to dine on their hats.

"We knew this would happen all along, but you wouldn't listen," smiled the Fianna Fáilers, wagging chastising fingers at the media.

In private though, some of the beneficiaries of this spectacular Bertie bounce were heaving enormous sighs of relief. There was little of the buck-lepping and hooting that normally accompanies a sure-thing return to power. The atmosphere was strangely muted. These were Fianna Fáil people who had gone to the brink, seen a glowing white light at the end of the tunnel, and returned to live and fight another day.

By midday, the implosion of the Progressive Democrats was already apparent, while the lack of tricolour-waving Sinn Féin supporters told a similar story.

In contrast, Fine Gael support was well up. Party handlers put on a brave face, consoled with the knowledge that their party had pulled off a marvellous recovery after the devastating losses of 2002.

As the twists and turns of a gripping count reached final seat territory, Fine Gael held to the slim hope that they might still muster the numbers to fall across the line. As night fell, Labour leader Pat Rabbitte arrived at the RDS and all but conceded his party would not be needed by Fianna Fáil.

"I expect people were concerned about the fragilities of the economy," he mused philosophically. Thoughts of coalition were not uppermost.

"So where does this leave you?" he was asked. "Outside the RDS."

Then the Fianna Fáil train hit the buffers. Martin Brady, who had seemed a certainty in Dublin North East, lost out to Fine Gael first-timer Terence Flanagan. Next door, Ivor Callely's expensive love-bombing of Dublin North Central was losing out to Independent Finian McGrath's shoestring campaign. Key seats were in the balance.

A couple of hours later, and Pat Rabbitte was on RTÉ, talking about "the hand of history" and "the national interest".

As the afternoon progressed, Fianna Fáil candidates, confident of victory, began entering the RDS in managed bursts of mayhem. Stacked like aircraft in the sky, they waited outside until they got clearance to land. Pat Carey – his seat said to be in mortal danger – was the first to taxi up to the waiting cameras, followed by Seán

Haughey and Chris Andrews.

Carey's supporters were jubilant. The quiet and courteous Pat modestly thanked the voters of Dublin North West, while a campaign worker shouted from the sidelines. "Is it time for a ministry, Pat?" Junior Minister Seán Haughey was similarly modest. "I'm willing to serve," he said, realising this maybe wasn't the best time to do a repeat of last year's "make me a minister" performance.

As for Chris Andrews, a first-time deputy from a family steeped in FF tradition, all he could do was smile and hold up his children. Then he found his mother and smiled some more for the cameras.

But as the Fianna Fáil seat tally climbed, the PDs saw their chances evaporate. Party leader Michael McDowell was in dire trouble from early on. He braved the RDS and conceded defeat in a generous and dignified manner. As his campaign workers wiped away the tears, he announced he was leaving public life.

Love him or hate him, Michael McDowell is a formidable political performer, and he will be missed. His leave-taking, as one would have expected, was not without incident.

Unfortunately, he was not allowed his moment without heckling from a number of men, who also held up hastily written signs celebrating his demise. "Bye-Bye Michael 'Paris' McDowell", read one. "Michael McDole", read another.

A PD supporter asked them to take down the signs. "Show the man some respect," he said, as the media crush around the former Tánaiste reached hysterical proportions. The supporter then tried to pull down one sign.

A slight scuffle took place. "No need to assault him. This is a democracy," bellowed a political opponent. "You're not in the special branch now." Then he joined in a gleeful chorus of "cheerio, cheerio, cheerio". The jeers came mainly from People Before Profit activists, with a smattering of Sinn Féin supporters among them. The electorate, rejecting Sinn Féin, chose a more gracious method to wave cheerio.

Apart from this unsavoury incident, Sinn Féin's performance was a world away from the intimidating, triumphal performance of five years ago, when they swaggered into the RDS behind Gerry Adams, holding tricolours in the air in a show of smug superiority.

Yesterday, Mr Adams still got the frantic media treatment. A female supporter had to be dragged from the throng, shouting she was going to faint if she wasn't given some air.

Both Adams and Mary Lou McDonald, who failed to get a seat in Dublin North, said the election had come down in the end to "who the people wanted as Taoiseach". In the war between Enda Kenny and Bertie Ahern, they argued, Sinn Féin ended up as collateral damage.

"Tiocfaidh Fianna Fáil" shouted a Soldier of Destiny, coming to terms with the extent of his party's success.

Bertie Ahern, meanwhile, was at home, watching the results unfold on television with his mobile phone turned off. Such was the extent of his vote, pulling in nearly two quotas, his favoured running mate, Cyprian Brady remained in the race despite polling a derisory 939 votes.

"Bertie Ahern could have Lassie as a running mate and it wouldn't matter," snorted a disgruntled opponent, disgusted that somebody who provoked such resounding indifference might end up in the Dáil.

Dublin Central may still be in love with their electoral phenomenon, Bertie, but first-timer Cyprian turned out to be no infant phenomenon.

As midnight approached, there was still no sign of the Taoiseach at the count centre. Some said he was in one of his locals, Beaumont House, having a pint.

May 26th, 2007

Hard to keep up the Nancy Reagan gaze when a rugby hero undresses

Whatever about the election, Labour is winning the battle of the backdrops.

Last week, the party set out its election stall in the impressive setting of the Guinness Gravity Bar – its commanding views over Dublin city provided a stunning setting for the publicity shots.

Yesterday, they went one better for their manifesto launch.

The location, high up in the Aviva Stadium, provided an equally inspiring venue, but it came with an unexpected sporting bonus that had Labour's spin doctors ecstatic.

As Eamon Gilmore, Joan Burton and Brendan Howlin stood in front of a glass wall, the hallowed Lansdowne turf beckoned thrillingly below.

But it got better. The Ireland rugby team – they play France tomorrow – was training on the pitch.

Where to look? "Today, we are publishing our manifesto for the direction Labour wants our country to take," said Eamon. "Ireland is a great country, and I believe, with every fibre of my being, that our best days are yet to come." Brian O'Driscoll was removing his tracksuit bottoms. Donncha O'Callaghan was doing warm-up exercises.

Joan's attention appeared to be wandering from her leader. Instead of fixing him with the requisite Nancy Reagan gaze, she kept sneaking glances out the window. "This is the time," quivered Eamon. Up went Jamie Heaslip in the line-out.

The rugby people got very concerned before the launch began. An official was dispatched to the third level to have a word with photographers and camera crews. The IRFU had no problem with them filming shots of the players, but requested they show none of the moves being tried out for the big match.

And then there was Hervé Amoric, France 24's man in Dublin.

He was seen talking on his phone "in urgent French" while the lads were doing their thing. Hervé was only discussing the general election, but the patriotic Labour boys fretted.

You can never be too careful.

Brendan Howlin addressed the issue of tax. Joan looked a bit distracted. Advisers kept finding excuses to potter in the vicinity of the glass. Eamon took over. "There is a big black hole in the figures published by Fine Gael." Was that Peter Stringer nipping across in the far corner? He's back in the squad. Plug that black hole, O'Connell, er, Noonan.

Joan Burton joined the line-out. She was amused at something she heard Brian Lenihan say on radio. "He referred to himself as one of the 'magnificent seven'," said Labour's finance spokeswoman, explaining that Lenihan had been referring to the remaining cabinet ministers. That got a laugh.

There were balls flying everywhere. "Will you take that one, Brendan?" "That's one for you, Joan." "I'll take that one."

Labour insists its policy on the bank bailout is not to walk away from the EU-IMF agreement. "We are not talking default. We are talking renegotiation," stressed Gilmore, adding that since they suggested taking this course, other parties "have entered the renegotiation space". The lads converged, chasing a garryowen. Hervé got in with a question about the game, exuding Gallic confidence.

"I have absolutely no doubt at all that Ireland will win very convincingly. . . as you know, we have a song called Ireland's Call and on February 25th, this day two weeks, it literally will be Ireland's call. And I hope that on that day Ireland will call for Labour," declared Gilmore, delighted to have been asked and going for the three points.

Then everyone piled out to the stand for a photograph. "I've never been here before in my life – this is my first and only time," harrumphed Emmet Stagg, indicating a solid working-class aversion to rugby. Just as well he isn't standing in Limerick.

The signs on the Havelock Square end exhorted "Bring Back the Roar!" But Gilmore has left his roaring behind in the Dáil chamber. For the election, he is trying to ditch the Mr Angry image. But had they listened carefully enough, they might have heard faint strains of Enda Kenny, who, at that very moment, was below in Wexford and bellowing for Ireland on his soap box.

The Happy Gilmore vibe continued after lunch, when Eamon followed in the footsteps of Enda and went to Paddy Power's betting office to place the traditional charity bet in aid of Guide Dogs Ireland. He arrived with more handlers than the two dogs there to meet him. The photographers formed a ruck.

"You see, I knew we could get a three-way debate," smirked the Labour leader, with a golden Labrador on one side and a Labrador/German shepherd puppy on the other.

Which one is Enda? "The quiet one." Eamon was on his knees. Frisky Micheál gave him a slap, following up swiftly with a head butt. Enda picked a spot on the wall and stared at it, saying nothing. (Micheál was a hefty pup called Hector and Enda was eight-month-old Chenna.) There was a big difference between Kenny's performance at the same gig last week and Gilmore's approach yesterday. Enda hammed it up for the cameras, dancing with a goldendoodle, cradling a big puppy in his arms and pretending to place a bet with another.

Not so with Eamon, who knelt beside the dogs, looking slightly embarrassed. Hector, all gangly legs and puppy fat, was scooped up by his proud owner in preparation for the handover. But Eamon stayed on his knees until Hector nearly fell on top of him.

"He is not going to pick up a dog," said a senior adviser.

In fairness to deputy Gilmore, he was wearing a new navy suit and red tie and it'll have to do him for at least the next four years (like the last one).

The photographers begged as Chenna/Enda sat in a huff and Hector/Micheál belted him with his oversized paws and rolled around the carpet.

Finally, Micheál got bored and went off to eat a betting slip. What's the point? He'll be in opposition anyway. Eamon stood and tried to get Enda's attention by force feeding him a biscuit.

He'll have to do a bit more of that in the coming weeks. The rift between Fine Gael and Labour is turning sulphurous.

The Greens' manifesto launch around the corner was much less fraught. They showed a DVD of a man patting trees in a forest and a woman talking about how she got her house insulated.

"We believe that a Green voice in the Irish parliament is essential to hold others to account," said party leader John Gormley. "Dáil Éireann is a failed political entity." They sound bruised after their experience in coalition. Eamon Ryan said they "spent 3½ years fighting the system" and now "have to pick ourselves up, dust ourselves down and fight an election". They did everything they could when in government with Fianna Fáil, said Gormley. "It was a baptism of fire and brimstone." Lie down with dogs . . .
February 12th, 2011

A rejuvenated Enda Kenny impressed voters on the campaign trail in the 2011 general election

NOBODY IS IMMUNE FROM THE BONHOMIE OF THUMPER KENNY

Brace yourselves! Inda's getting huggy. In a major policy statement yesterday, the Fine Gael leader announced he will be "putting the arm of politics about people who are disillusioned".

(Obviously, Kenny hopes the arm of politics is attached to the hand of history. And the fingers of fate.)

This was no idle threat. The declaration sent a chill through journalists covering his press conference. Should they write a straightforward report on his plan to hold referendums on political reform after one year in power, or should they issue an immediate alert to innocent voters about the danger lurking in their midst?

Because Enda, you see, is a bit too enthusiastic when it comes to putting his arms about. When the handlers told him it was possible for Fine Gael to come home with a thumping majority, they didn't mean him to take it literally.

On Saturday, we watched as he punched, prodded and walloped his way through the shopping centres of north and west Dublin.

Nobody is immune from the bonhomie of the Thumper Kenny.

After his party's good showing in the latest opinion poll, Enda is in buoyant mood – which can only mean one thing: danger here!

"We had a brief chat, and as we parted, I got three wallops on the back. I nearly coughed up a lung," a female political correspondent said. "Enda just punched me in the chest," reported a male counterpart. "It hurt."

You have been warned.

Cheesy sound bites and hearty wallops aside, following Enda over the weekend was an intriguing exercise. The campaign has a long way to go – not least, tonight's five-way debate on RTÉ and the eagerly awaited three-way tussle in the final week. Even so, there was something a bit different about Enda this time.

There was something different too, in the way the public reacted to him. Yesterday morning, he was more relaxed and assured than we've ever seen him.

He was asked, for example, about his relationship with Gerry Adams. "I don't get on with him that well, actually," came the startlingly forthright reply.

After the briefing, Kenny went for a photocall in front of the Four Courts. He had to cross two busy roads from the Clarence Hotel. There were lots of beeps of recognition from smiling motorists and only a couple of hostile reactions.

It almost mirrored the reception he received in six busy shopping centres around Dublin on Saturday.

We really didn't expect that.

Why? Because in our experience, mention of Enda has always provoked a reaction ranging from derisory to downright dismissive.

It was straight into the belly of the beast with a visit to Artane Castle Shopping Centre in Dublin North Central – the happy hunting ground of Charlie Haughey and Bertie Ahern. A teacher from Clontarf cornered Enda in the frozen food aisle and grilled him over his plans to abolish compulsory Irish. He was in front of a big display reading "battered cod".

Yvonne O'Toole conversed with him in Irish for nearly 10 minutes. "I just thought that battle had to be fought," she said afterwards. "I didn't give in to him, but he has lovely Irish."

A mother told him about her son with a master's in international relations who can't get a job. "Is he on the dole?" asked a solicitous Enda.

"No, he's in Sweden."

On to the Omni Park centre in Santry. Enda went to his favourite canvassing spot – a café. He whacked a man on the back to announce his presence, moving swiftly on as the man removed his fork to check if he still had any teeth. He sat beside a couple having their breakfast and cooed at their baby. Then he left them, bewildered, in his wake.

What did he say? "The beans and the rashers," replied the Dad. "He just said 'the beans and the rashers'." But there was a gorgeous, photogenic little tot that Enda couldn't pass. Four-year-old Christian Bodie was with mother Karen and Suzanne Treacy, who is chairwoman of Heart Children Ireland.

As the man most likely to be taoiseach held Christian in his arms, Suzanne and Karen asked him to give a commitment that the new children's hospital will be built. They don't care where, they just want a facility. Christian has a heart condition and has had two operations already.

"It will be built," said Enda. Within the hour, an e-mail lands from Fianna Fáil's Barry Andrews. "Kenny's hospital promise is deeply cynical," is the heading. In this election, Fianna Fáil is monitoring, rather than campaigning.

Kathleen Friel, who runs a small business, BDF Commercials in Lusk, buttonholes Enda. She is angry. She tells him her back is to the wall and she is fighting to keep her employees. They engage. And talk. And talk. And Enda rolls out his five-point plan again.

What did she think? "To be honest with you, I've changed my opinion. He has impressed me on the one to one. He hasn't impressed me on television. I would have always voted Fianna Fáil, but they've done nothing for me. I'm like a tiger in the long grass, waiting for one of them to knock on my door."

On to Blanchardstown. Enda is in deep conversation with taxi drivers at the rank. He is sympathetic. Leo Varadkar stands to one side as a driver harangues him. He isn't sympathetic.

Enda beetles off, probably satisfied with a job well done. He doesn't hear the man shouting "Did you hear what he said, Leo Varadkar? He said we need part-timers at the weekend, he said . . ."

A hairdresser comes out of Peter Mark. "I've a massive mortgage and bills coming out of my ears." Enda outlines a number of measures which may help her. It's a long conversation. "That's good" says Carolann Cantwell. "I'll have a think about it."

She heads back. "He's good. He changed my mind slightly. I liked Bertie though." Have you not got a client waiting inside? "Ah no, she's grand. She's getting shampooed."

Leo seems relieved when the canvass is over. "I find them very difficult. I think I'll go home and read a book."

Senator Frances Fitzgerald and Derek Keating wait at Liffey Valley. These two could end up killing each other before the election is out. By the end of their sweep through the centre, there were fears the pair of them would have to be surgically removed from Enda's shoulder.

A woman puts her daughter's case. "She has the oldest windows that's in Dublin. They're a health hazard." Enda takes control. "Emer, will you take this woman's number?"

There is a long engagement with a woman who has lost her job. She argues with Kenny. What the hell would he know about being unemployed? He perseveres. Eventually, they seem to reach a sort of truce.

"I have to say, he was more approachable than I would have thought from seeing him on the TV. He's more personable than I thought. That he stayed, instead of walking away, meant something." It happened again and again. No rows. No insults. No abuse. Not even for the sake of balance – can't say otherwise.

February 14th, 2011

ENDA TAKES A CALCULATED GAMBLE ON NIKITA AND THE GOLDENDOODLES

"Let's get Ireland working!" exhorted the leader of Fine Gael before sloping off to the bookies, where they were expecting him.

Tell that to the women in Paddy Power's.

"Which one of you will be taking Enda Kenny's bet," we asked the two cashiers behind the counter.

They shrugged their shoulders. It turned out neither would be dealing with the man most likely to be Taoiseach.

"We're being replaced by a dog."

Sure enough, when the time came for Enda to place his charity wager, a shaggy dog by the name of Clive popped up behind the bulletproof glass and plonked his substantial paws on the counter in a businesslike fashion.

Enda didn't bat an eyelid. That's what years of dealing with the Fine Gael front bench does to a person.

He presented his completed dockets to Clive – thus immediately marking himself out as a potential customer of Guide Dogs for the Blind, who stand to benefit to the tune of €5,000 as a result of yesterday's joint publicity wheeze for Enda and the bookmaker.

Calm despite extreme provocation, a stoical Clive gazed dolefully at his owner through the partition and refused to recognise the scary man who kept hitting him on the snout with betting slips.

Clive is a goldendoodle – which makes him a cross between a Labrador retriever and a standard poodle.

He is a working dog and he has his dignity.

Enda is a strawberryblue – which makes him a cross between a strawberry blonde and a Blueshirt.

He is a working politician. He is fighting a general election. There is no such thing as dignity.

Eamon Gilmore posed with a dead halibut in Cork last week, studying it in smiling wonderment as if it had just told him the third secret of Fatima.

As we are seeing, all sense of decorum and reality goes out the window when it comes to politicians and general election photo opportunities. It's a very crowded market out there and a leader will do what a leader has to do to get noticed.

Also in that photo was Gilmore's colleague Ciarán Lynch, outgoing deputy for Cork South Central. Other local representatives didn't make the frame. Afterwards, one of them complained about being cut out of the picture and wondered why this happened.

The experienced Lynch gave him some invaluable advice. It is advice that all aspiring deputies would do well to remember when they hit the trail.

"Stay close to the fish," counselled Ciarán. "Always stay close to the fish."

This is exactly what Enda did yesterday, except Clive was his halibut, ably assisted by Nikita the Labrador puppy and three young goldendoodles.

The Paddy Power charity bet has become something of a general election tradition. Bertie Ahern would pitch up in the Merc and plunge inside, causing mayhem as he shamelessly hammed it up with the ever-so-photogenic doggies. During the last election, a photographer was injured in the melee when the Bert brandished a stunned baby retriever in front of startled punters.

This time, with no taoiseach to speak of, it was interesting to see that Enda Kenny was the one in the limelight this time around.

"Other politicians will be coming here as well," said a spokesman for the bookie. "But in fairness to Fine Gael, they were first out of the traps."

Kenny arrived late, having given journalists all the time they needed to ask questions at his morning briefing. This followed a very fractious press conference the morning before, when some of our more thrusting journalistic stags decided it was time to lock antlers with Fine Gael and put a bit of manners on them for ending the session far too quickly.

Yesterday morning, the party leader put in his best performance yet when launching his jobs-development strategy.

With Richard Bruton on one side of him and Leo Varadkar on the other, Inda sounded authoritative and assured. It was a good morning for him. You could see his team of handlers relax as the press conference progressed.

With Enda, so much has been written about his propensity to combust under media pressure that one began to wonder if it was becoming a self-fulfilling prophecy for him. Self-belief is all for people who aspire to lead. Could we discern the doubts creeping in? The team surrounding Enda Kenny look perpetually haunted. They will worry for the rest of this campaign. But yesterday, despite the best efforts of those of us employed to look for weaknesses, the Fine Gael leader did extremely well.

He knocked everyone for six when he delivered an understandable explanation of "cloud computing". The question had been asked to catch him out.

He got a round of applause from the media and weak-kneed handlers for his ability to learn and his aplomb.

The other two, Richard and Leo, also did a lot of talking. "If I say so myself, this really is a good document," said Leo.

Which brings us back to the bookies.

Enda pulled up in a big black Merc. (Just in case anybody thinks he isn't serious about this taoiseach thing.) As soon as he got in the door, he was handed Nikita. She wore a little jacket. It said: "Pup in Training". You could see Enda was very taken by the jacket. Maybe he could get one made up for Leo? The man who may be taoiseach clutched the shell-shocked pup and simpered for all he was worth.

"She'll give you a kiss if you turn into her." She didn't.

"If you give her a bit of a blow, she'll kiss you on the face." Cripes. She didn't.

Enda didn't care. He knelt on the floor, knee joints cracking, Nikita in his arms.

Lovely. His handlers wept for joy.

Then Clive was produced. Curly golden hair. Mature. Clive wouldn't kiss him either.

"Can he show his teeth?" asked Enda, pawing at poor Clive's handsome muzzle. He wouldn't. Admirable reserve.

So Clive was persuaded to get up on his hind legs and put his paws on Enda's shoulders and the two of them waltzed around the floor of the bookies.

Clive, by the way, is not a guide dog. He is a valued companion to an autistic boy and is known as an "assistance dog". He knows his business, as a grateful Enda can attest.

A grizzled punter watched from the sidelines as they danced. "That Eamon Gilmore's let himself go."

February 4th, 2011

WHAT DO WE WANT? MORE GUARDS – SHINNERS' UNLIKELY NEW RALLYING CALL

And first, the fallout from that Leaders' Debate.

We looked out our window at midnight to find Micheál Martin barely clinging to the lamppost outside – completely buckled – and Eamon Gilmore lying face down in next door's garden.

Enda Kenny was trying to hold Micheál up, but as the Fine Gael leader was half cut and listing alarmingly, he wasn't making a very good job of it.

By early morning, the pair of them had slithered to the ground. This is the stress of politics.

But the poster boys were back in action soon enough: Micheál and Enda out West and Eamon only an hour from Dublin in Navan.

Marvellous stamina on display under such dreadful pressure.

The voters of Sligo, Mayo and Meath are to be commended.

Back in Dublin, Sinn Féin launched its proposals for "community safety and tackling crime".

The Irish Times was hoping Gerry Adams might be there. He's a Lord. This reporter is a Lord. Sure we're practically family now. Alas, he wasn't.

But Gerry is in town today, though, for the launch of the Sinn Féin manifesto. It's happening this morning in Cassidy's Hotel. Fianna Fáil Senator Donie is neutral when it comes to renting rooms for party political purposes in his fine establishment.

Sinn Féin's combating crime launch was held at an interesting venue – the Department of Justice.

A British journalist tootled along to St Stephen's Green for the event, through the door (revolving, of course) and up to the reception desk.

"I'm looking for the Sinn Féin policy launch. I understand it's in here," said the visiting correspondent, not unreasonably.

"Oh, no it's not," replied the man from the Department of

Justice, with a thin smile. "I think they may be outside."

Sure enough, there was Aengus Ó Snodaigh and fellow Sinn Féin candidates moving into position on the bottom two steps of the Department of Justice, over to one side so they wouldn't block the entrance.

Cllr Dessie Ellis, who served a lengthy prison sentence in the 1980s for possession of explosives, was initially down to attend, but was delisted in a subsequent notification.

A solitary garda stood on duty, a few steps above them, near the door. She paid little heed to the Shinners. Times have changed since those occasions when SF only came to the Department of Justice to have a protest. You could hardly move, for all the policemen.

Back then, who would have thought the day would come when they would gather there and call for more gardaí on the streets – the same gardaí who spent years chasing their republican forebears/ associates around the same streets?

In order to combat the problem of crime and antisocial behaviour affecting many communities, the party's justice spokesman Ó Snodaigh proposed an increase in the number of gardaí and community gardaí on the ground "while also focusing on building better relationships between the community and the Garda".

We wondered whether his words outside the Department of Justice yesterday were in keeping with his actions last November outside Government Buildings, when he was among a group of Sinn Féin protesters who forced their way through the gates, causing gardaí to draw their batons.

They can be clearly seen in television footage, pushing the automatic gates open.

His photograph was on a lot of front pages, in the thick of things.

"I've a right to protest but, if you look at the footage, I was trying, in fact, to help the gardaí," explained the outgoing deputy for Dublin South Central. "If the garda had've calmed himself down we would not have had those pictures."

But was Ó Snodaigh not in the vanguard of the people who pushed through the gates?

"They were open."

He added he was trying to make sure people didn't go through and this was borne out by video footage.

Helen McCormack, who is running for Sinn Féin in Dublin North East, said the gardaí had used "unnecessary due force" in restraining what was "a peaceful protest" when "20 or so people walked through".

There was no law against them doing this.

Also present was veteran republican Larry O'Toole, who is a candidate in Dublin North East. The hardworking Larry is a popular figure around the constituency and this will be his fifth attempt to win a seat in Dáil Éireann.

"I think we'll make the breakthrough this time," he tells us. He might well be right, this time.

February 10th, 2011

Angry electorate coldly voted to liquidate Fianna Fáil

Finally, the tall grass parted. By God, but this was no rush job. It was a long time coming.

When the verdict came, it was crushing. Moreover, it was thoroughly considered.

For this is the new politics; history, tradition, old allegiances and overweening presumption hold no sway anymore.

The Irish people looked back in anger this weekend and then they coldly voted to liquidate the party that plunged their country into liquidation.

After decades of Fianna Fáil dominance, they turned and taught Fianna Fáil a devastating lesson: You call yourselves a national movement? Now, let us show you the real meaning of a national movement . . .

And with that, they emerged from the long grass and gutted the Soldiers of Destiny. Extraordinary.

Unthinkable, once.

The general election of 2011 will be remembered as the one which shattered another of the three great pillars of old Ireland. It was always a proud boast of the faithful multitude that they belonged to the Untouchable Trinity of the Catholic Church, Fianna Fáil and the Gaelic Athletic Association.

No more. Only the GAA remains, standing proud and rightly cherished.

FF big beast after big beast falling, as the ticker-tape pulsing across the bottom of television screens announced the end of political dynasties and shell-shocked household names watched stronghold constituencies desert them. It made for compulsive viewing.

The winners were almost overlooked as the compelling story of Fianna Fáil's momentous meltdown unfolded.

But not in Co Mayo, where Enda Kenny led from the front, bringing home an unprecedented three running mates.

Fine Gael fought a brilliant election. Kenny, the underestimated man from Mayo, is now taoiseach-designate. He stepped into his new role on Saturday night with a refreshing humility and a pledge to restore public trust in the debased currency of Irish politics.

You could see how much he wanted the job. His energy and passion undeniable; his determination to make a difference an encouraging contrast to the jaded nature of what went before.

Given the level of public expectation surrounding him and the scale of the task facing his new government, it's hard to know whether to feel happy or sorry for the man.

The Labour Party put in its best electoral performance ever, exceeding the seats won in the Spring Tide of the early 1990s. When Eamon Gilmore ties the knot with Kenny – don't expect a long engagement – their union will produce a government of well over 100 TDs.

Labour's campaign was a rollercoaster ride, from the high expectations of the "Gilmore for Taoiseach" days to a worrying slide in the opinion polls and a final-week rally that pulled them back to respectable territory.

Sinn Féin's Gerry Adams romped home in Louth as his party returned a record number of TDs and post-election Tricolours. They will be a major Opposition force, within touching distance of Fianna Fáil. How the two parties will rub along together on the very much depleted Opposition side of the Dáil will be a fascinating feature of the 31st Dáil. Drawing up the seating arrangements should be an entertainment in itself.

The Green Party won't figure in those plans, as none of their TDs made it back.

Adding their considerable bulk to the fascinatingly diverse make-up of the Opposition will be a large assortment of Independent deputies from the right, the left and the whatever you're having yourself wing of Irish politics. The stuffy and prissy powers that be in Leinster House must be having palpitations over the imminent arrival of the flamboyant likes of Luke Ming Flanagan and Mick Wallace.

Whatever else happens in the coming months or years, it won't be boring in Dáil Éireann.

If it won't be easy for Kenny and his incoming administration, heaven only knows what it will be like for Micheál Martin and his traumatised little band of Fianna Fáil survivors. No women in their ranks, the much vaunted Ógra generation almost wiped out, the party in a shambles at local level.

Dara Calleary, the only outgoing junior minister to retain a seat, began the fightback on Saturday night in Mayo.

"This is our darkest hour, but we will rebuild and I will roll up my sleeves and work for our party." Fianna Fáil will regroup, but things will never be the same.

The shape of Irish politics is changed forever. And it was the people, no longer passive in the tall grass, who did it.

February 28th, 2011

SINN FÉIN'S CAPITAL COUP LEAVES PARTIES REELING

Sinn Féin showed this weekend there is more than one way to stage a "spectacular". Not even halfway through the count and party leaders were already admiring their handiwork.

"That landscape is changed, and changed utterly," marvelled Gerry Adams.

"Something profound has happened," declared Mary Lou.

Gerry tried to hug us. It's the new dispensation.

On a national level, the party didn't do as well as might have been expected. But that's a minor inconvenience when set against an absolutely stunning performance in Dublin.

Sinn Féin (screamingly mainstream now but trying desperately to hide in the closet) had the other establishment parties reeling. Fine Gael and Fianna Fáil supporters were shocked.

These would be the ones you see at counts: wheezingly amiable men in well-pressed smart-casual attire and expensively handbagged women dressed for gossip and a cocktail party. "They topped the poll in Dundrum, for God's sake!"

Seasoned party hands passed around the latest results; each fresh communication bringing further bad news. Dun Laoghaire had fallen. Clontarf, Howth and Malahide too. And it was touch and go in Rathmines and Rathgar.

They wandered shakily around the count centres like a contingent of Bishop Brennans after Father Ted kicked them in the arse.

Something dreadful had happened. It really shouldn't have come as a surprise to them, but it did. The middle classes were turning to Sinn Féin. Dear God, it was as if Gerry Kelly and Martin McGuinness crept into the golf club during Captain's Prize and defecated on the carpet in the members' bar.

Their obvious discomfiture only deepened the delight for the simmering Shinners.

As a group, they weren't the biggest success of these elections; that honour went to the Independents and, in particular, Ming Flanagan.

There is no truth in the rumour that the Ceann Comhairle was witnessed doing cartwheels down Dún Laoghaire Pier when word came from Castlebar that his Dáil tormentor is headed for Brussels.

Eamon Ryan, leader of the Greens, was chuffed to find himself in the mix for the final seat in Dublin. His party all but disappeared from the political scene after the last election. Now, they're sprouting again.

Party colleagues were triumphing in the locals while former junior minister, Paul GoGo Gogarty, running as an Independent, took a seat in Lucan.

Ordinarily, the Greens aren't the type to take pleasure in the misfortune of others, but they made an exception. When they were ingénues swimming in a Fianna Fáil government, Labour gave them a terrible time. So as Gilmore's crew were getting kicked up and down the country by the electorate, there was no sympathy.

Eamon was at the count in City West to watch as the ballot papers were sorted. "I love the collegiality of the tally," he said. He seemed pleasantly surprised and gratified by his good showing.

Fianna Fáil's revival around the country was good news for Micheál Martin, but it was eclipsed by the Sinn Féin onslaught in Dublin. Mary Hanafin and Kate Feeney both emerged with seats following their highly publicised selection shambles in Blackrock. A tearful Hanafin got in on the first count, with Feeney following at a later stage.

Seán Haughey (hardly a new face) did the business in Clontarf. He fought an interesting campaign. We'd love to tell you more about it but, as he adopted a Greta Garbo strategy and refused media requests to accompany him on canvasses, we can't.

The lord mayors of Dublin and Cork got the heave-ho: both members of the Labour party. The claims by Independent Senator Rónán Mullen that the "Dublin media" have it in for him were sadly compounded by the realisation that voters in Midlands/North West don't need the Dublin media to tell them what way to vote. They gave him the boot all of their own accord.

Labour struggled to find any silver lining in its black cloud. Joan Burton sent out mixed messages about the state of her tiresomely fluctuating confidence in the party leader while Pat Rabbitte talked about "refurbishing" the programme for government.

And everyone sniffed that nobody gave them credit for all their "heavy lifting".

Joe Higgins worried about fellow socialist Ruth Coppinger winning the byelection in Dublin West. She eventually took the seat, but it was a close call as Sinn Féin romped up on the inside.

"It's the national surge," Joe explained. "You can't fight it. I had a national surge in 1992 in Ballyfermot, when Joan Burton was elected on the Spring Tide. Nobody knew who she was."

Enda Kenny was in Longford on Saturday night. He was in the worst of humour, doing himself no favours during a petulant telephone interview with Newstalk's John Keogh.

Contrast that with Gerry Adams, who strolled into the count centre with Mary Lou McDonald by his side. On Saturday, the votes weren't even half counted but Gerry and Mary Lou were in full general election mode, the events of the last few weeks merely a pit stop along the road of the Sinn Féin Project.

Things will change now, says Gerry. How? "The parlance will change to include the word 'citizen'."

And there's a freshly minted catchphrase too; Sinn Féin is "rooted, relevant, republican". Ah yes, Gerry and his disciplined, community activists/candidates are on a roll.

The Government parties say this Sinn Féin coup in the capital is a good thing. They will have to take tough decisions at council level now. They dismiss the results as a mid-term wake-up call from the people. When a general election comes, they will shy away from the Sinn Féin brand. Mary Lou was talking conditions for going into coalition yesterday.

Swathes of the electorate crossed a boundary with their punishment voting. The sky didn't fall in.

They know they can do it now. Sinn Féin know that too. The project is on course.

May 26th, 2014

135

PRESIDENTS AND
PRETENDERS

No brass bands as McAleese makes last official engagement at homeless hostel

And now, the time had come and so she faced that final velvet curtain. For Mary McAleese, there was just one more plaque to unveil, one last cord to draw. After 14 years of splendid service as President of Ireland, she had reached her closing engagement.

Where would it be? What would it be? An opportunity to roll out the concluding canapés and champagne flutes, perhaps? Or maybe some farewell hobnobbing beneath the chandeliers for the great and the good?

But that was never Mary's style, even if she did shine on major State occasions. She made her decision months ago, when a letter arrived requesting her to formally open a refurbished block of long-term accommodation units for homeless men.

"We invited her, but she named the day," explained Larry Toumey and Tommy O'Reilly of the St Vincent de Paul. "She pointed out that this would be her last engagement and she wanted it to be here." There were no brass bands to announce the President yesterday morning, just the bells of nearby Christ Church Cathedral chiming the 11th hour as her car drew up outside the Back Lane Hostel in Dublin's Liberties.

There wasn't a big crowd either; a mere handful of locals and a group of delighted primary schoolchildren from nearby St Audoen's. Business as usual, really. Much of the President's work during her two terms of office has been done beneath the radar.

Yesterday was different. The residents, volunteers and support workers inside the Back Lane Hostel were joined by at least four camera crews, a battery of photographers and a large contingent of reporters.

This was a very happy occasion, if tinged with some inevitable sadness. But it was a nice sadness, entirely appropriate for her perfectly pitched departure.

The children cheered when four Garda motorcycle outriders zoomed into the narrow street ahead of the car with its flags flying from the bonnet. They held up a big yellow card: "Mary McAleese. We will miss you" was the multicoloured message.

"Thank you, lads," smiled the famous lady in the crimson suit and red shoes as she accepted it.

"We love you!" shouted one little boy.

McAleese and her husband Martin were taken on a private tour of the building, where she met many of the residents. The refurbishment, which cost €800,000 and was financed entirely by the SVP, provides permanent accommodation and support for 18 clients whose physical or mental health means they cannot live independently. Another part of the old building, managed by Depaul Ireland, houses a 42-bed emergency unit for homeless men.

The ceremony took place in the hostel's simple chapel. "I'm moving home today, as you know," began Her Excellency, using her own circumstances to talk about the importance of home in our lives.

She said it was through places like the Back Lane Hostel that the homeless can rediscover their sense of worth and rebuild their lives. While it is somewhere no parent imagines their child will ever be, there will always be those who, through circumstances, become "frail people" and put their faith in the hands of strangers.

The President thanked the men and women, the loving strangers, who make it their business to care for them. "They may be down, but they are certainly not out," she said of the men.

Although McAleese has been fortunate to have always lived in happy homes, she recalled her childhood in Belfast when sectarian threats rendered her family temporarily homeless.

In the audience were some of the people she stressed are "worth investing in". Men like Noel Fitzpatrick, who shyly presented her with a bouquet. And men like Frank Brady, who composed a poem for the occasion. He read in a faltering voice, drawing inspiration from sources such as Star Trek and Simon and Garfunkel. The room hushed for him and exploded in applause when he finished.

Was that a tear in Her Excellency's eye? These are the sort of events that form the framework for the day-to-day work of a president. The days when people, who often work for scant reward or recognition, are honoured by the nation's first citizen. The head of State comes to say "thank-you" on behalf of all of us. It matters.

She brought pride to the faces of the men who now live in the new en suite rooms. The President of Ireland, out of all the things she could have done, chose to visit their home on her last day in office. She came so she could wish the best of times to those who have seen the worst of times. "This place is evidence that love exists." At 20 minutes to midday, Mary McAleese pulled the cord and parted the final curtain to reveal the plaque. Outside, she gave a brief press conference.

She agreed it was a sad day for her. "If you give me two seconds, I'll be in floods of tears, but I don't want to do that in public!" she said, paying tribute to the great team she worked with in the Áras.

Any advice for Michael D? "Oh, just to enjoy it. Enjoy being president. I woke up every morning full of joy. I loved every day on the job. He's a very lucky person, as I was."

Then, the soon-to-be private citizen posed with her husband for a group photograph with the children. She lingered perhaps a little longer than usual.

Sisters Catherine Fenlon and Eileen Kimmage waited by her car to wave her off. "See ya, Mary, bye bye!" called Eileen, who lives around the corner in John Dillon Street. "Ah, she's lovely, isn't she?" said Catherine, who is from up the way in Reginald Square.

"She's a proper lady and he's a real gentleman." A neighbour walked past. "Carmel, we saw the President" they shouted.

And what about the next President? "Aaah, Michael D. We love him," said Eileen. "He deserves a chance because he's the oldest." Catherine agreed. "My fella is the same age as him. He fell down the stairs a few years ago and is still hobbling around. But he's a great man all the same."

Back in the hostel, the excitement was dying down. Frank Brady, who read the poem, said he was honoured to meet McAleese and her husband – "magnificent people". Frank is one of the residents in the new wing. He plays guitar, harmonica and piano and is also a fan of Michael D.

"I wrote to him and told him I enjoy his poetry. I didn't think he'd write back to somebody like me but didn't I get a phone call from his PA? She told me he had read my letter and wanted to express his thanks. At the time, I hadn't as much as a shilling and she told me he was going to send me a few books. The way she pronounced it, I thought she meant 'bucks'," he laughed.

"Then a parcel arrived and it had two of his books. I was absolutely delighted. I have them in my room." A day, indeed, of happy endings.

November 11, 2011

David Norris abandoned his bid for the Presidency after letters he had written seeking clemency for his former Israeli partner were published

No way back as harsh political realities hit home

Beneath the vision it is vicious. For all the fluffy sentiment of Irish presidential campaigns, the race to Áras an Uachtaráin is not for the faint-hearted.

While the candidates may waft along on perfumed clouds, the behind-the-scenes machinations are far from genteel. Others are busy getting hands dirty on their behalf. It's called politics, it isn't nice, and it can leave a nasty taste for some.

The sad exit of David Norris from the contest had a certain inevitability to it. Not just because of what came to light last week, but also because of doubts raised previously about his suitability for the office.

Past achievements, limitless self-belief and force of personality were never going to be enough for the flamboyant Senator, who, for all his years in Leinster House, underestimated the ruthless nature of the business he is in. He learned that lesson the hard way yesterday.

As he mustered all his dignity and relinquished his long-cherished dream, it was impossible not to feel huge sympathy for him. David Norris bowed out in a welter of cliché.

Some were already comparing the manner of his downfall to a Greek tragedy. He fits the bill.

Others were talking about the best president we never had. We'll never know.

Our old friend, Shadowy Forces, entered the frame.

– Taken out because he is gay.
– Taken out because he represents the liberal agenda.
– Taken out because it looked like he might win.
– Taken out because he loved too much.
Maybe some, or all of the above, apply.
But the outcome stays the same: his campaign is over. Norris

will not be the next president of Ireland. In a contest where it seems that bland is best, he was always going to be a risky bet. He referred to "the recent frenzy" as his reason for withdrawing from the election.

But did he really not see it coming? Did he think that opponents wouldn't trawl his past? The weekend release of letters he wrote to the Israeli authorities seeking clemency for his former partner – who had been convicted of the statutory rape of a minor – followed the controversy over comments he made in a 2002 magazine interview on sexual activity between older and younger men.

His campaign, no matter how he explained it, was irrevocably tainted. There was no way back for him. The support he needed from Oireachtas members to get his name on the ballot paper began to crumble. After days of silence – that didn't help either – word came through at lunchtime yesterday that Norris would be giving a press conference in North Great George's Street. A large media contingent gathered at the foot of the steps leading to his ivy-clad Georgian home.

Was he inside? There was little sign of life. The "Norris for President" stickers were still in the window, while his basement campaign office looked deserted. A single, blue, "Norris" T-shirt was folded neatly on the desk.

At 3pm, his old Jaguar car pulled up outside the house. Immediately, it was surrounded by photographers. Norris made his way through the throng, smiling but silent.

Most unlike him. His hands, palms facing backwards, hung by his side as he walked. He looked strained. The steps were closed off with red velvet rope. A microphone and lectern had been set up in readiness. Some neighbours joined the crowd, clearly upset for him.

Norris took his speech from his pocket, his silver watch chain glinting across his grey waistcoat. His hands trembled ever so slightly. In that letter he wrote 14 years ago on behalf of Ezra Nawi, "a person I loved dearly", he said that he had been "widely mentioned as a possible candidate" for the presidency of Ireland. He wasn't running for the job this year on a whim – the idea clearly was in his mind back in 1997. Norris believed he could win. Despite the initial setback over the magazine interview, he remained, by far, the most popular of the potential candidates among voters. Until the Ezra letter was published, he had the nomination within his grasp.

Now, here he was, back in his beloved North Great George's Street, across the road from The James Joyce Cultural Centre where he enjoyed many a nutty gizzard on Bloomsday, bringing the curtain down on his ambition.

It must have been a hugely difficult statement for him to make. But it was a well crafted and emotional valediction – if short on detail. Not surprisingly, it was powerfully delivered. But up close, you could see the effort it was taking. "Here I am today outside my home where all my great journeys have begun to announce the end of my presidential campaign. This has been a most wonderful experience, despite the trauma and energy expended."

Directly across from where he stood is the former home of Sir John Pentland Mahaffy. "Scholar and wit" it says on the plaque outside the door. Just like the man over the other side of the road. There wasn't a hint of bitterness in his speech, just sadness at what could have been.

Among the ranks of the media were Vincent Browne and Sam Smyth. Norris was to have stood in for broadcaster Browne on his programme last night. Instead, Smyth stepped into the breach. It was a bit strange to see the trinity together in the one place.

When he finished his statement with a spirited quote from Samuel Beckett, he turned and slowly climbed the old steps to his beautiful front door. Then he spun on his heels, smiled and swept this arm in the air, like an actor at curtain-call. He gave a little bow, waved again and disappeared through the dark green door. There was applause.

Did the house lights dim when he went inside? Maybe not, but we know somebody put the kettle on because a neighbour rushed across minutes later with a jug of milk. Just around the corner in the Gate Theatre, Noel Coward's Hay Fever is packing them in. "A hilarious comedy of deliciously bad manners," says the playbill.

Which is what David Norris used to be - with manners impeccable if mischievous.

Another reason for his undoing.

August 3rd, 2011

PAST IS ANOTHER COUNTRY
FOR ÁRAS HOPEFUL

I SAY! We nearly choked on our pink gins in the Dáil bar yesterday (or GHQ as we like to call it) when we heard that Martin McGuinness was blaming "West Brit elements" in the Dublin media for daring to ask questions about his past. Honestly. It's simply not cricket.

That David Norris guy is different. He has been known to wear a bowler hat on Bloomsday and sounds like a West Brit. He deserves to be fully interrogated about his past – which he was recently, with disastrous consequences for his presidential ambitions.

But not Mr McGuinness, who is on a career break from his day job as Northern Ireland's Deputy First Minister and seeking to be the Republic's next president.

His past is another country and it appears he wants journalists from the adjoining jurisdiction to respect this.

Like hell they will. The DFM's wish to be designated a Special Area of Protection is unlikely to be granted in the coming election. Otherwise, those who would not ordinarily pull their punches might be accused of having an agenda.

Recent presidential campaigns have been characterised by a viciousness that contrasts with the affection and respect immediately afforded the new incumbent.

Candidates must face an equal opportunity onslaught and no-holds barred background check, with the eventual survivor deemed equal to the requirements of the highest office in the land.

They know this around Leinster House, where the saga of who will eventually be on the ticket continued to be one the main talking points. Martin McGuinness's preciousness about his background raised many eyebrows, both on the political and the media front.

Although it has to be said that some of the "West Brits" brigade arrived back after the weekend in such a state of drink-related All-Ireland final exhaustion that they could barely string two words together, never mind get worked up about the DFM's remark.

All this only serves to make Enda Kenny very happy. As far as the Taoiseach is concerned, the more distractions the better.

Having finally put the lid on Fianna Fáil's presidential election fiasco, Micheál Martin began the recovery, pressing Enda on what he saw as a possible U-turn on his Government's stated policy on income tax and social welfare.

The Taoiseach – with more than a touch of the DFM – said what he wanted to say and completely avoided the question.

Sinn Féin's Mary Lou, standing in for Gerry Adams, was impressive, asking what he intended to do about the massive payoffs and pensions being paid to retiring senior public servants.

"And please don't tell us that it's Fianna Fáil's fault – you're in charge now." The Taoiseach responded by outlining what had been done for low earners, before taking a swipe at Sinn Féin's past.

The fact that won't go away, he told her, was that his party had introduced changes to the minimum wage, VAT and employers' PRSI. "That fact won't go away, no more than the facts relating to your own party won't go away in a lot of areas."

Minister for Justice Alan Shatter piled in: "How many banks were robbed on your watch?" Sinn Féin's Pádraig McLoughlin retorted: "What about Michael Collins's record?"

Joe Higgins of the Socialist Party wanted to know why the Minister for Finance reversed his pledge to burn the bondholders.

"It would be like the heroic Stephen Cluxton on Sunday who, after a brave run forward, instead of kicking his county into history, had suddenly turned and booted the ball in the faces of his team-mates and into his own goal. Except this time it's €3.5 billion of the funds of our people that should . . . be going into investment and services."

Joe, whose late brother Liam won two senior All-Ireland medals for Kerry, scored the winning point of the day.

But the real action was taking place elsewhere. At the ploughing championships, the five presidential candidate massed like hungry calves after a bucket of nuts. Around Kildare Street, David Norris (still in with a slim chance of a nomination) and Dana Rosemary Scallon (with little hope of making the ticket now that Fianna Fáil will not be involved) made last-ditch attempts to enter the game.

As for Martin McGuinness, he took the opportunity later in the day to clarify his "West Brit" media conspiracy faux pas.

"No, no, I think there is a very tiny number of people who fit into that category, but there are undoubtedly a number of people out there who are very determined to try and undermine my campaign, but I'm not going to get fixated about any of that."

It was an "off-the-cuff" remark and if he offended people in the media, "it wasn't generally meant for the media". Top-ho, so. Pink gins all round!

September 21st, 2011

SURGEON REFUSES TO BURY MICHAEL D'S CROÍ AT WOUNDED KNEE

Gaitgate struck at the top of Grafton Street.

And it had all been going so well.

With the cameras and microphones closing in, the last thing Michael D wanted was a chance encounter with a knee surgeon anxious to inspect his limp. The man could have said anything.

To make matters worse, Labour's candidate for the presidency had just torn up and down the street like a hot favourite in the Galway Plate. But now, his impressive bilingual gallop was hanging in the balance thanks to the intervention of smiling Stuart from Pennsylvania.

Would the orthopaedic surgeon bury poor Michael D's croí at Wounded Knee? His backers looked on anxiously as their runner swivelled a fearful eye at the friendly visitor, not sure whether they were about to hear the all-clear or witness the screens going up around the presidential aspirations of their political thoroughbred . . .

It's been a relatively easy course for Higgins thus far. While other candidates have been subjected to a lot of tough questioning about various aspects of their pasts, he has maintained a statesmanlike distance from the debate.

The only issue that has been raised is his physical ability to do the job, much of it centred on a leg injury he sustained last year when he slipped on wet tiles during an aid agency trip to Colombia.

So the 70-year-old has been belting on and off his battle bus with all the energy he can muster, assuring everyone that his leg is on the mend and he's more than fit for the fray. It's a process of attrition and yesterday, at an impromptu press conference outside St Stephen's Green, nobody raised the subject.

This will have come as a relief to his handlers.

Instead, he was asked about his income.

It's getting ridiculous, as candidates fall over each other to account for every ha'penny they ever earned. It can only be a matter of time before they offer full details of their communion money.

Heaven knows how Bertie Ahern would have coped had he made it to the ballot paper.

Higgins outlined how much he got from his pensions, threw in the price of his house in Galway and what he earned from his literary endeavours.

"The two poetry books have been declared for tax purposes," he said, adding with a sad sigh: "The income was minimal".

Then, with his campaign team in place, he set off on a swashbuckling hobble through the city's premier shopping thoroughfare.

There was the obligatory stop at the flower sellers. At the first one, the woman fled. "Who is it?" she asked a bystander. "It's one of those presidential feckers."

There's a high recognition factor for the Galway politician, and yesterday, it spanned all age groups.

His team propelled him into a group of giggling Trinity students, who seemed pleased to see him, posing happily for photographs. Lynn Kenny from Glenageary, Julianne O'Sullivan from Dartry and Louise Flanagan from Rathmines reckoned they might give him a vote.

So you like Michael D then? "Is that his name, Michael D?" A shiny young Labour worker ran over to them. "Do you have something short and snappy to say that we can put up on twiduur?" Lynn rose unblinkingly to the Twitter challenge. "He's a really good speaker and really friendly."

American tourists were very taken by the twinkling little man causing the commotion. "Wow! And he's a poet too?"

The spoonplayer with the old wooden dancing dolls was guaranteed a visit. Hugh Murphy from Dunleer told Michael D that music and dancing is very good for people under pressure. He plays on Grafton Street because it's "a good pastime" and the wooden dolls are an old Irish tradition that should be kept alive.

The candidate threw a few bob in his hat. "Supporting the arts," remarked a Labour supporter, a touch smugly.

If they don't watch themselves they might start becoming cocky. Minutes away from the safety of the battle bus and Stuart

Gordon materialised. He's been on holiday here with his wife and they've had a ball.

He's an orthopaedic surgeon in Pennsylvania and saw Higgins on the Late Late Show. He wanted to talk about the gammy knee.

Michael D repeated the story of his big accident south of Bogotá.

"Did you have the kneecap tied together with wire?" "With wire, yes . . . the wire is still there, yes. It can be taken out later. Yes. I'm galloping along now." Stuart said he thought he was doing very well. He told us how pleased he was to hear Michael D's story and to see "how vital he is and how brave he was when he had the knee surgery". At this point, the handlers' knees gave out. With relief.

"This is because of the wonders of modern orthopaedic surgery techniques and because he has a lot of heart," continued surgeon Gordon.

And the prognosis? "He has a bit of a limp but he seems to have a good gait and he has a nice, nice cadence to his gait." (Never mind the poetry.) In his opinion, Michael D's knee is good for at least another six years.

Stuart's wife Marianne took a photo of the candidate. "He's so cute." She's a gastrointestinal doctor. "I look into people's colons." Whereupon cute Michael D sprinted for the bus.

October 5th, 2011

With a last gasp and at the 11th hour Dublin city allows Senator to try again

In the Rotunda, the air was heavy with expectation. Much juggling of phones and anxious men pacing around the pillars.

Finally, after a gestation period more suited to an elephant, a large bearded bundle of joy bounced through the front doors.

On Tuesday night, at City Hall, to Senator Norris, a nomination.

"Celebrate democracy!" he cried, just stopping short of handing out cigars.

At long last, after nearly two years of trying and some serious knockbacks, David Norris had arrived on the ballot paper.

Call it last gasp, 11th hour, under the wire – whatever way you look at it, he had cut it fine, with nobody to blame for his frantic, faltering lurch across the line but himself.

Eight weeks ago, after yet another setback, he had given up trying, thought he had tried everything to bring about his happy event but it was just not meant to be.

He stood on the steps of his home in Dublin and declared his presidential dream was over. "Ever tried. Ever failed. No matter. Try again. Fail again. Fail better," he said then.

Now he has been given the chance to try again.

There were jubilant scenes in the imposing Rotunda of City Hall when councillors voted by an overwhelming margin to facilitate his bid for the presidency.

A long list of terms and conditions applied to their assent, but they concern the campaign proper. For the moment, after a long and fraught journey, it was enough for Norris to heave a long sigh of relief and go home to bed, still in the race.

His hopes seemed, as they say, dead in the water, until Michael D Higgins came along and gave him the kiss of life. What a thought. We'll move on. But yes, his triumphant rebirth came at the hands of Labour's Michael D, his crucial intervention at a meeting with his party's councillors (they have a large majority) resuscitated Norris.

To say the Senator was grateful would be an understatement. At a suspiciously choreographed chance meeting between the two in the Rotunda – Michael D on his way out after meeting his colleagues and high-as-a-kite David on his way to observe the imminent vote – the Senator fell upon his saviour and rival.

"You're a generous, a decent and a good man, and I thank you!" he gushed, taking the Labour man by both hands and looking into his eyes.

Michael D responded with grace. "It's about democracy, David, and I hope you have a good campaign."

There wasn't a dry eye in the house as, to the distant gnashing of teeth from the other five candidates in the caring stakes, the pair outdid each other in sincerity and magnanimity.

"You're a real democrat, Michael," emoted the Senator. "Thank you very much. I'm dee-lighted we met, I'm not sure you got the message – it should be on your machine."

"I did," smiled the man ahead in the polls.

"Good," smiled the man in pursuit.

Such graciousness.

"Give my love to Sabina and the family," said David, and with that, the saintly Michael D wafted off, his job done.

David said he was "deeply moved" by his fellow academic and former Seanad colleague's selflessness. "Michael D Higgins is a gentleman. He's a scholar. He's an old friend of mine," said the deeply moved Norris.

"You have to hand it to him, he pulled a master stroke there," sniffed a Fine Gael councillor, watching the Labour group retreat.

Mannix Flynn proposed the motion to support the Norris candidature "on behalf of the thousands and thousands" of signatures gathered in his support.

"It has been a very hard and harrowing time for this candidate," said Mannix, hoping the council would give the Senator "a warm welcome and comfort".

Not all councillors were in favour of giving the nod to Norris. They cited what they saw as his ambivalent stance on adults having sex with minors.

Fine Gael's Bill Tormey was particularly forthright in his criticism. "Senator Norris has smeared himself . . . because he doesn't believe in an age of consent."

In the public gallery, the Senator shook his head slightly, then looked straight ahead, expressionless.

As some of his colleagues flinched, Independent councillor Damien O'Farrell talked of "grooming" and "buggery" and "underage sex" and said: "I have no doubt as to where I stand on the issue."

He said Senator Norris had many questions to answer.

Overall though, the view was that councillors have no right to stand in the way of democracy. Most said they were in favour of putting Norris on the ballot sheet, but that did not necessarily convey support for him in the campaign.

Fine Gael's Gerry Breen summed it up: "We're endorsing his candidacy tonight, we're not actually voting for him."

Norris knew he had it in the bag. The indications in the chamber pointed to success. With each pledge of a vote, he seemed to relax a little bit more, the dimples growing ever deeper above the beard. With each favourable contribution, the cheers from his supporters in adjoining room could be heard in the chamber.

Finally – the vote. More cheers. Their man, at long last, had made it to the final round of judging.

Andrew Montague, the Lord Mayor of Dublin, announced the result. Thirty in favour, six against and 11 abstentions. Dublin had seen their man right.

Earlier in the day, he suffered a reverse when Cork City Council didn't deliver a nomination.

Soon afterwards, we got tongue-in-cheek text confirmation of the reason from a proud Corkonian: "Cork councillors did extensive checks into Norris's background before the vote. They were appalled by what they found and voted against when they heard he had no Cork connections whatsoever."

When the result was announced, as the roars intruded from next door, Norris stood and gave two little bows. It was just after 7.40 pm and he had made the cut with just over 16 hours to the deadline.

Talk about making heavy weather . . .

The press withdrew to the Rotunda with its statues of Grattan and O'Connell and the rest. Norris descended in the lift with

Mannix Flynn and into a frenzy of cameras and microphones and elated supporters.

He made his way to the podium, sweating in his sensible grey three-piece suit, white hankie billowing from his breast pocket.

There was no better place to make a speech kicking off a campaign. With his words echoing under the domed roof, he thanked the councillors for their kindness.

"This is the spirit of the nation!" he cried, getting somewhat carried away.

Then he invoked Daniel O'Connell. "At another time, he was reviled and yet, he came through."

Soon, with that presidential wave – the one thing about his woefully inept campaign that he seems to have perfected thus far – he exclaimed: "Celebrate democracy!" Then it was outside, in an unmerciful scrum, to a waiting car.

"Will you release the letters?" journalists shouted. At first he said he couldn't hear them, then he said the issue had been addressed, then his minders quickly shepherded him to the car.

"Well done Ireland, never mind the bloody letters," cried a supporter.

We'll see. But for now, he's on the ticket. That's good.

The rest is yet to come . . .

September 28th, 2011

TV DEBATE PUSHES THE ENVELOPE AS BATTLE FOR PRESIDENCY FINDS ITS BITE

The envelope is mightier than the sword. Just ask Seán Gallagher: a man selling a story with more holes in it than a string vest. He was caught out last night. It was riveting stuff.

This was The Frontline – in name and in bruising reality. Pat Kenny, running the war office, delivered an hour and a half of compelling television.

It's a pity they didn't have this debate at the start of the campaign. Then again, nothing concentrates the mind like imminent defeat or tantalising victory.

The battle for the presidency reached endgame last night and, for the first time, you could feel the passion and sense the fear.

Two front-runners fighting for the ultimate prize. Both petrified to put a foot wrong. One, striving to make up lost ground. The other, trying to cling on in the face of mounting, damning, evidence.

The perceived no-hopers cut loose. Playing their hearts out on the decks of their sinking ships, hoping, perhaps, to catch a place in a life-raft by hitting the right notes.

Finally, a merciful release from the touchy-feely meanderings of the Áras aspirants.

The tone for the final debate was set at the very start with a question about Seán Gallagher's connection with Fianna Fáil. He fielded it well, at first, as he has throughout the campaign. It has played well with voters, who appear to have discounted his political past.

Why? Because he was merely a grassroots member and it's unfair to demonise the decent grassroot.

None of the candidates disagreed. Then David Norris and Martin McGuinness powered in with less palatable facts from Gallagher's Fianna Fáil CV.

It ended, as these things tend to do, in envelopes, and an account of a €5,000-a-plate fundraiser for Fianna Fáil. Gallagher maintained he played a peripheral role in the event.

McGuinness produced evidence to the contrary.

"I would caution you Seán at this stage, you're in very murky waters." A chilling moment. He said he knew a man who paid over a cheque to him when Gallagher delivered photographs of the event to him.

Prove it, countered Seán.

He denied receiving a cheque.

Martin cautioned him. "I have to say, you're in deep, deep trouble."

Prove it.

Later in the evening, Pat Kenny demanded clarification. "Sinn Féin are going to produce the man who gave the five grand."

Gallagher recalibrated. "I may well have delivered the photograph, if he gave me an envelope . . ."

The audience hooted.

Norris, who did himself no harm at all last night, was asked if he had a view. "Not much, except I think the reference to the envelope is a bit unfortunate." Gallagher, under heavy bombardment – which continued for the rest of the night in relation to his much-vaunted business credentials – began taking on water. He was listing badly by the end of the night.

A game changer?

McGuinness was strong, but he too was holed badly below the waterline when condemning IRA atrocities was considered.

At lunchtime, by the way, the seven had gathered in Google's headquarters for yet another airing of issues which have precious little to do with the role of president. Newstalk were the facilitators this time.

But it was Dana who came out with the most bizarre intervention during the Newstalk debate.

Host Ivan Yates asked a question about gay marriage and same sex adoption. She took grave offence. Why does she always get these questions? Whereupon she turned – she was at the end of the row – and looked across at the other six.

"Are you all practising Catholics?" There was a stunned silence, followed by some affronted yelping.

Norris (Anglican) said he went to mass in Christ Church on Sunday and Mary Davis, clearly at a loss, murmured that her husband is a member of the Church of Ireland.

Gallagher said he was "unsure" about the issue of gay marriage and same sex adoption because "I don't know about the research".

Back to brass tacks on The Frontline. The most interest was in the two front-runners – Higgins and Gallagher.

Michael D remained resolutely presidential – he could do that, because the others did the hard slog for him. Gallagher strove to remain "above negative campaigning" but could not credibly answer the questions about his political past and business achievements.

And the others? Mitchell was feisty and sensible; Mary Davis did well, but far too late; Dana was very sweet but of no consequence; Martin McGuinness shored up his support. Norris went a long way to demonstrating why he has a unique attraction in Irish life.

At one stage the discussion got bogged down in commodes. (Emptying them in the interests of the people.) A race to the bottom? Or did one candidate manage to rise above? Friday will tell.

October 25th, 2011

FAREWELL, OLD COMRADE, AND YES, WE'LL TRY TO GIVE UP OUR AUL CYNICISM

It was only when his friends began to say goodbye that Michael D really realised his life is changed. "But where are you going?" the ninth president of Ireland said to his election agent. "What are you saying goodbye to me for?"

So many people: Kevin O'Driscoll, the agent, who has been with him, on and off, for over 30 years; his campaign driver, Kevin McCarthy; loyal team members like Mags and Tony; countless Labour party colleagues who have been a constant in his life over the years.

All bidding him farewell. Everyone could see they still want to mind him, but can't anymore.

These were special, emotional, moments, when their Michael D went from private citizen to President-elect.

Col Joe Dowling arrived at the entrance to his city centre apartment on Saturday evening and presented him with a scroll which formally confirmed his election.

A uniformed garda was already in place at the front door. His close protection team stood discretely in the background.

Michael D's life was not his own anymore.

"There was a fleeting moment on Saturday morning when you could see a shadow of panic cross his face. The reality of his achievement sank in," recalls O'Driscoll. "But then there was worry when he thought about having to share a platform with people who would be very downcast. We've been there before, we've lost elections more than once, and he was acutely aware of how they were feeling." The Army officer saluted his new commander-in-chief. In a nice twist, Col Dowling was also saluting his former university lecturer – he was a sociology student of Michael D's back in the 1970s.

It was a whirlwind day in a momentous weekend.

After a quick bite to eat, the President-elect's official driver drove him in the official car to the Mansion House, where supporters gathered for an impromptu celebration. After the exertions of the previous 48 hours, they didn't expect to see him. So when he arrived, their cheers lifted the ceiling of the Oak Room.

"Yes, there were tears, and lots of them" said director of elections Joe Costello. "He stayed for the best part of an hour and made a rousing speech. There was huge excitement."

After a good night's sleep, Michael D was out and about again yesterday. He did a radio interview at lunchtime, coining a slogan in the process which may well go down as the phrase of his presidency. He eschewed quotes from Emmanuel Kant and Friedrich Von Hayek, drawing instead from an Oscar-winning Irish cartoon.

"I think cynicism is of no value to us at all; we must all now be positive and we must also be practical. And to the people who find it difficult and are cynical, I say, just like the film said: Give up your aul sins. It's about 'Give up your aul cynicism'." That made listeners give a little cheer.

Then it was off to Eyre Square and his homecoming. "Welcome Home to Galway, Mr President" read the banner draped across the Meyrick Hotel. There were flags waved and brass bands and dancing in the rain and a huge musical hooley afterwards.

President Michael D (and he'll be known as nothing else) knew on Friday morning that his hour had come. He spent much of the day in his apartment working on the speech he would make in Dublin Castle after the official declaration. He had a long wait. It was late on Saturday afternoon before the result was announced.

In the meantime, Michael D drafted his address. His apartment is full of books and papers, but he wanted to write his main points on note cards. He couldn't find any. His family turned the place upside down, but to no avail.

In the end, the next president had a brainwave when he saw his new shirt, there, ready for the next day. He unwrapped it, removed the cardboard insert and cut it into neat rectangles. Problem solved.

Finally, it was time. Michael D and his wife Sabina arrived in the central count centre with their daughter and three sons. Labour activists were beside themselves. All the men seemed to be wearing red ties. There was an outbreak of red roses among the women.

If the President-elect had been worried about the other

contenders, he needn't have been. Mary Davis and Gay Mitchell were not in attendance – a genuine mistake on Mary's part and a conscious decision on Gay's.

It fell to the Taoiseach to do the speaking for him, something one suspects Enda wasn't too happy about. But he was pleased for Michael D. In fact, everyone was pleased for him. David Norris looked so happy people could have been forgiven for thinking he was the winner. His speech was vintage Norris – and thoroughly gracious.

Martin McGuinness was wonderfully magnanimous. So, too, was Dana. For Seán Gallagher, who came so near, his address was, perhaps, his finest hour. Still exuding positivity, his sincerity and magnanimity was touching. "I know that you will do us all proud as the ninth president of Ireland," he said to the winner. "Go well, Sir."

On the platform, Enda Kenny stood next to his nominal boss. Hugs and kisses all round.

The Fine Gael Taoiseach asked his Labour Tánaiste if he wanted to switch places and stand next to the man his party nominated.

Eamon Gilmore said he was fine where he was. Had he been any happier he would have spontaneously combusted.

Michael D's speech was passionate and eloquent, building to a crescendo as his supporters held their mobile phones aloft and recorded the occasion for posterity. He swam seamlessly between English and Irish, like an otter slipping from river bank to water.

It was stirring stuff, none the worse for having been crafted on the cardboard from the middle of his shirt. And as he spoke, we thought: winner alright.

When he embraced his former party leader, both men seemed close to tears. Gilmore's happiness and pride was plain to see. They are old friends.

"As a party, we have been very proud of Michael D all down the years. He is the life and certainly the soul of the party" said the Tánaiste, his voice thickening. "Go n-eirí leat, a Micheáleen... you are our Head of State and we are enormously proud of you."

There wasn't a dry eye among the Labourites.

"I'll have to let him go now. My Michael D. I don't want to," quivered a misty-eyed woman from party headquarters.

When returning officer Ríona Ní Fhlanghaile announced the

final figure, the crowd whooped and applauded. He had smashed the million-vote barrier.

There were kisses, then some more from his wife Sabina, elegant in a Frank Usher outfit. "I'm so happy" said Sabina, beaming at the side of the man who called her "my comrade in life". There won't be a dull moment with them in the Áras.

Yesterday, during his RTÉ radio interview, he was asked what his father, who died many years ago, might think about him becoming president. Michael has written movingly of him in his poetry.

They had little money; his father suffered from poor health. He didn't answer the question. "It's still too painful for him," explained a close friend.

But it's the future that beckons now. "Give up yer aul cynicism" was his rallying call. Some day, perhaps, we will. Go n-éirí an bóthar leat, Michael D.

Uachtarán na hÉireann.

October 31st, 2011

IF YOU'RE A PRESIDENT, COME INTO THE PARLOUR

It's a long way from Clare to here, he must have thought, as he walked along the Francini corridor towards the State reception room.

A life's journey for Michael D.

President-elect Higgins looked a little overwhelmed when he arrived at Áras an Uachtaráin yesterday to view the place he will call home for the next seven years.

It is always a slightly awkward occasion when the new owners come around to survey their house before the sitting tenants have moved out.

Michael D and his wife Sabina waited at the edge of the corridor for their hosts to appear. A small group of photographers and reporters watched them from behind a velvet rope.

Nobody said a word.

The atmosphere was hushed and a tad tense.

Then a door opened and the woman of the house came bustling from a side room with a cheery, "Good morning to you all!"

She wore an elegant crimson suit, but nobody would have been surprised had Mary McAleese emerged wiping floury hands on a floral apron. We imagined a Victoria sponge cooling on a wire rack in readiness for the visitors.

Everyone relaxed.

If you're an Irish President, come into the parlour. There's a welcome there for you . . .

President Mary McAleese and her husband Martin, who move out of the old mansion next Thursday after 14 years in residence, welcomed the Higgins family with open arms.

"Thank you. We so appreciate this," said the president-elect, as the President incumbent gestured to the rest of the Higgins clan to come in.

"Fáilte isteach," cried Mary, clucking them into place for the official photo.

But Her Excellency – old hand that she is – was ever mindful of the occasion. While she effortlessly put the incoming first family at their ease, the one thing she might have been expected to say, but didn't, was: "Don't stand on ceremony."

Because ceremony is what they are all about in the Áras.

So Mary and Martin marshalled Michael D and Sabina and their four adult children for posterity, chatting away as if the cameras and notebooks weren't there.

Then, to our left, a serious-looking man in a dark suit who had been watching from the sidelines, nodded towards the presidential party. On his signal, Mary and Martin turned to leave and the Higgins family followed their cue.

Still, not a peep from the media, some of whom had no compunction about roaring the most awful impertinences at presidential candidates a couple of weeks earlier.

We know the drill in the Áras.

But Michael D, bless, was clearly nonplussed. He had already shot a few quizzical glances at the mute press paragons when standing in strained silence on the corridor.

With the rest well on their way to the Council of State Room, he hung back for a moment, turned and attempted to say something to the hacks.

You could see he was mad to talk.

But all he managed to say was "Good morning!" accompanied by a happy wave.

One emboldened soul called out to him. How was he feeling?

"Great," gurgled the president-elect, as he was swept up and out with the rest of the party before he could hear the follow-up questions.

And that was it.

He'll be a martyr to the protocol.

In the room beyond, we could see bottles of champagne and jugs of orange juice and a tray of crystal glasses.

They sat down to lunch: tomato tarte tatin with prosciutto; seared fillet of black sole on a bed of celeriac purée with basil cream sauce and parisienne potatoes in a straw basket; and lemon soufflé with shortcrust biscuits and fresh raspberries.

Then the President and president-elect retired for a brief meeting in the private study.

While they discussed the job, the secretary general to the President, Adrian O'Neill, took the family on a tour of the building. Afterwards, Rosaleen McBride, the head of household, brought everyone over to the private living quarters – the Wesht Wing.

What was it like there yesterday morning, before the guests arrived? Was Her Excellency rushing around plumping up cushions and straightening pictures?

"Martin, I won't tell you again. Get those socks off the radiator. They'll be here in a minute."

We rather hope so.

At Home with the McAleeses. Soon to be At Home with the Higginses.

In the end, it's pretty ruthless. Mary and Martin will be gone by Thursday morning, with their bibelots and whatnots in the boot of the car. (The OPW owns the furniture.)

Michael D and Sabina will move straight in after Friday's inauguration at Dublin Castle.

The first pups have already been chosen. Soon, the Áras will resound to the romping of paws – the president-elect and his wife love Bernese mountain dogs and have successfully bred them in years past.

Lovely big slobbery lumps they are too. The sofas will be ruined.
November 4th, 2011

EVENTS

CUTE HOOR/FAST BUCK GENE TO BE REMOVED FROM NATIONAL HERD

The greens have embraced the concept of genetic modification, and with remarkable results.

That's a turn-up for the books.

The party doesn't do things by half measure. Their conversion isn't down to some namby-pamby tinkering on the fringes of the allotment, or attempts to grow a pig from quorn.

John Gormley, Eamon Ryan and their ecologically motivated Frankensteins have only gone and engineered a change to the basic genetic make-up of the Irish people.

Using a secret procedure (which has been fully approved by their frightened partners in Government because they fear an agonising political death if they don't), the party has succeeded in removing the cute hoor/fast buck gene from the national herd.

"We've actually taken away that whole speculative impulse," Eamon Ryan announced at a press conference yesterday.

Thanks to new legislative engineering to be introduced by the Greens in the "post Nama period", profit-driven land hoarders will lose their amoral desire to squeeze as much cash as they possibly can from hard-pressed fellow citizens.

The Greens – Eamon says it should have been done 30 years ago – think they have discovered the formula that will curb the baser instincts of the Irish wheeler dealer.

They will neuter the loophole merchants before they become swashbuckling entrepreneurs and beggar another generation. They will temper the national tendency towards greed.

Their windfall tax will make us good people. And net a Nobel Prize for John and Eamon.

If it works, it will be a stunning triumph for the science of genetic modification. The speculative impulse is deeply ingrained and for some, impossible to resist.

Having a ball with somebody else's money is a major symptom of the speculative impulse. That, and lack of shame.

Again, the Greens were ahead of the curve yesterday in this regard. Following further revelations of lavish overspending in the State training agency Fás, party leader Gormley said the board of directors should resign.

This was in contrast to the Taoiseach, who shrugged his shoulders and said they were due to be replaced shortly anyway so why cause a fuss, while his Tánaiste said she would accept their resignations, if they were of a mind to go.

Was this, perhaps, evidence of a rift between Gormley and Cowen? One man looking for resignations, the other a noncommittal step behind.

In light of the Government's abject standing with the electorate, Gormley was asked: "How satisfied are you with Brian Cowen's leadership style?"

The reply was baffling in one way, but perhaps, rather telling in another.

"I think personalising it is not good. I mean, I find that some of the questioning can be quite intrusive. I don't like that. I don't like the way that a person can be pushed in that way and, you know, intruding into somebody's personal life and some of the questioning I find, I don't like it, but you know, it's up to the media and if they want to go down that particular route, it's up to them."

When the question was put a second time, he said he has "a perfectly good relationship with the Taoiseach."

But in his first answer, Gormley appeared to be indicating that the Taoiseach might not be coping well with the media's fascination with his personality and delving into his personal life.

Still on the subject of speculative impulses, and the modification of same, the subject of the expenses regime in Leinster House was also given an airing.

John thinks it should be overhauled. "I also believe that it will be one of the items that will be up for review in our programme for government."

They're all in favour of doing something about their expenses down Leinster House way, but it's a very slow process. And a bit embarrassing to have to discuss it in public, like they were ordinary folk. They'll just have to take their time with it.

Meanwhile, as the Greens patted themselves on the back for having such a major influence on the Nama legislation, a large group of farmers protested outside over cuts in the sector.

"On your bike!" they roared at party members when they appeared, reserving the loudest abuse for Minister for Food Trevor Sargent.

"Ye're lookin' at bicycle sheds in Dublin and light bulbs, but you've abandoned rural Ireland. Ye should be ashamed of yourselves!"

A large number of gardaí arrived at the hotel doors, but the protest went the usual way of farmers' demonstrations.

There was a lot of noise, a demand to be met by the most senior political person present, protests about being snubbed, an eventual meeting, a bit of banter with the gardaí outside, distribution of leaflets, the arrival of the ham sangwitches followed by tea and orderly dispersal.

It'll be noisy for the Greens again today, when proceedings switch to the Sheraton Hotel in Athlone for a party discussion on Nama.

September 12th, 2009

A VERY IMPORTANT JOB,
AND A VERY PUBLIC ILLNESS

Smiling, Brian Lenihan bounds over for a word. He apologises. "I don't know what more I can say, but fire ahead."

This is just terrible. "Jesus Brian, I don't know what to say."

The Minister for Finance has cancer. He starts chemotherapy on Thursday. His is a very important job and his is a very public illness.

Around Leinster House, people were inordinately focused on doing their job. Everyone was so businesslike, but too obviously so. Even the banter sounded strained. All in a day's work and all that – except they knew it wasn't.

There was Lenihan, facing up to difficult and very personal questions about his health and ability to carry out his duties. His advisers remaining as resolutely upbeat as their boss. The journalists asked what they needed to ask, but many were feeling really uncomfortable.

"I'll be totally focused on doing my job," was the Minister's message, as in newsrooms around the city reporters were dialling the nearest friendly oncologist to take soundings on whether that message could be relied upon.

Leinster House is a small place. The cut and thrust of politics is reported. People fall out. People make up. Reputations are burnished or dismantled. Headlines come and go. That's business. But on a personal level, Brian Lenihan is a popular politician. Which is why yesterday afternoon, as everyone went about the necessary task of covering a story of undoubted national importance, the tone of sadness could not be dissipated. There was a surreal air to the proceedings.

It was a tough day for Lenihan. He got his diagnosis in Christmas week. It was made public, without his approval, on St Stephen's Day. On his second day back at work (he was back at his desk on

New Year's Eve), he spoke publicly about his medical condition.

The dogs in the street have been talking about it for a week now. Yesterday, in a series of interviews and press briefings, he confronted the reality, sounding upbeat and confident.

First, he spoke at length to RTÉ's Seán O'Rourke for the One O'Clock News. Immediately afterwards, the Liveline switchboard went into meltdown as listeners rushed to commend him on his openness and bravery.

The interview took place in the conference room of the Department of Finance, under the gaze of his 24 predecessors whose photographs line the walls. Afterwards, Lenihan said he was glad O'Rourke didn't shirk the hard questions about his illness.

"I didn't want him to hold back."

He had to sound confident and competent. Soon afterwards, he met the political correspondents. But it was a meeting that many more wanted to attend, so before he went into the inter sanctum of the pol corrs' room, he did a question and answer session.

How did you hear the news? How did it feel at the time? Was it a shock? How do you feel now? Are you up to working? Have you thought about the effects of chemotherapy?

Lenihan answered with a sense of calm and a lightness of delivery which knocked many off balance. He went from talking about a blockage at the entrance of his pancreas to discussing the budgetary estimates. He made little jokes at his own expense and everyone laughed a little bit too hard. It was unsettling stuff in its ordinariness. And God, but it seems like everyone is an expert on the pancreas now.

"Long term, how do you think this might affect your political future?" he was asked by one of the pol corrs.

"I haven't really thought long term in that sense. I mean, I'm very focused on the long term in the department and the economy, and I'm thinking that way."

Then he paused and mused: "But I'm not really . . . I think ambitions somewhat fade when you're in a position like this and you focus on survival yourself and doing your job right."

Then he made a little quip about people who get so caught up in thinking about the next promotion they "make a bit of a balls of the job they're in, but I'm not going to give you any examples of that!"

Again laughter.

There was much talk about the economy, naturally. "The position is stabilising in economic terms," said the Minister.

But really, the story wasn't about the economy, despite the dutiful performances all round.

A pattern emerged after the first couple of briefings. Lenihan's lines, even the humorous ones, didn't change much as the day wore on. He knew what he was going to say. More detailed questions about the precise nature of his condition were skilfully deflected.

He won't be giving further bulletins about his conditions. There is now other work to do.

And so, he beetled over to The Irish Times, loitering at the edge of the pack. "Fire away!" says Lenihan. But we can't. What to say, apart from the obvious?

So he says he had a wonderful Christmas at home with his family and he's rearing to go. "Ah, don't be worrying now," he soothes, saying he'd love to come out with an interesting new angle for us, "but there's only so many angles you can take on a pancreas!"

Finally, he leaves the subdued media behind and heads back to Leinster House. His opposite number, Fine Gael's Richard Bruton, approaches down the corridor. Lenihan reminds him to keep up the tough opposition. "Aggressive intervention!" he says to Bruton, who laughs and nods and keeps moving so fast he nearly mows down a stray hack.

The Minister is now doing the comforting. "Is the bar open? C'mon, I'll buy you a drink."

There is nobody else in the bar. Lenihan orders a green tea and tells the barman to order in plenty of it. He leans back on the stool. He looks very tired. He read a lot of interesting books over Christmas, and he's read a lot about cancer. This one, he vows, is not going to beat him if he can help it. People have been wonderful. He had to clear 500 messages from his phone on St Stephen's Day. Holy relics have been arriving in the post. A butcher in Cabra sent spiced beef.

His two advisers arrive as he talks about all the people he's only found out now have cancer. And he was amazed how many people thought he smoked. "Never smoked in my life."

The Minister gently ribs one of the advisers, saying he was in tears on the phone to him on Christmas Eve. "No need for that sort of carry on!"

No, everybody is upbeat now. We still don't know what to say to him. The Minister is yawning, clearly drained. There's a junior Minister wanting to speak to him on the phone. Lenihan says he can wait. He can do those sort of things now. Then he drains his teacup and sighs. "God, I'm glad that's over."

January 5th, 2010

Planet Dáil in turmoil as Fine Gael's shooting star turns out to be an alien

Irish politics is in deep shock. A blue fireball blazed across the political firmament yesterday and plummeted into the heart of Leinster House.

Everyone was stunned. Politicians from all sides couldn't believe what happened.

"Is it true?" they asked each other.

"It's incredible!" they cried.

And so it was that the meteoric career of George Lee fell to earth. It was blinding, it was brilliant and it was over in a flash. Fine Gael's shooting star shines no more.

They were utterly astounded. Because for politicians – who would sell their grannies for a safe seat in the Dáil – what George did defies reason.

TDs couldn't understand why a newly-elected deputy, with an adoring public and a national profile they can only dream about, upped and walked away.

The idea of doing such a thing is alien to them. George and his principles? No, they will never get it, because it is beyond their ken.

And as the smoke cleared, and Fine Gael prepared to assess the damage and Fianna Fáil danced, all parties agreed on one thing: George Lee was never really one of them. Which is why he got elected in the first place.

The news broke at lunchtime. Few deputies and Senators were about, for the House doesn't sit on Monday.

For those Fine Gaelers who were there, the same word kept cropping up: "Gutted." George – The People's Princess – had buoyed their spirits and cheered them. And now he was gone. Maybe they should have minded him a bit more.

He said they never included him in their plans. He was Inda's plaything, paraded around the country for his celebrity status. But he had "zero impact or influence" on formulating economic policy.

As George put it in one of his many interviews yesterday: "If this was a relationship, it would be irretrievably broken down – I'm off!"

He stopped short of saying there were three people in the marriage – George, Enda and a clutch of frontbench heavyweights who are no respecters of Georgie Come Latelys, even if they arrive on the scene with an excellent pedigree, a stellar TV career and a landslide majority.

Now, in the wake of the departure of his South Dublin rose, all a devastated Inda can do is take comfort in the words of Sir Elton John: "Goodbye Georgie Lee, although I never knew you at all . . . "

He issued a brief e-mail to mark the embarrassing departure, then stayed behind closed doors back in Castlebar. House private.

But George was talking. A lot.

He looked despondent. He sounded shattered.

His dream – the one he spoke about so eloquently nine months ago, was dead.

"I had to be true to myself . . . I've decided I'm not going to be fake . . . I am not prepared to live a lie."

Congratulations to all those interviewers who resisted the urge to ask: "But what about the children, George?"

A bit late for that now. And did nobody in Fine Gael see this coming? Everybody else did.

The novelty of his new job would have kept deputy Lee going in the early months. But as time passed, that eagerness and enthusiasm visibly waned. Many commented on the regular sight in the Dáil chamber of finance spokesman Richard Bruton, in conclave with his deputy, Ciarán O'Donnell, while George, weighed down with folders and documents, looked on from a few rows behind.

Deputy Lee's resignation will be no surprise to the "I told you so" brigade. They forecast it would end in tears from the start, knowing how the system works.

"He'll need counselling within the month," commented one Leinster House sage after George was received in triumph on his first day.

From the afternoon he was first unveiled to the public, Fine

Gael treated Lee like a trophy wife.

At the time, the party leader joked they would have to employ a tour manager to organise George's diary, such was the clamour from the grassroots to meet him. They put together an economic roadshow, with George as chairman, and blitzed the country.

But it was Richard and Ciarán, along with Leo Varadkar and Simon Coveney, who got to deliver the speeches. And when the platform speakers did their thing, they departed to continue formulating policy and thinking deep thoughts while economist George was left behind to press the flesh, sign autographs and pose for photos.

He didn't like it. He wanted to have an input into that policy. He said his sole purpose for putting himself forward for election was to get his teeth stuck into shaping the party's economic strategy.

What made him go? Innocence and ego or courage and principle? It's probably somewhere in between. But George did a brave thing nonetheless.

Ironically, in those starry-eyed days, he said he went into politics because he felt "constrained" by his job in television. Little did he know.

We wished him the best when he said, "I am going to speak out and I don't care if they don't like it." Noting the raised eyebrow he insisted: "I WILL!" It didn't happen.

George Lee says Enda Kenny misjudged him. He wanted to be involved in formulating policy, but he was cold-shouldered. His boss was more interested in using him as a show pony. "I'm not there to be used just for my celebrity or to draw a crowd."

The jokes have started already: RTÉ is to air a new reality show staring Charlie Bird and George Lee. It'll be called Celebrity Big Baby. It's a cruel world outside Montrose.

February 2nd, 2010

Richard Bruton led an unsuccessful coup to unseat Fine Gael leader
Enda Kenny, and was sacked as FG deputy leader

A FIASCO THAT BEGGARS BELIEF AS PARTY PUSHES SELF-DESTRUCT BUTTON

Death Wish: you've seen the movie. Now marvel at Death Wish: the political party.

Not for the first time, it's all about to get very bloody.

Is Fine Gael addicted to disaster? If you gave them a car, they'd crash it.

If you gave them a pool, they'd drown in it.

If you gave them a cake, they'd choke on it.

Yet, even by their own high standards, this latest Fine Gael fiasco beggars belief.

After an eight-year absence, when there was reason to believe that its people had finally been weaned off their propensity to politically self-harm, the nuclear button has been activated again.

It happened in such a sudden and spectacularly ill-judged way that audiences all over the country – regardless of political leaning – are absolutely astonished.

They can't believe their good luck in Fianna Fáil. Instead of a weekend of bad publicity for the party, culminating in an embarrassing Dáil motion of no confidence in Brian Cowen today, they've been watching Fine Gael self-destruct in front of their eyes.

For the last few days, as Richard Bruton conducted a masterclass in how not to unseat an incumbent leader, the Fianna Fáilers have been wallowing in their rivals' startling lack of political common sense.

Biffo spent yesterday gadding around Dublin doing nice little gigs like having his photo taken in an electric car, launching a new kind of hurley in Croke Park and making a speech in the sunshine of the Botanic Gardens.

Motion of no confidence? What motion? And no, he wouldn't be so rude as to comment on the situation in Fine Gael, God bless the poor crathurs.

Meanwhile, back at the ranch, plans were already well advance for the gunfight at the FG corral.

There are two principals in this latest production: party leader Enda Kenny and Richard Bruton, who used to be deputy leader until yesterday afternoon, when Enda sacked him.

Enda's leadership has been under pressure for some time by a faction within the party known as "the mutterers". But while they have belly-ached for a long time among themselves, no attempt was made to remove him.

At issue is Deputy Kenny's leadership style – lack of media skills; poor Dáil performances; failure to benefit from a historically unpopular Fianna Fáil government; and a consistently poor personal showing in opinion polls.

As they see it, Enda served them well in bringing the party back from the brink of oblivion, but now a new phase and a new leader is needed for the party.

Richard Bruton, Baby Bruton, brother of former FG Taoiseach John, is their choice.

Matters came to a head on Thursday night, after the publication of the latest Irish Times poll. Another little decline for Fine Gael and a dreadful rating for the party leader.

So the mutterers got a-muttering with all the mumbling they could muster and somehow, word got around that Richard Bruton was challenging Enda for the top job.

What followed yesterday and on Sunday has been nothing short of high farce.

Richard went to ground, along with a number of his front bench colleagues. A flurry of statements supporting Enda Kenny started to flood into newsrooms. Party chief whip Paul Kehoe did his best Gerry Collins impression and pleaded with Richard to "look into his heart" and turn back from the dangerous road upon which he was embarking.

Not a word from Baby Bruton and his embedded but incommunicado frontbenchers as the Kenny supporters grew more vocal.

"I believe it is totally, totally, car-crash politics" wailed Kehoe, in the one indisputable statement of a surreal day.

This was no night of the long knives; more a long day of

competing soundbites, rumour and silly silence.

Joe Duffy got in on the act and party members around the country rang in to support Enda. But a phone poll showed more support for Richard.

Back around Kildare Street, Fianna Fáil was Fianna falling around the place laughing at Fine Gael's self-inflicted crisis.

What was Richard Bruton thinking? How did he ever imagine that it was a good idea to go to war with his leader at the same time as the party was bringing a no confidence motion against the Government?

If Enda Kenny is a weak leader, what confidence does Baby Bruton engender? Through his actions, he's let the Government off the hook and plunged his party into chaos, displaying a truly awful sense of timing and political judgment.

If mild-mannered Richard wanted a nice, civilised transition of power, he's managed to engineer the complete opposite. Enda, back to the wall, charged out fighting from his corner.

And Fine Gael – within sniffing distance of government – are in flitters again.

You're supposed to shoot yourself in the foot by accident, not, as in the case of Baby Bruton and the mutterers, strap it down and fire indiscriminately at your toes with a blunderbuss.

Enda called a press conference for 5.30pm, thus getting in before Richard, who was to go on the 6pm news.

Bruton, hearing the Enda was about to make a declaration of war, nipped in live on the TV3 news, saying he was going to contest the leadership.

Cue Enda, statesman-like, firm of voice and playing the wronged party, on the steps of Leinster House, party banners flying behind him.

He'd supported John Bruton three times in leadership heaves. "I was that soldier!" How could Richard do this, after all Enda had done for the party?

"I've been a great friend of Richard Bruton for 25 years and politics will not interfere with that friendship" sighed Enda, before giving him the bullet.

As for the former deputy leader, he said he had to put his country above loyalty to his party. Enda had fallen short on too many occasions and it was time for him to go.

Battle lines are drawn. A split looks inevitable. Some of the moderates and older heads in the party are aghast at what is happening.

There will be blood.

And they're breaking out the beer in Fianna Fáil.

Will they ever learn?

June 15th, 2010

An autumn Fianna Fail think-in in Galway turned into "Gargle-gate" after Taoiseach Brian Cowen gave Morning Ireland an interview in which he sounded "hoarse"

Singing Taoiseach hits bum note as critics lap up 'Gargle-gate' in Galway

It was the Morning Ireland after the night before.

The Taoiseach sounded dog rough. Wheezy. Groggy. Muzzy. A bit slow.

Around the breakfast tables of the nation, butter knives hovered above toast and and tea-cups paused mid-air as people listened, then mused: "God, but Biffo sounds like he had a right skinful last night."

Whereupon all hell broke loose and the roof caved in on Brian Cowen and Fianna Fáil. So began an extraordinary day in Irish politics and media.

Here's your simple guide to Gargle-gate:

Was The Taoiseach out way past his bedtime drinking pints?

Yes.

How do we know?

Because we were there.

Should he have left the pub before half three in the morning?

Yes.

Did he belt out a song for a cheering crowd and do a few funny impersonations?

Yes.

Was he any good?

Yes, actually. He was a hoot.

Did he look drunk?

No.

Did anyone whisper to him that it was time to go?

Not that we saw.

Has he only himself to blame?

Yes.

Is he utterly mortified now?

Yes.

Does that matter?

No. The genie is out of the bottle now.

By the end of an incredible day yesterday, a sore head was the least of Brian Cowen's problems. He was a humiliated man with a badly damaged reputation, a laughing stock in the international press and an embarrassment to his appalled colleagues who had to rally to his defence.

In the Ardilaun Hotel, party handlers and the Taoiseach's closest allies wandered about, stunned, whispering into their mobile phones.

The skies have opened over Fianna Fáil and the party is sinking. The Taoiseach took his demoralised troops to Galway in an effort to put some steel in their souls, but in his accident-prone fashion, he managed to insert it between their shoulder blades instead.

The politicians should have been returning to their constituencies yesterday afternoon with a clearer outlook and a bit more pep in their step.

But if they were fragile before they arrived, they were shattered when they left.

All because their boss sounded hungover during his interview on Morning Ireland. This led to a bizarre chain of events as the media went into overdrive and Fianna Fáil went into meltdown.

Why such a frenzied reaction to this 13 minutes of airtime?

Because in the media, it has often been hinted that our sociable Taoiseach is overly fond of a drop, but nobody had ever said it or written it straight out.

When radio shows and the internet began buzzing and tweeting about Cowen's woeful performance, and one of those questioning his level of sobriety included an Opposition frontbench spokesman, the journalists had legitimate grounds to broach this sensitive issue.

Some have been waiting for this opportunity for a long time – Cowen gave it to them on a plate.

Had the storm not erupted, Monday night's very pleasant and relaxed gathering in the bar of the Ardilaun would not have been reported in any great detail.

Think-ins are a blend of business and socialising. Some say the bonding element is every bit as important as the speeches and the workshops. There is usually a sing-song in the bar after dinner. The leader usually circulates. Pints are bought. Gossip swapped. Contacts cemented.

We're not talking Sodom and Gomorrah here (although we had a snigger yesterday morning when an attractive young female journalist told us how one Fianna Fáil backbencher (a noted letch) bought her six gin and tonics and then promised to introduce her to the Taoiseach.)

In fact, only two major incidents come to mind in the history of the think-in drink-ins. Fianna Fáil's Peter Kelly once juggled a pitcher of water on his head while juggling his shoes and then sang a medley of Elvis numbers into his upturned tie.

On another occasion, Enda Kenny said in an interview that he looked better in cycling shorts than Bertie Ahern – images that still give us nightmares.

On Monday, there was the usual dinner in the ballroom. This was followed by an address from former GAA president Joe McDonagh, who finished his contribution with a rousing rendition of The West's Awake.

After the meal, some deputies went into the city for a drink. Some retired for the night and more headed for the hotel bar, Cowen among them.

Senior Ministers – interestingly enough, the ones who would be spoken of as leadership contenders – schmoozed journalists at the small bar in the ballroom, but the lure of the sing-song was impossible to resist.

Two non-drinkers, Senator Donie Cassidy and MEP Brian Crowley, were directing the entertainment. Brian played the piano for a while. Donie was MC, beating people up to sing.

He pleaded all night for a representative of the media to sing. It was by the grace of God that nobody took him up on it.

It was well after midnight and nudging 1am when the Taoiseach was prevailed upon to perform. He did a very funny routine, mimicking Micheál Ó Muircheartaigh along with a famous Kilkenny hurler and a quintessential Dub.

He brought the house down. Encouraged by the ovation and as the crowd called for more, he agreed to do an encore.

Wagging a finger at the journalists – also enjoying a drink and enjoying the show – he cautioned them not to get him into trouble by reporting his performance.

He then did an extremely funny impersonation of former Ryder Cup golfer Philip Walton who had a rather high-pitched voice, and his then team captain, the gruff Scotsman Bernard Gallacher.

He swung an imaginary club as he spoke, then exhaled to give impression of a ball flying through the air. It was very good.

Cowen sang just the one song, a passionate rendition of The Lakes of Pontchartrain.

The Taoiseach joined some friends for a drink. From what we saw he was having a few slow pints.

Various people sang. A man played the tin whistle. It was a bit like the afters of a country wedding. Cowen chatted for a while with Batt O'Keeffe.

We left as the time neared 3am. At this stage, Cowen was talking to people in the lobby. He didn't have a drink with him. We hear he retired at about 3.30am.

It was a good night. Nobody went mad, at least from what we could see. Which brings us to what happened next. That awful interview – it wasn't what he said, but the manner in which he said it.

Calls flooded into radio stations. Was Cowen still drunk? Hungover? Did he realise how bad he sounded?

Suddenly, the atmosphere in the Ardilaun became highly charged. When the Taoiseach arrived, TV3's Ursula Halligan asked the question crackling over the airwaves: was he drunk or hungover during the interview?

The Taoiseach looked shocked, as his minders pushed Ms Halligan out of the way and steered him into the hall. He took grave offence at the question and, highly indignant, absolutely denied the charge.

A media frenzy ensued, although some of us were stranded in a strange place between sanctimony and complicity.

As the morning wore on, reinforcements arrived down from Dublin newsagencies. Already, the Taoiseach's denial had made the Wall Street Journal.

The price of Irish bonds jumped, ratings agency Standard and Poors pronounced.

An air of hysteria took hold. Two senior Ministers were trotted out to rubbish the allegations. Inside the hall, they were talking about Nama and the €30 billion Anglo bailout. Outside, Micheál Martin was insisting "clearly, that the issue seems to be he was a little hoarse".

Then Noel Dempsey (both Ministers were nearly driven through the backdrop by the advancing media) declared: "I think Brian was a little bit nasal" before saying: "I often have a frog in my throat in the morning."

Dermot Ahern said on radio that it was widely known "the Taoiseach suffers from congestion". "I understand he has a cold," said Seán Haughey. Tony Killeen blamed the clattering of cutlery in the background for putting Cowen off his stride.

Seán O'Rourke, meanwhile, on the lunchtime news, was getting stuck into Simon Coveney. "Do you stand over your tweet?"

"A man is being knocked back because he is hoarse in the morning and congested," said Mary Hanafin. On and on it went. Until finally, with the hacks on the brink of exhaustion and the handlers on the verge of a nervous breakdown, the Taoiseach came out. He apologised for being hoarse. He attacked Fine Gael for playing dirty politics. His grim-faced Minister colleagues flanking him.

Then, the question that made his fellow politicians wince. "Taoiseach, are you worried about your drinking, do you ever think you drink too much?"

There was a low hum of disapproval from the TDs and Senators. "Shame!" said one. But Cowen silenced them with a wave of his hand. He was happy to take the question. And he answered – "everything in moderation, including moderation".

That moment evoked another electric scene involving a Fianna Fáil leader – when Bertie Ahern, new leader, was asked about his marital status. His supporters loudly booed, but Ahern silenced them and took the question.

They cheered his answer and cheered him from the room. Cowen was cheered too, but not half as sincerely.

A little hoarse and a storm in a stirrup cup? Or the beginning of the end? Time will tell.

September 15th, 2010

THE DAY O'BAMA STORMED MONEYGALL

If home is where the heart is, then Barack Obama became a true son of Ireland yesterday. And we all walk a little taller today.

But none more so than the villagers of Moneygall, who welcomed the president of the United States to their tiny village in Co Offaly and fell head over heels for his irresistible charm.

It is a day they, and we, will never forget. Yet another day that will go down in song and story after a remarkable week of historic milestones for the country.

Did it also mark a turning point for the 44th American president? If so, that point can be traced precisely to Main Street, Moneygall.

Obama was a revelation: this guy who is not supposed to do sentimentality; who reputedly finds it difficult to jettison his bookish reserve and become "a man of the people". It's a desirable quality for a politician.

From the moment he stepped from his armoured Cadillac SUV, he had the air of a man who meant business. One side of the long street was lined with people, many with babies and young children, who had stood and waited for more than five hours in atrocious weather to see the president.

"They're like emperor penguins huddling against the Antarctic winter," remarked a man from Foreign Affairs.

But suddenly, the cold was forgotten. For finally, after all the planning and talking and hoping, Barack Obama had finally arrived in the village.

The cheers that greeted him shook the very summit of the Slieve Blooms. And then the sun came out.

The honoured guest was met by Henry Healy, his Irish cousin (eight times removed) and two magnificently bechained council leaders from Offaly and Tipperary.

The hug for young Henry was wide and warm and it set the

tone for what was to come. After the pleasantries, Obama loped across to the swooning, screaming, singing crowd.

He plunged in – grabbing hands, grabbing babies, kissing babies; grabbing grannies, kissing grannies, getting kissed by grannies; hugging blushing farmers, embracing swooning teenagers and high-fiving simpering young fellas.

He posed for photographs, flashing that famous smile. Crowd-surfing toddlers were bumped over adult heads and into his hands.

He talked and he listened and he laughed. The delirious crowd broke into song.

"If you're Irish, come into the parlour/There's a welcome here for you/And if your name is Timmy or Barack/as long as you come from Ireland there's a welcome on the mat . . ."

It was cruel weather for May. Obama may have lived in the Windy City but it had nothing on Moneygall yesterday afternoon, when a vicious and icy wind drove the rain in sheets down Main Street.

He didn't appear to notice, despite the concerned looks of members of his entourage – a shivering scrum of slate grey suits and beige macs.

"I think he'll be going for another while," shouted one of them into his sodden shirt-cuff as Michelle Obama thrust a crying infant into her husband's arms.

Gorgeous Michelle, smiling in a shimmeringly elegant silk coat which was absolutely soaked with rain.

The crowd sang again: "On the 23rd of May/Barack Obama arrives that day/To our little village home in Moneygall . . ."

Even the secret service agents were celebrities.

"Shake my hand! Shake my hand!" squealed teenage girls to the beefy minders as they padded past.

The White House press corps, who've seen it all, were beginning to take notice. "This rope walk is slower than usually. He would normally make it through one of these things pretty quickly." But Barack was taking his time. There was no way this outing was going to take just the allocated 45 minutes.

A little girl held up a sign: "Did you bring Bo?" (The Obama family dog.) Then groans of disappointment from the rest of the line as the president went back across the road and into his ancestral home to meet the current occupants, the Donovan family. He stood in the doorway. "Michelle! Michelle!" And the missus tore herself away.

But he was quickly back, jogging up the street, working the crowd. It was pouring from the heavens. He wasn't wearing a topcoat.

An anonymous figure in the crowd was Brian Cowen, the man who first invited Obama to Co Offaly. He stood quietly at the back of the cheering crowd as the president passed him by.

Just past the midway point, Obama drew level with Ollie Hayes's pub (which is opposite Hayes pub, which is next to Hayes Bar). The crowd groaned again as he made for Ollie's place.

The president turned at the door and waved a cupped hand under his mouth – the traditional sign that says "I'm going for a pint". And a big farmers' cheer went up, with hoots from the ladies.

Inside the cosy bar waited his extended family (many times removed). Generations of the Donovans, the Benns and the Healys waited nervously to greet Obama. He breezed in and put them at their ease.

Shouts to Michelle to get into the photograph. Hugs and kisses all round. He behaved like a man who had all the time in the world, relaxed and at home with his people.

Then came the big moment – the pulling of the pint. Would he or wouldn't he? The smart money said the president would do a Queen Elizabeth and look but not taste.

Ollie Hayes gave it the big build up. Barack played along with gusto, asking serious questions about the perfect pint. Ollie, with a steady hand, put up a pint for the president and a glass for the first lady.

Frankie Gavin and the band burst into a rousing jig. The extended family, friends and media waited. Barack picked up his glass and Michelle raised hers.

They drank the Guinness.

"He gave that a right wallop," said a local in the back bar, approvingly. "Sure he inhaled it!" said his companion.

"That's good stuff. Delicious," said the president.

Stuffy? Reserved? Awkward? Not this fella. He could have given lessons yesterday to Bill Clinton.

Back outside, the crowd waited for Barack's return. Ten minutes later, still wearing their damp clothes, the presidential couple emerged and they worked their way right to the end of the line.

This was pure gold from Mr and Mrs President.

Finally, they took their leave, but they took their time. Obama, waving goodbye again and again and, just before his motorcade took off, he stood on the running board of the SUV, turned to the people and waved again.

What he left behind was like the aftermath of a benign whirlwind.

People excitedly discussing what happened. What he said to them, whom he kissed, what he said. Re-enactments of split-second encounters that will live forever in the memory.

"He held my hand, then he touched my hat, then he pulled me forward and kissed my cheek," said Anne Maher, like she was describing the final chapter of a Mills and Boon novel.

Publican Ollie Hayes describing how Obama threw down a €50 note – "the president pays his bar tab" – and producing said note from his pocket. How the parish priest drank a pint pulled by Michelle and retired in triumph with the empty glass.

The family members in their finery, reliving the moments again and again for friends who couldn't hear enough.

"He called me Sweetie," said Margaret Gally, Henry's auntie.

"I called to him 'Bwana Uhuru' and he came over and asked if I used to live in Kenya," said local man Frank Heslin, who once worked in Tanzania.

Stories. Everyone had a story.

As Obama's helicopter was landing in Dublin for phase two of this fantastic journey, Moneygall was calming down. But just a little.

The mist cleared and you could see the sheep again on Liar's Hill above the town. People clustered around their phones and cameras to see their photos. "We'll have to get them blown up." There was a little queue in the Irish accordion shop to see the Sam Maguire and Liam McCarthy cups which had been on display during the visit.

Two gardaí, in their fluorescent jackets, posed with them, beaming. "One's from Westmeath, the other from Wexford. Sure when will they ever get the chance again?" said an Offaly man.

And they queued up in the shop for ice-cream cones, happily licking their 99s, oblivious to the cold.

A perfect day.

The day O'bama came home to Ireland and a president found his heart again.

May 24th, 2011

SEANAD'S BATCH OF NEW TALENTS BECOME DUBLIN CITY RAMBLERS

"When a man knows he is to be hanged in a fortnight, it concentrates his mind wonderfully." Not strictly true.

If Dr Johnson were around today, he might be rounding off his famous observation with an important qualification: "unless the condemned man is a member of Seanad Éireann". Concentration is beyond a lot of them.

The Senators sat in full sight of the gallows yesterday afternoon after Enda Kenny channelled his inner Pierrepoint and prepared the trapdoor and noose. The Taoiseach told the Dáil his Government intends to hold a referendum next year on the abolition of the Upper House.

So when the 24th Seanad held its inaugural meeting, the members were acutely aware that they were sitting on the political equivalent of death row.

But they hold out hope that the voting public will come to their rescue and grant clemency to their jaded institution. They will pitch their appeal by making the Seanad indispensable to the democratic process and this they will achieve by changing their ways.

Senator David Norris, the new Father of the House, led the charge with his trademark eloquence. "To put it bluntly, we are confronted with the possibility of extinction," he informed his colleagues – old and new.

A ripple of nervous laughter greeted this statement of fact.

But old Fr Norris has no intention of quitting the field without a fight and he wants to take his legions with him.

Drawing inspiration from ancient Rome – "Senatus Populus Que Romanorum, The Senate and the Roman People" – he issued his call to arms: "Like an army, the Senate should be reorganised, drilled and disciplined, keeping ourselves honed in mind and body for the coming conflict. This is a task to which we, as Senators, must pledge ourselves today." In order to survive, cautioned Fr Norris, members must reconnect with the people. The old ways will not do anymore.

It'll be sword, sand and sandals stuff from now on.

The new intake – including Enda's Eleven – sat back and watched the old guard to see how it's done. And they duly rose to the challenge with all the bounce of a punctured inner tube.

But first, Fine Gael's Paddy Burke was elected Cathaoirleach. The smooth Mayoman is Enda's eyes and ears in the west and he slotted seamlessly into the vacancy left by his predecessor, Fianna Fáil's Pat Moylan, who was Brian Cowen's eyes and ears in Offaly.

Reflecting the redrawn battle lines in the chamber, Fine Gael's Maurice Cummins took Donie Cassidy's old job of Seanad leader, with Labour's Ivana Bacik his second in command. Maurice and Ivana nominated Paddy for the chair. Fr Norris was delighted with this turn of events, reflecting, as he saw it, a wonderful example of cross-party co-operation. Or coalition, as others might see it.

He was over the moon when Darragh O'Brien, the new Fianna Fáil leader in the upper house, indicated that his party would also support the popular Burke.

"I see this as an even greater example of cross-party co-operation," trilled David, as Darragh waved his hands to indicate that this might not be an ongoing arrangement.

Then the talking began.

For nearly an hour and a half, the old guard (mostly Fianna Fáil) showed that they still have a great welcome for themselves. As the clock moved on, they talked about how great they are and why abolishing the Seanad would be a terrible disaster for the country.

At one stage there were fears that Labhrás Ó Murchu and Paschal Mooney might have to be taken down with elephant guns. Paschal waxed nostalgic, recalling "my late father, senator Joseph Mary Mooney, who served in this house in the Sixties . . . " Long-time Senator Labhras said he had "a vision and a belief". The new Cathaoirleach had a bell. A pity he didn't use it.

Maybe he was afraid what effect it might have on former athlete Senator Eamonn Coghlan. A couple of tinkles might have seen him tearing off in search of a last lap. There were pleas for "respect" and pleas to the media for more coverage. New boy Trevor Ó

Clochartaigh of Sinn Féin managed to use Obama's "Is féidir linn" at least four times.

Ronán Mullen spoke twice.

"If he doesn't shut up soon, I'm voting for abolition," sighed one of the journalists tethered to the press gallery.

Senators shouldn't be rushing "lemon, er, lemming like" over the cliff, urged Ronán, before he cried to the weeping hacks: "Don't be strangers!" One of the Enda's Eleven (we have high hopes for them) appeared to be asleep.

And Prof John Crown could have cleared at least three trolleys in St Vincent's during the time the old guard were bigging themselves up.

He made himself useful when another of the Taoiseach's nominees, Senator Mary Moran, sprained her ankle during a photocall on the plinth.

But where does this sit with Fr Norris's lean, mean, fighting machine? Finely honed minds do not ramble.

Terry Leyden, back again, declared the Seanad to be "a home for all talents". Then he managed to slip in a reference to meeting the Queen last week.

Fine Gael's Fidelma Healy-Eames declared: "This may be the last session, but it also may be the best. Are we worth keeping? Are we worth saving?" We were saying nuttin'.

Louth Fine Gaeler Jim D'Arcy was the first of the much vaunted Eleven to speak. He was short and to the point and got a round of applause.

By and large, the new intake kept quiet. Broadcaster and educationalist Marie Louise O'Donnell looked fascinated and, occasionally, bemused.

One grizzled old stager whispered to the press gallery: "I've a few verbose colleagues, haven't I?" Senator Mary White singled out the new Senator Martin McAleese for special mention. (She's after his wife's job). Quite what Enda's Eleven and the other first-timers made of it all is anybody's guess.

Going on yesterday's proceedings, the future of the Seanad is in their hands.

May 26th, 2011

HEALY-PREMIUM-RATE TO PAY €2,600 WHILE NATION ENJOYS PRICELESS GAIETY

"Celebrities DO go wild," remarked the Taoiseach before breakfast, wearing his voice-of-experience face.

But he didn't elaborate.

Whatever did he mean? How does he know? Is he hanging out with Bono's peahens? Then, just before elevenses, Enda told the Dáil: "I have every sympathy for the people of Gaza . . . I've been there." This was refreshingly honest from Taoiseach Kenny.

He probably treated them to one of his famous motivational speeches. As if they haven't suffered enough. They certainly deserve every sympathy.

Sympathy, it has to be said, was thin on the ground for Independent celebrity deputy Michael Healy-Rae, battling to explain how 3,636 votes he got in a TV reality show originated from Leinster House. Records show that the premium-rate calls could only have been made from phones assigned to TDs and senators or their personal staff.

Deputy Healy-Premium-Rate's father, Jackie, was a TD at the time.

You can see how people might get suspicious.

"I am being scapegoated," said Deputy Healy-Premium-Rate yesterday evening.

The Taoiseach entered the fray early yesterday morning.

"It might be funny if it weren't as serious as it is. Celebrities do go wild. This money should be paid back, full stop." Good old Enda. No sooner had he said this, than the Leinster House rumour mill cranked into action. Deputy Healy-Premium-Rate was apparently going to conduct a press conference out on the plinth and tell us all to go to hell, he wasn't about be giving any money back.

The shame of it.

Journalists rang his office for details to be greeted by the pleasing lilting tones of a Kerryman. "Is that Deputy Healy-Rae?" "No. He's not available at the moment." "Oh, right. Who's that?" "This is Jackie." "Jackie!" "That's right. Jackie. His son." It was surreal.

While the Dáil discussed the European economic crisis and the situation in Greece, the media gathered outside, listening to Michael Healy-Rae as he did an interview on the one o'clock news.

Seán O'Rourke was in sparkling form, coming up with a new class of misdemeanour which he termed "incitement to phone". Finally, the man of the moment arrived, with young Jackie (16) by his side. When building a dynasty, it's never too young to blood the young fella in the rough and tumble of politics.

Michael wore his trademark cap. Young Jackie has no need of one, with his youthful head of black hair.

Back in the homeplace of Kilgarvan, Jackie snr was being chased by journalists for comments.

He didn't want to talk, taking himself and his cap away from the microphone as fast as his big Merc could take him. "Go to Hell!" he told TV3's Paul Byrne.

His son can't afford to be so blunt. He has a Dáil seat to look after. Certain standards are required. He read out the letter he had written to the Ceann Comhairle setting out his side of the story.

"I write in response to the relevations [sic] that Oireachtas phones were used for the purpose of raising Funds for People in need. Obviously, raising funds for charity is very worthwhile but should not be done at the taxpayers' expense . . ." he began.

"I had no hand, act or part in these calls," he said, which is fair enough, as he was in the wilds of Connemara at the time.

It is possible that whoever was responsible for them also had no hand in the enterprise. Looking at the timing sequences of the calls, they could have been generated by a preset fax or an auto-dialler.

The deputy is of the view that the calls "came from all over the houses of the Oireachtas . . ." Fianna Fáil Senator Ned O'Sullivan from Listowel, got the ball rolling for his countyman by putting on the record that he could have voted for him at least a dozen times.

But that was about it.

However, Michael does not want this story to distract from the pressing national issues of the day. So he is selflessly picking up the tab.

"Every person who made those phone calls, I'm paying for every one of their phone calls now. I'm the only person in Ireland that's paying for other people's phone bills." This is not true. The people of Ireland are paying for Deputy Healy-Rae's phones, and phone bills, at the moment.

Muddying the waters, he added that he thinks the issue of the use of Oireachtas phones should be investigated.

As for those anonymous deputies and senators who voted for him, "other people did what they did and they should answer for it . . ." Who would they be? "I'm not going to go naming people." In fairness, the calls cost just over €2,500. But the episode added much to the gaiety of the nation and provided a welcome distraction for a couple of days.

Compare that with €20 million or so spent on the Queen of England and Barack Obama for delivering the feel-good factor.

The bottom line for Deputy Healy Premium-Rate was clear: "Remember, this was a misuse, but it was for charity".

June 30th, 2011

CARTRIDGE NUMBERS JUST DON'T ADD UP FOR DELL BOY Ó SNODAIGH

Dell Boy and The Cartridge Family aggressively market themselves as the font of political virtue.

They have thrown out the old stylebook and adopted a fresh typeface for the new politics.

At least that's what Sinn Féin has been trumpeting since entering the Dáil last year with the average industrial wage in one hand and a lucrative surplus in the other.

But the moral high ground is a dangerous place, as the party discovered to the taxpayers' cost yesterday.

Deputy Aengus Ó Snodaigh's insistence that the €50,000 worth of Dell printer cartridges he took from Oireachtas supplies were solely for personal constituency use was far from convincing.

As he stood on the plinth and sought to justify a two-year printing spree that would have put a small publishing house to shame, shades of the Michael Healy-Rae's "Ring of Kerry" phone vote escapade returned.

And we were transported back to tribunal territory, when the likes of George Redmond said he had large cash accumulations in his hot press because he was "a very heavy saver". Or when Ray Burke described his personal and party operations as "seamless".

This is an unfortunate turn of events for Dell Boy Ó Snodaigh, who would take great umbrage at being bracketed with the likes of Redmond and Burke.

He finds himself in this embarrassing situation for two reasons: he was a victim of the system, innocently taking many multiples of the average number of expensive cartridges used by all other deputies, because nobody told him to stop; and because he is "a prolific leafleter".

But for all his protestations about putting together brochures for the poorly informed people of Dublin South Central and sending out crack delivery squads "morning, noon and night", the numbers didn't add up.

Even accounting for the average industrial page, Dell Boy must have been bathing in the printer ink to go through the amount he said he took for his legitimate personal use.

At the very least, he could have shared them with his Sinn Féin colleagues around the country, with their pressing printing needs coming up to their breakthrough election.

But no. He used them all for himself. Certain of that.

Some people say something smells about the whole story, that there's a bit of a pen and ink about it.

Sinn Féin did very well at the polls last year. The party went from four Dáil deputies to 14. Undoubtedly, their mail-bombing of the electorate helped take them out of the realm of the Rank Xerox outsiders.

Mary Lou McDonald, who came out to do some cheerleading on his behalf at lunchtime, was lost in admiration. "Unrivalled" in the field of handing out pamphlets, she marvelled.

After his many media performances yesterday, Deputy Ó Snodaigh is also up for a gold for defending the indefensible – now that Bertie has retired, undefeated.

As Sinn Féin toppled down Dell Boy's paper ladder, people in Leinster House quickly became experts on printing costs and paper runs and inkjet versus laser.

And given their own knowledge of the Dell cartridges in question and how long they last, few were willing to buy the deputy's story.

He is, of course, the victim here. As his deputy leader said: "I think if Aengus had been given a tap on the shoulder by the management in here, people with an eye on expenditure, to tell him that those were the kind of costs involved, I believe that those type of expenses wouldn't have been run up."

Ah yes, the tap on the shoulder. It can work wonders, in some circumstances. Mary Lou was right, it may have been just the wake-up call Dell Boy needed.

Then drink reared its ugly head.

The cartridge debacle has already been dubbed "inkgate". Suddenly, we were staring down the barrel of "garglegate II". There is a venerable hostelry not far from Leinster House, much beloved of politicians and hacks. Ears pricked up when Deputy Ó Snodaigh was asked if he might consider reimbursing the taxpayer the cost of some of his printing accoutrements.

To which he replied: "If the Houses of the Oireachtas ask all of the TDs to pay back the money from Toners, I have no problem looking at that. I wouldn't have that type of money to hand but . . ." What's that? How many pints would he have had to drink in Toners over two years to run up a €50,000 bill? A journalist put the question: "Your use of Toners was excessive compared to other TDs." Mercifully, in Ó Snodaigh's case, his excess was lower case.

And then there was the question of his €3,000 cartridge bill outstanding from 2009, when the rules were changed and a cap was put on the number of free Dell cartridges given out to politicians.

Deputy Ó Snodaigh's appetite for them seemed to have dulled considerably at this point. It seems the Twitter was a more attractive proposition now.

When will he pay back the money? "Now that this furore has come about it will be paid back tomorrow. I can guarantee that." You bet it will.

Luckily for Dell Boy and The Cartridge Family, the Taoiseach and Tánaiste kindly did them a favour yesterday afternoon by coming into the House and announcing that a referendum will be held on the EU fiscal treaty.

But the Sinn Féin font of political virtue is badly damaged – even the sanctimonious blot their copybook.
February 29th, 2012

TD's TAX EVASION BOMBSHELL RENDERS TECHNICAL GROUP SPEECHLESS

Joxer Wallets from Wexford is off to Poland today, where he is sure of a welcome on the VAT.

"I'm going to the three Irish games and a couple of other matches," the broke deputy told broadcaster Matt Cooper on Wednesday evening, having nipped over from Dáil Éireann to talk about his passion for football.

He was on radio again yesterday, this time admitting on Morning Ireland that he knowingly made a false VAT declaration, underpaying to the tune of nearly €1.5 million.

But the Independent TD for Wexford is a lucky guy. The Dáil, where he is currently employed, is in session during the European Championships. Happily for him, he has an understanding boss – the Irish taxpayer – and can take the time off to join Ireland's travelling band of Joxers.

And if Mick Wallets is stopped by customs at the Polish border, he can tell them: "I have nothing to declare but my substantial property portfolio and a vineyard in Italy."

The bombshell news of his tax evasion was the talk of Leinster House. It came as such a shock to Mick's colleagues in the technical group that they were unable to speak or answer their telephones for most of the day.

Not a peep out of the permanently indignant socialist-leaning wing of the group, of which deputy Wallets is a member. They went to ground.

Yet here they were, with a cast-iron opportunity to stand up and fulminate about one law for the rich and another for the ordinary Joe. But they had nothing to say. Very strange.

The irony wasn't lost on the main parties. They asked what would have happened in the Dáil if one of their number – a property developer to boot – was found to have lied to the taxman and deprived the State of a huge amount of money? They were pretty sure that the likes of Joe Higgins and Richard Boyd Barrett and Ming Flanagan would have been screaming blue murder and demanding a head on a plate.

After Leaders' Questions, a large contingent from the technical group repaired to the members bar. A Fianna Fáil deputy later reported that they were huddled in conversation with deputy Wallets.

"Maybe it was an emergency meeting of their ethics committee" he snorted.

Meanwhile, Mattie McGrath, who would consider himself part of the group's capitalist rump, spoke of his unease with situation. An uncomfortable Boyd-Barrett surfaced on teatime radio, striking an uncharacteristically weak tone.

Slowly, some of his colleagues put their heads above the parapet to mutter that it was not their place to pronounce on a fellow deputy's suitability to hold elected office.

What could they do? Take a stand, perhaps.

A number of them finally issued a statement last night indicating they did not condone their colleague's action

The Fianna Fáilers – routine targets for the moral outrage of Mick's comrades – thought it a hoot. The mortification of the Technical Group was matched by their amusement.

It was left to deputies from Fine Gael and Labour to denounce deputy Wallets in the house.

By late afternoon, word swept Kildare Street that Deputy Wallets had already left on his Polish odyssey. In fact, he had gone out to RTÉ to reiterate that he had been a very good boy until he withheld his VAT. "The idea that I'm a serial tax defaulter, I think, is very unfair," he whinged. Anyway, he did nothing wrong on a personal level . . .

And so what, if Joxer Wallets wants to take off now for the European Championships? When he comes back from the soccer beano, his colleagues will have a welcome on the VAT and a ready-made defence.

Sure we all partied . . .

June 8th, 2012

ELEPHANTS IN ROOM TRAMPLE WILD FANTASIES OF REBUILDING

It was all terribly awkward.

An excruciating comedy of manners where the anxious principals were petrified they might say the wrong thing and upset the whole country, again, while simultaneously fretting about bumping into embarrassing old acquaintances who would make a show of them.

The tense undercurrent made for an odd atmosphere – quite unlike anything experienced at party conferences down the years.

And yet, on the surface, Fianna Fáil's 73rd ardfheis went off very well. It looked great. The delegates turned out in force and were on their best behaviour. Nearly everyone tried to smile and sound positive.

But it's difficult to put the best foot forward when you're walking on eggs.

On Saturday, it was like Dublin zoo on tour in the RDS, such was the number of elephants in the room being studiously ignored by the top brass.

This ardfheis may have been badly needed to boost Fianna Fáil's sagging morale and begin the rebuilding process, but there was a sense that the party leader and his backroom team just wanted to get it over and done with without any major mishap.

Micheál Martin's relieved smile at the end of his keynote address spoke volumes.

He had performed well. He got through it. But that's about all the comfort he can take from the day.

He still remains shackled to his recent past. Two searing reminders of it – one ridiculous, the other damning – will stand as the defining images from his first ardfheis as leader.

If Bertie Ahern's arrival early in the day delighted the media, it sickened the party's new brooms, working hard on their programme of "renewal". One TD, when told the former taoiseach was nearby, loudly cursed his presence and did an abrupt about turn.

At one point, Martin had to cross Bertie's orbit to get to a radio interview. He moved like greased lighting to avoid his former boss, who he had criticised from the platform the night before.

Brassneck Bertie hasn't missed a Fianna Fáil Ardfheis since 1972, we were told on his behalf. (The excuse for turning up.) He didn't speak to the media.

It made no difference whether he said anything or not. Just being there was a gesture of defiance and provocation to the party leader.

He stood around, exchanging inanities with grinning grassroots, fully aware of the convulsions he was causing among the handlers and fully aware he was being photographed and filmed.

A great help for a party trying to make a break with the past.

In the main, Bertie attracted two types of delegate – there were the old-timers, perhaps nostalgic for the good days but probably more inclined towards the view that you don't kick a man when he's down. And there were the giggling younger members, crowding around for photographs because it'd be a hoot to have a picture of themselves and the notorious Ahern up on the Facebook page.

But lest it is forgotten, delegates in their thousands cheered Bertie to the rafters at the last ardfheis in 2009, when he was already in disgrace.

The other image was of a long, long line of people outside the building next door, waiting to get into a hiring fair. Queuing in their thousands to leave the country that Fianna Fáil left them.

"Be part of the renewal" was the slogan chosen for this ardfheis. "Be part of the diaspora" might have been more appropriate.

The proximity of the Working Abroad Expo was another embarrassing reminder of the past but everyone averted their eyes and said nothing.

This is because the weekend was all about forgetting the recent past and moving on. But how could anyone forget the excesses and arrogance of the boom-time years when the two faces of Fianna Fáil were on full display? And which one does Micheál Martin see when he looks in the mirror? The one which was in cabinet for over a decade with Bertie Ahern and Brian Cowen – or the one apologising for having been a part of it? This was the perpetually puzzled-looking Martin's problem before the ardfheis began and it was still his problem when it finished.

Behind the party leader on his swish octagonal podium sat the younger members of the party and those deputies who survived the general election cull. The shiny and fresh-faced ones were cleverly framed in the backdrop.

Off to Micheál's left sat the old guard – his former cabinet colleagues and former Taoiseach Brian Cowen. Ahern, despite rumours that he was due in the hall, stayed away. An astute move. He got what he wanted earlier.

Bertie – once adored – is now the party's pantomime villain. Brian Cowen, on the other hand, was viewed with sympathy and affection on Saturday night. He got a huge, lengthy ovation when his presence was announced from the platform.

The grassroots appear to see him as a victim of circumstance. Cowen looked embarrassed by their response, reluctantly rising to his feet to acknowledge their noisy tribute.

He was always a loyal party man. However disastrous his management of the country may have been, Cowen always had Fianna Fáil's interests at heart. They don't think that of Bertie Ahern anymore.

First time TD Robert Troy of Longford Westmeath did the warm-up speech, and did it well. Then it was Micheál's turn. His delivery was polished and he made all the right noises.

The delegates were pleased. But the public will have seen those images of Bertie Ahern, and the crowd lustily cheering for Brian Cowen and the smiling former ministers trooping into the RDS.

It was always going to be very awkward for Micheál Martin – the old broom among the new.

Then up pops Dick Roche yesterday morning with words of encouragement, to help him deeper into purgatory.

"I think he got the zeitgeist of the moment just right," opined the former junior minister, as radios were hurled out of windows all over the country.

One step forward. Two steps back.

Very awkward.

March 5th, 2012

ALL SORTED AS MING THE MEEK
MAKES HIS POINTS

A new political cohort has emerged in Leinster House – The Technicality Group.

These are the deputies who may have transgressed (think Mick Wallace and his tax affairs) but manage to escape censure on a technicality. Group members are distinguished by their brass necks and fantastic ability to turn a blind eye.

Hypocrisy and victimhood also come with the territory.

At the moment, The Technicality Group has three leading lights – Wallace, Clare Daly and Luke Ming Flanagan.

Its members were to the fore last night when the Spent Convictions Bill came up for discussion.

By the time Ming finished speaking, listeners could have been forgiven for thinking they had wandered into a debate on the Compromised Convictions Bill. Although, in fairness, it was a case of being in the wrong place at the wrong time for Flanagan. He just happened to receive his penalty points when there was somebody in a position of influence around to have them wiped from the record.

In another unfortunate twist, he just happens to be in Leinster House this week. If he were in the Vatican instead, Ming would surely be a front runner in the race to the papacy.

Thanks to his wonderfully self-serving performance last evening, the holier than thou Roscommon deputy presented a most immaculate set of credentials to the House. (At least according to himself.)

Others may enter into the distinctly dodgy practice of actively seeking to have motoring penalty points quashed while others may find themselves sucked into a world of corruption by domineering Garda sergeants and sinister senior county council officials, but

Ming the Infallible can do no wrong.

He may be part of a crusade against certain members of An Garda Síochána for sorting out people's points problems, among other things, but when he turns out to be the beneficiary of such carry-on – not once, but twice – Flanagan has no problem standing up in Dáil Éireann and bleating about the incidents as if they represent an injustice perpetrated against his own pristine character.

What was he to do?

The first time, Deputy Flanagan was forced by a sergeant to write to the station and request that his offence be wiped because he was entitled to do so under an antiquated rule which states that TDs cannot be snared by the police on their way to or from Leinster House.

This was after the officer heard that Ming had been done for using his mobile phone while driving.

What did this custodian of the law do but "insist" that Flanagan put pen to paper to avoid the fine?

Listening to Ming in the Dáil yesterday evening, you'd believe that policeman all but frog-marched him to the biro and Belvedere Bond.

Ming the meek – just ask all those people who have protested with him down through the years – always does what the local constabulary tell him to do.

But "that's not all" he told the Dáil, anxious to show how innocent people can be drawn into this murky world where "corruption is like rust", starting out unseen but soon corrupting everything it touches.

But not Ming, of course.

On this second occasion, in December 2011, six months or so after he endured the first atrocity, Deputy Flanagan was stopped again for talking on his mobile phone while driving.

This time, he mentioned it at a county council meeting and soon afterwards, a senior official got in touch to say he had sorted out the matter for him.

As you can imagine, Ming was outraged. On the spot. On both spots.

As outraged as any ordinary crusader for the little man trying to combat "systemic abuse" by shadowy establishment forces would be.

As outraged as only Ming can be, and frequently is.

And he did nothing. Said nothing.

Until the whole penalty points thing blew up and the Technicality Group ran with it.

And until the newspapers got wind of the penalty points that were turfed under the carpet for him.

Well, of course, it was the Garda's fault for leaking the information. That's "illegal" he told the Dáil, stung that such a thing could have been done to him.

And he would have said something (if not at the actual time, which some might consider the right moment to act) sooner, only he was keeping his powder dry so he could use his story to ambush the Minister for Justice.

No such thing as points getting quashed? At which point he would astonish Alan Shatter with his news.

"Whatever about the case whereby the points were removed on the grounds of travelling to the Dáil," he told the House, there was no case for the council official doing him a turn.

He's been terribly hard done by.

Ming is now hoping he will be allowed to pay the fine which "should have been imposed on me as punishment in the first place".

He believes 15 other parliamentarians were let off penalty points.

They should make amends too, he sulked.

(The TDs and Senators we met last night were moaning about their points and how nobody ever told them how to have them scrapped.)

Wallace, Flanagan and Daly spoke one after another, then left the chamber together.

Another mortifying night for the Technical Group. But, by the look of the Independent trio, a triumph for the Technicalities.

March 12th, 2013

JUST A CHANCE ENCOUNTER BETWEEN BERTIE, CHARLIE AND ME

Last Saturday, two days after the publication of the Mahon report, this reporter and a dog called Charlie set out for a walk in St Anne's Park.

Crossing the road to enter, I recognise a photographer friend getting out of a car. He is joined by the driver, a man in a navy overcoat with a baseball cap pulled low over his eyes.

As I walk towards my former colleague, realisation dawns. The other man is Bertie Ahern.

We smile at each other. It's a bit awkward.

He extends his hand, sheepishly. "Am I allowed to do this?"

"Of course you are."

I try to think of the right thing to say, only to blurt out: "You've been a bold boy . . ."

Bertie shrugs his shoulders and says nothing.

"So what are you going to do now?"

He says everything is in the hands of "the legal people". He shakes his head. He says how expensive it is going to be. Hundreds and hundreds of thousands. You wouldn't believe how much.

He speaks quietly, sounds almost bewildered by what has befallen him. I want to be sympathetic, but can't. "Well, you know where I stand on all of this."

Bertie stops, turns and looks at me from under the peak of his "FDNY" baseball cap.

"No. What?"

So I tell him. "I don't believe you, Bertie. I don't f***ing believe you."

He shrugs again. Smiles, head down. "Ah, well . . ." More awkward pleasantries and more sighs about the legal costs until it's time for me to take a different path.

He suddenly says: "You made the right decision. You're good at your job . . .", his voice trailing off so I couldn't hear the rest. I'm not sure what he meant. He didn't explain.

"I wish you luck" I say, as we part. "I really do. You were always good to me."

He nods, then walks on, head bowed. Nobody recognises him and he doesn't try to be recognised.

His photograph is on the front page of the Sunday Independent the next day. He has resigned from Fianna Fáil.

And he has already left the country for a speaking gig in Nigeria.

Just a chance meeting – Bertie, Charlie and me.

March 31st, 2012

POOR OLD DICEY REILLY, SPINNING HIS YARN TO STROKE POLITICS EXPERTS

It's been an awful political week.

Infuriating, unsettling and – probably worst of all – disappointingly inevitable.

But in a happier turn of events, most of the Cabinet was able to escape to Brussels on Wednesday, thus avoiding the embarrassment of having to sit beside James Reilly while he struggled unsuccessfully to convince the Dáil that he hadn't been caught pulling a major political stroke.

Neither did they have to endure the discomfort of knowing that practically everyone in the chamber was of the view that Reilly wasn't the only Coalition Minister in on the wheeze.

The Minister for Health may be relatively new to national politics, but even he must have realised he was spinning his convoluted yarn to an audience of experts who weren't going to buy his story for a minute.

You don't climb the greasy pole to a seat in Leinster House without knowing how pork barrel politics operates, even if you don't partake yourself.

His fellow Fine Gaelers and Labour colleagues will have known the score, along with the inky-fingered Sinn Féiners across the floor. But, in a lovely irony, the loudest protests about the mysterious appearance of two towns in Reilly's constituency on a coveted list of places to get primary healthcare centres came from Fianna Fáil.

Pulling strokes? Fianna Fáil wrote the manual.

Micheál Martin and his health spokesman, Billy Kelleher, were all over Reilly as he tried to talk his way out of trouble.

Their killer line hung in the air, unspoken: Minister, you don't teach your granny to suck eggs . . .

So why was it such a terrible week? It was terrible because, away from the scandalised shouting and indignant waffle, Minister

Reilly's little divvy-up of prized places on this national list wasn't such a big deal around Leinster House. The big deal was the fact he was rumbled.

To paraphrase Bertie: he only went and upset the apple tart.

In fairness to some of the new intake, they are horrified by the events of the last two weeks. Their Government promised to be different from all the rest. Their Government swept to power with a promise of reform – operating by the rules and ending the pernicious reign of nod-and-wink politics.

And now it turns out their crowd is just as bad.

Overall, though, we found the general reaction very dispiriting. It was a shrugging acceptance that this is the way things work. Much of the Opposition included.

"What's wrong with a bit of patronage? Isn't that what we're elected to do?" argued one Government TD.

Across the airwaves, hapless backbenchers polished their brass necks and blustered for Ireland, seemingly unaware that Joe Public isn't entirely made up of gullible half-wits. The big guns went missing.

But talking to people around Leinster House, we didn't find anyone rushing to convince us that the shuffling of the care centre locations was anything other than a classic example of stroke politics.

Not one.

So, we had the Minister for Health, unable to produce a shred of documentary evidence to explain how certain locations were fast-tracked up this important list of health centres.

But Enda is happy with James. And Eamon is happy with James. And that's all that matters. In the interests of stimulus and stability.

Then we had the original list of places earmarked for these facilities, ranked in order of need and fully backed up by a substantial document outlining the methodology used to select them.

Róisín Shortall's list, all done above board, fully transparent and in accordance with the programme for government.

When Dicey Reilly added to and tinkered with that list, but couldn't adequately explain why, the junior minister resigned. "Stroke politics," she declared.

But in Kildare Street, we detected a strange air of sympathy for the embattled Reilly.

Fine Gael's deputy leader may not be the most popular person in his parliamentary party – no track record with Fine Gael, headhunted by Enda and made opposition health spokesman on his first day as a TD in 2007 – but if there was to be a villain in this piece, it wasn't him.

It was Róisín.

We were struck by the underlying message that James Reilly was very unlucky to have ended up with Róisín Shortall as one of his junior ministers.

You see, politics is about the art of compromise – and Róisín can't. And sure, what harm was Reilly doing only pulling a few strokes? This scandal was all that bloody woman's fault.

Well, maybe not all her fault, because we mustn't forget the media, trying to "drive a wedge" between Labour and Fine Gael. That's what one Labour deputy said was the real reason for the furore.

"A man wouldn't have resigned like that," said another, in all seriousness. We forgot to mention Willie Penrose. But then, Willie resigned on a matter of principle.

Whereas Róisín . . . well, she's difficult to work with, apparently.

One Minister privately expressed his disgust. He was apoplectic over the cheek of Fianna Fáil trying to give his party lectures on probity and good government.

As the week went by, Fine Gael and Labour sat shoulder to shoulder with Dicey Reilly and brazened things out. Who could point the finger anyway? Not when there were whispers that an aspiring Labour TD, who just missed out on a Dáil seat in the last election, had been gifted one of the primary care centre plums.

In a lucky twist for Calamity James, there was fleeting talk of possible corruption when it emerged that his friend and political associate owned one of the sites in Balbriggan. It was just coincidence, but it gave the Government the chance to fume about baseless allegations of corruption, while conveniently ignoring the fact that their man still couldn't explain the rejigging of the list.

On Thursday the Tánaiste, out of the blue, came over all decisive. He summoned the head of the Department of Health, along with the head of the HSE, to his office. They assured Gilmore that Calamity James had nothing to do with choosing the sites.

But there was no mention of why certain locations were bumped up the list. And no documents.

You want to see some? Put in a Freedom of Information request, he told a gobsmacked Opposition.

But Eamon was satisfied. Because he has to be. For the sake of keeping the show on the road. Which is understandable.

Our Minister isn't corrupt. He was only pulling a stroke.

Time to move on. Nothing more to see.

It's only those disappointed and disillusioned eejits who thought this Government was supposed to be different, who won't let go.

Now. Have a look at the lovely photograph of Enda Kenny looking chiselled and handsome on the cover of Time magazine.

What an honour. Aren't we great, all the same?

Truly, it's been an awful political week.

October 6th, 2012

TRIALS AND TRIBULATIONS

Bertie Ahern spent several sessions in the witness box of the Mahon Tribunal trying to explain movements of money when he was Finance Minister in the early 1990s

MASTERFUL BERTIE LEAVES
GALLERY BAFFLED

"The reason I probably can't give you a better reflection of what I was doing on the 19th of January is because I didn't do it." Oh, dear God. Make it go away.

Bart Simpson meets Samuel Beckett by way of Alice in Wonderland.

Allez le Bert! The man is a genius.

The Taoiseach put up a barnstorming performance in the tribunal witness box yesterday. He baffled all before him with a masterful display of how to talk your way around difficult questions, with any amount of different answers.

In years to come, Japanese students will be writing dissertations on the Taoiseach's Mahon transcripts. Bloomsday will be forgotten.

Tourists and scholars will gather in Dublin on September 26th to mark Dig-Out Day, that special day in 2006 when Bertie Ahern opened his heart to Bryan Dobson, setting in train a remarkable odyssey through the English language and the human imagination.

It's almost a year to the day now since a tearful Taoiseach went on national television to set the record straight on his curious personal finances for once and for all. But he didn't set the record straight. He's still explaining.

But back to Dig-Out Day, when aficionados will wear anoraks, stand outside 44 Beresford and declaim excerpts from the House Purchase chapter.

They will sit in parked cars outside the AIB on O'Connell Street and read pertinent passages from Celia Larkin's soliloquy.

"Yes, Yes, I said Yes, I will take the briefcase and give it to the teller and not look inside and I will say Yes Bertie to the curtains and the carpets and the gold spun drapes! YES!" Lunch will be a humble pint of bass in Fagans. No burgundy and Gorgonzola in

Drumcondra.

Then, as the day's festivities (sponsored by Dublin Tourism) draw to a close , they will repair to luxury hotels and not eat the dinner.

Poor Senator David Norris will be out of a job. For Senator Eoghan Harris will be on hand, the world's foremost interpreter of Ahern's glorious canon of work.

Yesterday, at the end of the Taoiseach's third gruelling day on the stand, his exhausted and confused audience spilled from Dublin Castle, brains buzzing as they tried to make sense of what they had just heard.

Bertie had managed to get through five hours explaining in bewildering detail how he couldn't remember what he agreed were "memorable events" involving money he might have converted into foreign currency, while "contemplating" how contemplations made him withdraw £50,000 in cash, which he hadn't needed to do, upon mature contemplation.

Wha? Exactly.

After a long day, people struggled to work out the Taoiseach's convoluted and ever evolving explanations of how he nearly didn't rent a house, leading him to withdraw a huge sum of cash from his bank, converting some of it into sterling in a transaction he can't recall, and for which the bank has no documentation.

They tried to reconcile their Michael Walls with Bertie's talk of Chinese walls. In these pre-Northern Rock days, they tried to work out why he preferred his "safe safe" in Drumcondra to an interest-earning account in the bank. They tried to imagine how he fitted in house-hunting expeditions with never-ending trips around Ireland building up Fianna Fáil. Then they tried to understand how he forgot those snatched weekend and night-time house-hunting exercises until friends got in touch this summer to remind him of the fact.

As for that £50,000, it seemed to enjoy more peregrinations through the banking and non-banking system than Daisy the cross-border cow during the worst days of the beef tribunal.

Then again, in 1995, it was only a forgettable £50,000, not far off Bertie's gross annual salary as minister for finance.

"I wouldn't have thought any big deal of taking the money out of the bank and keeping it in cash," said Bertie yesterday. He was just withdrawing it so he "would have it handy". People are always quick to think the worst. It wasn't like the money he spent on the house he eventually bought from Michael Wall – we'd need to print a special supplement to explain the ins and outs of that – was spent abroad.

"All of the work on the house was spent in Ireland." Indeed, he explored that theme again, when explaining how he decided to repay Michael Wall his stg£30,000 from his own funds, rather than just closing the account Celia opened for him and returning what was in it.

"There were no Chinese walls." No, rather like Ray Burke and his personal and political money, his accounts and Celia Larkin's accounts were seamless. After all, Celia Larkin was his then partner.

"My life partner." When he uttered those words, it caused a sharp intake of breath in the public gallery, followed by a very audible, and very female "Oooooh!"

He had an answer for everything. When The Irish Times reproduction of the opening statement he made to the tribunal last Thursday was displayed to point out discrepancies between what he said then and what he was saying yesterday, he talked his way around them with confidence.

So much confidence that the newly established Fianna Fáil Dublin Castle cumann applauded yet again. The chairman reminded them that applause was forbidden.

Whereupon the claque against clapping for Bertie clapped their approval.

It had been a long, complicated day. The anoraks in the media section had added another page to their growing list of contradictions in the Taoiseach's story. But, such was the amount of dust kicked up by the voluble Bertie, it's difficult to know if the general public is exercised enough to bother with the essence of his evidence left behind.

Perhaps it was a touch of cabin fever, but a giddiness took over at the end. A crowd gathered outside to watch the Taoiseach leave.

The three tribunal judges left first, and they were treated to a rousing round of applause. It was like first curtain call at the Gaiety.

Finally, Bertie made his exit. The Dublin Castle cumann –

Drumcondra on tour – cheered loudly, in an effort to drown out the boos.

A beaten-down media hung over the crash barriers. There was just one question: "Any message for the Irish rugby team?"

And a smiling Bertie, full of beans, leaned over his car door and replied: "I wish them well. You know, they should keep up the confidence and just keep going." Never mind Eddie O'Sullivan. Listen to the master, lads. Allez le Bert!

September 21st, 2007

CELIA'S MASTERCLASS IN HOW TO GET AHEAD WITH JUST A BRASS NECK AND BLUSTER

Two large piles of complimentary newspapers rested on the reception desk yesterday at the Woodlands House Hotel in Adare. "Celia faces tax probe over €30,000 house 'loan'" screamed the front-page splash.

But Celia Larkin, "highly regarded image consultant and personal branding consultant", was in no mood to talk about the personal branding implied in the headline or the effect it might have on her image.

She refused to consult on the matter.

Ms Larkin was the main speaker of the morning at a one-day Personal and Business Branding Workshop, hosted by the Limerick County Enterprise Board and aimed at women in business. Sixty women had signed up to hear her insights on the subject, lunch included.

A handful of journalists paid their €20 registration fee too, although they came in search of a different set of insights from the Taoiseach's former life partner.

Namely, what are the facts behind Bertie Ahern's astonishing Mahon tribunal revelation that Celia emerged from their relationship with sole ownership of a fine house in Dublin, financed by an undocumented loan of £30,000 from Fianna Fáil funds? And can she remember any more details of their joint financial dealings when he was minister for finance? Given that the combined might of the Mahon tribunal had severe difficulty making much headway in either department, it was highly unlikely that a handful of curious hacks were going to be treated to any further explanation. Which, predictably, turned out to be the case.

Nonetheless, the exercise was not a fruitless one. The morning yielded a fascinating glimpse into why "Brand Bertie" has been such a runaway success. It was impossible to come away from the event without thinking that Ms Larkin played a very significant role in making "Brand Bertie" work.

Celia drove her 08-registered Mercedes into the hotel car park at half past nine. As she walked towards the building, she received a call on her mobile phone, looked across and saw the small knot of waiting journalists. Whereupon she returned to the car and removed her coat, thus allowing the thrilled cameramen to photograph her in her exquisite beige fitted suit as she made her way to the front door.

A radio reporter fired questions about the controversial Dublin house and possible tax implications, but Celia kept her head bowed, continued walking and said nothing. The reporter filed his story, his voice interspersed with the loud clickety-clack of her heels.

Celia looked fabulous, every inch the successful businesswoman in her chic designer suit and elegant shoes.

Her audience of businesswomen gave her a warm welcome. She was introduced as "a lady well known for her entrepreneurial skills" and the owner of three beauty salons. Celia said she intended to talk about "personal branding". She spied the journalists in the back row and, cooler than a cucumber in an eskimo's fridge, she smiled down in recognition.

"A strong personal brand is of vital importance – it takes control of the process of how others perceive you," she counselled. "It is much better to take control, as it places you in a strong leadership position and helps you increase your earning potential."

The businesswomen scribbled away; the reporters' notebooks nearly went up in flames.

Creating a brand requires a mix of elements, including excellence, visibility, lifestyle, leadership, personality, persistence and goodwill, she said. Find your niche and specialise in it.

As she spoke, Celia walked up and down the main aisle of the hotel ballroom. She stopped near the back row and turned to the journalists.

"Now, Miriam," dripped Bertie's former life partner, who has been coming in for a ferocious amount of stick from this column, "how do you specialise?"

The obvious answer, were one as together as Celia, would be to reply "by writing about the Mahon tribunal, unexplained large sums of cash, Bertie Ahern and your part in the story". But we muttered politely about writing colour for The Irish Times.

Celia spun on heels and told the ladies that "Miriam specialises as a colour writer within a newspaper". (Just like in the tribunal, Celia makes a big thing about first names.) Miriam, she pointed out, is an excellent example of branding.

However, she went on to cruelly dash my hopes of getting a start on the Wall Street Journal by declaring that, were I to "write in a serious way about economics and business", I would "dilute the brand".

These were real Bertie Ahern tactics. He is notorious for the way he seeks out journalists who have just written the most awful stuff about him and being mortifyingly nice to them.

But then, in the words of Celia, "when somebody complains, it is how you deal with the complaint that matters". Goodwill is important too. She also stressed that "good judgment" is vital – unfortunately, it went out the window with Bertie when he took cash from private sources for his personal use when in ministerial office.

The famously closed Drumcondra Mafia came to mind when she advised her audience that it is not necessary to be famous, or have wide appeal, when developing a brand. "Just keep it within a small domain," she said. "Keep it tight." The similarities with "Brand Bertie" and the woman behind "Beauty at Blue Door" just kept coming.

Crow over your achievements, be professional, increase your visibility, your popularity and your earning potential. Two people might do the same job, but everyone automatically assumes that the one they see more is doing a better job.

And remember, ladies, "every penny counts". (And in no time at all, you too could be lodging large amounts in the bank.) Be distinctive – it could be the way you look, or the way you speak. Like Madonna, remarked Celia, or Cilla Black.

Or Bertie Ahern, we thought.

Sometimes, though, it is hard to follow the rules. "Avoid confusion by keeping it simple," declared Celia. She obviously didn't pass that one on to You Know Who.

It was quite the strangest morning, as an unfazed Ms Larkin questioned this reluctant journalist and RTÉ's Cathy Halloran time and again about their jobs. She was clearly enjoying herself, although the same can't be said for the one man in the audience, a young reporter from the Irish Independent doing his best to melt into the carpet at the top of the room.

Her motivational spiel is very good: all buzzwords and the blindingly obvious, but delivered with confidence and panache. As the relieved Indo man pointed out afterwards, he could apply the same principles to his football team.

When it was all over, the woman at the centre of a tribunal storm walked back to her car, tight-lipped, refusing to return the favour by answering the questions of those she had questioned earlier.

Should Celia Larkin ever consider closing down Beauty at Blue Door, she has a great career ahead of herself in Bluster at Brass Neck.

Excuse the language, but the lady had more balls than the entire Fianna Fáil parliamentary party. How on earth is Bertie managing without her?

February 29th, 2007

After his resignation as Taoiseach, Bertie Ahern continued to appear before the Mahon Tribunal, trying to explain where he got money he received while Finance Minister in the early 1990s

BERTIE BARED HIS SOUL IN THAT RTÉ INTERVIEW AND WE SHOWED HIM COMPASSION – WORSE FOOLS US

It was a Tuesday evening, September 26th, 2006, when Taoiseach Bertie Ahern gave that interview.

It was a powerful piece of television. Even at a remove of nearly two years, it remains etched in the memory of all those who watched it. And many, many people did.

There was much at stake. Bertie Ahern's political career was in the balance, and so too was Fianna Fáil's future in government. A general election wasn't far away, and Bertie, the party's prime electoral asset, was in deep trouble.

The Irish Times had run a story that he got €50,000 from businessmen when he was Minister for Finance. He couldn't deny it, because it was true. Nor could he ignore the rising media and political clamour for an explanation.

In a make or break appearance on the RTÉ six o'clock news, he began the fightback. It was a high-risk strategy, but the master politician gambled on his reputation as a simple and honest man of the people, and on the fact that the public liked him.

He bypassed the Dáil, he bypassed the media and he made his pitch directly to the people. He asked for their understanding. He played on the emotions of the decent men and women of Ireland. He gambled right.

More fools us, as we discovered in the Mahon tribunal yesterday.

Let's go back to that interview. It's important.

Sure, it was wrong to take the money, he said. Sure, with hindsight he would have done things differently. But he had a story to tell – it pained him to have to do it, because it was very personal and embarrassing, but he had to clear the air.

"It's best that I just give the true facts and you know, from the position of the Irish public, they've always been kind to me about being separated. They've always been understanding and, em, if I've caused offence to anyone, I think I have to a few people, em, I'm sorry," he said.

He sat in St Luke's and told his difficult story to the nation. Eyes brimming with tears – for he is a proud man, swallowing hard, pausing now and then to regain his composure, he relived the "dark period" in his life.

He gave all the details, for "correctness" and "completeness". How, as part of his separation agreement, he agreed to provide €20,000 for his children's education. "I also had to pay off other bills, so the money I'd saved was gone. So my friends knew that. I had no house, the house was gone so they decided to try and help me."

God almighty, but it was terrible hard to watch. You could see the emotional turmoil Bertie, our Bertie, was going through, having to say this stuff in public about his marriage breaking up, having no roof over his head and strapped for cash in Christmas week.

His pals got together on two occasions and had whiparounds for him. They were "friends at a time of need when they knew I was in difficulty", said Bertie.

He said he wasn't "impoverished" at the time, but what does that mean? He wasn't on the dole, or unable to eat. But his solicitor knew of his financial situation and tried to do something to help him. "It's not for me to plead how hard my life was then . . ." said Ahern, having painted a picture of personal desolation.

What a performance. He bared his soul to the people, and they showed him compassion and understanding in return. Worse fools us. He took advantage, pure and simple.

And in the tribunal witness box, Bertie Ahern tried to insist yesterday that in the Dobson interview he had not tried to put across the idea that he had been on his uppers. (Because, as has been shown in the last two days, and in Ahern's previous appearances, that was definitely not the case.) "I don't think that was the impression I gave," he told lawyer Des O'Neill.

"I made it clear to Mr Dobson that I wasn't impoverished after my separation . . . but I equally made it clear that I didn't own a home." O'Neill took the view that his interview gave the impression "he had been in straitened financial circumstances". Bertie didn't know where he got that impression from.

"We've been through this before," replied Bertie sulkily.

Deathly Des wondered if the former taoiseach, in that emotional interview, had been seeking to "create the impression" of "financial impecuniosity" in order to justify getting payments?

"I don't think, I mean, I haven't looked at this for a while," mumbled Bertie.

And this after a morning of farcical evidence about him routinely carrying around a "float" of a few thousand pounds in his hip pocket when he went over on a trip to Manchester. Of how he didn't think it "a significant" amount of money to be carting about on his person in the early 1990s.

How he, as minister for finance, was using his millionaire pal (deceased) in England as a bureau de change. How he was thinking of buying himself a pad in Salford – a two-bedroom house or "mewses" property – as an investment. How he changed £30,000 into sterling in one transaction, but didn't do it himself and can't remember who ran the financial errand for him. How he was betting on the horses in England and homeless in Ireland.

It's ridiculous. And Bertie knows it.

But the worst thing of all is that he used the public, his public, to get himself out of a tight spot. And now he's denying the import of what he said.

That interview, the one that saved his bacon, was a sham.

Worse fools us.

June 6th, 2008

Flynn stonewalls in eyebrow-raising fashion as he puts his trust in the hands of a higher judge at Dublin Castle

Smug, self-regarding, arrogant and patronising – there is nothing quite like Pádraig Flynn in full flow.

The former schoolteacher spoke very slowly to senior counsel Patricia Dillon, emphasising each word, like she was his very special project in a class of very slow learners.

Sometimes he raised a long index finger, indicating he wanted quiet because he hadn't yet finished speaking.

When he wanted to make a really important point, Pee simply ignored Patricia, swivelling to talk directly to the judge.

His performance brought to mind the quivering words of Mr Collins in Pride and Prejudice, when he spoke glowingly of his patron, Lady Catherine de Burgh: "Such condescension!" Nobody condescends like Pee.

Compared with Bertie, he has a different approach to tribunals.

Whereas the Taoiseach strives to assist with hilariously complicated excuses, Pee Flynn deigns to entertain their tiresome questions and then grants them the honour of a reply. Terse, monosyllabic answers, delivered with overweening confidence.

Different approaches, same scenario: large amounts of unexplained cash piling up in their safes when they were government ministers.

There was an added piquancy to Pee's reappearance in Dublin Castle yesterday. It dovetailed nicely with the return of his daughter, Beverley, to the Fianna Fáil fold last night.

A timely reminder of the reason she was kicked out of the parliamentary party in the first place. It happened after she lost her libel action against RTÉ when a jury found she encouraged people to evade paying tax by selling them financial packages involving offshore accounts.

Bev, even if she was acting on the instructions of her banking superiors at the time, does not accept to this day that what she did was wrong.

No matter. Hours after Père Pee's shiny shoes flapped their way out of the castle courtyard, his daughter was readmitted to the FF club by the unanimous vote of her elected colleagues.

She figured in tribunal dispatches, as we were reminded how she opened various investment accounts for her parents, kick-started by very large cash deposits taken from her father's well-stocked safe at home.

Pee can't remember removing the money and giving it to Bev, and during an earlier hearing she testified that she can't remember the details of the transactions either. Her financial acumen – one lot of the family money went through the Chemical Bank of New York – has never been in question. Just her memory.

A chip off the old block.

This might seem a little suspicious to people who might be of a suspicious nature. But in the interests of fair play, it must be pointed out that Pee was anxious to stress on a number of occasions that he was giving sworn evidence. "Everything I say here is on oath, and I know what that means," he declared.

At one point, he looked at Judge Mahon and, with the greatest of respect, said he was also testifying before "a greater judge". When Pee speaks, God listens.

The £50,000 he got from developer Tom Gilmartin in 1989 was invested into a non-resident account with an address in Chiswick, London. Flynn never resided there.

However, the tribunal's use of the phrase "non-resident account" offends Pee's rarefied sensibilities. He insisted throughout the day that what he had was an "external account". He was also unhappy at the use of the word "paid" to describe the manner in which he was given the money by Gilmartin. "I dislike the inference of the word 'paid'," he sniffed loftily to Ms Dillon. He got a "contribution".

Furthermore, in further echoes of Bertie, that money was a "personal political" donation.

Fianna Fáil never saw it that way, but Pee insists this is the case.

Anyway, he lodged it in his non-resident account in June 1989, then withdrew it in two cash lots of £25,000 in October and November of the same year.

Here again Ms Dillon offended Pee. He didn't withdraw the money. It was his wife. Not the same thing. But did Dorothy not take out the cash on his direction? Pee levitated with annoyance, his voluminous eyebrows taking off towards the ceiling.

"I'm not in the practice of giving my wife directions!"

But she operated the account, didn't she. He had to agree.

Ms Dillon pressed on. So he had "no hand, act or part" in operating the account?

"That's a wild accusation," bridled the former minister for the environment and EU commissioner.

But true, he eventually conceded.

He couldn't remember how he gave the cash he took from his safe to Beverley so she could invest it. "One's daughter does occasionally come home," he told the lawyer.

There was always a lot of money in cash in that safe. Roll on to 1993, when she invested £33,000 for him. He's no idea where it came from, but he was a commissioner then, and reckoned a lot of it "was brought back from Brussels". The mind boggles.

Was it Belgian francs? wondered Patricia. Pee wasn't too sure. "Well, I brought it back and Mrs Flynn brought it back." To the busy safe in Casa Flynn in Castlebar.

The thing is, the money that kept building up in his safe over the years was "a confluence" of cash, streaming in from various strands of income. Politics is an expensive business, and when he wasn't spending money on getting re-elected he had other expenses, like putting tarmacadam on the driveway and buying furniture.

"I want to tell ya, there is nothing normal about an election." Pee would have the tribunal believe, for example, that in 1989, he spent over £40,000 in election expenses. His gross income was £51,000.

You wouldn't believe the size of Mayo.

There are no records of how he spent the money he kept in his safe. The lawyer wondered if he ever considered doing "a cost benefit analysis" of what an election cost? Pee never did. But he was a martyr to the accretions. That money just kept washing into his safe.

Then the story of Gilmartin's "contribution" hit the newspapers. It was in September 1998. On the day the first story appeared, Pee rang Gilmartin. Only to make sure that Gilmartin was as certain as he was that the cheque he gave him was for his personal political use. "I just wanted to check that my memory was the same as his."

Some of the calls went on a long time, but this was because Tom had personal problems, and he wanted a sympathetic ear. Pee Flynn hardly got a word in edgeways.

Fortunately for him, Commissioner Flynn kept a detailed note of some of their conversations, where he said the money was intended personally for him. Unfortunately, Ms Dillon showed two documented instances of where Gilmartin, years before their telephone conversations, had insisted the money was intended for Fianna Fáil. He said this again, just days after they had spoken, in a sworn statement to the tribunal.

Pee raised a finger, silencing Patricia. He turned to the judge and accused Gilmartin of telling "a litany of untruths and inaccuracies".

At the end of yesterday's proceedings, Judge Gerald Keyes snapped. Why didn't he acknowledge the generous contribution in writing? Pee said he just didn't. Hadn't he thanked Tom in person when he handed over the cheque? What about courtesy and good manners? Thanked him there and then, insisted Pee. "Astonishing, extraordinary," spluttered the judge.

"Sure I wanna tell ya, I thanked him on the spot," said Pee.

He's back this morning for more.

April 9th, 2008

Tom Gilmartin, the businessman who blew the whistle on planning corruption by developers and politicians, died in 2013 and was buried in Urris, Co Donegal

A QUIET FUNERAL FOR A BRAVE MAN THE BIG BOYS COULD NOT BURY

He was the man the men in charge could not bury. Yesterday, with love and pride, his family laid him to rest. For Tom Gilmartin had done the State some service – and undone some preening servants of the State in the process.

He was a young lad from Sligo who went to England in the 1950s, made his fortune and came home with the dream of creating jobs so other young lads might not have to follow that same emigration trail.

But it was 1980s Ireland and Tom was soon swallowed up by the resident political sharks.

Unlike countless others broken by the greed of this powerful elite, he refused to let them away with it.

Tom Gilmartin spoke out about the corruption he encountered in the system. His evidence to the planning tribunal opened up an ugly seam of patronage and payback involving individuals at the highest levels of public and business life in Ireland. And they didn't like it.

He spoke from bitter experience in the witness box at Dublin Castle, doggedly sticking to his guns as top politicians, business smooth-talkers and grasping hand-greasers with pristine cuffs tried to take him down.

The indomitable Sligo man stuck to his guns – at huge personal cost – and emerged with his reputation enhanced.

The ordinary people in the public gallery applauded him.

But he got precious little thanks from the State for his trouble. It was a quiet funeral for the man the big boys couldn't bury.

No ringing oration after his coffin was lowered into the ground in a tiny graveyard overlooking the Atlantic at the northernmost tip of Donegal.

Just prayers, a poem and a song.

Tom died last Friday. There were no Dáil tributes when the House reconvened yesterday after the weekend break.

Bloody tribunals. Embarrassing old relatives the two biggest political parties in Ireland would prefer to forget. They dismissed him and talked him down in Fianna Fáil. Tip-toed around him in Fine Gael.

But when the final report was published, Tom Gilmartin's story was the one the tribunal believed, because when he spoke of large sums of money going to named politicians, those same amounts surfaced in the myriad of accounts maintained by these paragons.

He brought down Bertie Ahern, the most successful taoiseach ever in electoral terms and he brought an ignominious end to the overweening arrogance of Pee Flynn.

His evidence brought the likes of Liam Lawlor, George Redmond and Frank Dunlop to book, along with a supporting cast of strutting suits willing to spin any old yarn to support their threadbare testimony.

Tom is dead now. But he's left a legacy more valuable than any plot of land ever fought over by the rezoning vultures.

Gilmartin reared his family in Luton, but he never lost touch with his home country, not even when it turned on him.

At midday, he was interred in the cemetery next to St Michael's Church in Urris, a speck on the edge of the Inishowen peninsula. It is his wife Vera's home village, the woman he nursed through her illness while fighting his own battle with the powers-that-be in Dublin.

Vera was home too yesterday, burying the man she married from just down the coast in the village of Lislarry.

The night before in Sligo, at the church in Grange, a huge crowd turned out to pay their respects to Tom before he made his final journey.

The funeral was a normal Irish funeral – for family and community. A proper Mass, nothing fancy, but plenty of reminiscing before and after.

It is winter bleak and desolate now on the headland at Urris: breathtakingly beautiful but bitterly cold. The warmth in the small church embraced mourners as they crossed the threshold.

Before the Mass, Tom jnr delivered a eulogy to his father. He was always by his side on the days he travelled over from England to appear at the tribunal.

His words were well pitched as he painted a picture of the father he knew – how he loved telling stories of his childhood in Lislarry and how he liked his tea so strong that the spoon would nearly stand up in it. How he loved Vera and was a great dad. How he loved Ireland and Sligo and Donegal.

Tom jnr's pride shone through his words as he told of how his father had to emigrate to find work and how he became a successful businessman in the UK. The usual stuff.

Except there was an edge. A sadness beyond the heartbreaking loss of a parent.

"Dad's stubbornness could be an asset too," remarked Tom, describing how his dreams of building major developments in Dublin ran into insurmountable obstacles.

"Unfortunately, my father was let repeatedly down by men for whom morals – moral scruples of the type my father lived by – were viewed as a weakness," he told the mourners.

When he told the tribunal about his experience, "he never wavered in his commitment to the truth, even when subjected to an extraordinary campaign of vilification. He would never perjure himself – even when it was disadvantageous for him to tell the truth, such was his honesty, so strong his religious faith. Dad loved his country as a proud Irish man. It truly grieved him, as the son of a man who fought for his country's independence, to see the sacrifices of his father's generation discarded by lesser men."

In the church, people nodded. And Tom continued, as his siblings wept.

"It is a source of great sadness to us, his family, that Dad was never truly given the credit he deserved for what he did or the apology he was owed for what was done to him."

Then he paused, and looked out over the congregation.

"He deserved better."

The mourners hesitated at first. Then they burst into applause for Tom Gilmartin.

They said a decade of the rosary in biting cold in the shade of the Urris Hills and the family placed red roses over the coffin.

No amount of rezoning could replicate Tom Gilmartin's burial plot with the mountains around it, Malin Head and Tullagh Bay below and, on these winter nights, a celestial show from the Northern Lights.

Because he deserved better.

November 27th, 2013

Move along, there's nothing to see here, says Garda Commissioner

Before the most powerful committee of the national parliament, the Garda Commissioner stood his ground and all but told the representatives of the people to keep their noses out of police business.

"My force. My officers," he said, at one point.

Martin Callinan was correct, in as much as he is the commander of the force. But it is not his force. They are not his officers. It is our force. They are our officers.

Which is why his evidence to the Dáil Public Accounts Committee yesterday was so troubling. He finds the actions of "so-called whistleblowers" who chose to take their grievances outside the blue brotherhood nothing short of "disgusting".

There is nothing, it seems, that cannot be sorted within the confidential confines of the organisation. There is a system in place. Whistleblowers should use it. To do otherwise, to step outside "the system" is a step too far.

The commissioner conjured up the sort of appalling vista which could unfold if so-called whistleblowing caught on in the force.

"We can't have a situation where 13,000 members can start making complaints against each other," he told the PAC members. The view of the top brass, it seems, is to keep those whistles for nothing more than a bit of refereeing at weekends.

The meeting was investigating the alleged wiping of penalty points by some members of the force for favoured individuals. The committee has boxes of information that came from two whistleblowers.

But the country's top lawman appeared not to understand the nature of this whistleblowing lark in large organisations.

"Isn't it extraordinary that it's just two people that are making huge allegations," he mused aloud. "Why isn't it dozens? Hundreds?"

Everybody else in the room probably knew the answer. But not the commissioner. So Shane Ross patiently explained the obvious.

"People who make these allegations are always very rare because they are fearful of their positions." (It's also why there are regular discussions in the Dáil and Seanad about the need to protect whistleblowers).

Some of them, to be sure, are making vexatious or mischievous complaints. Others though – for a variety of reasons – are doing a very valuable public service, if their information stacks up.

As the committee went about it work, deputies Clare Daly and Mick Wallace sat in the back row of the public gallery. They have been making all the running on the penalty points issue, and judging by their reaction to what they were hearing, they didn't think much of it.

Meanwhile, commissioner Callinan wanted to make it very clear that he wasn't there to "circle the wagons," while stressing that any retired or serving officer who takes the "disgusting" decision to go outside the circle would likely face disciplinary proceedings.

Any garda contemplating such an action now will not have been comforted by what the boss had to say. "I cannot be usurped by subordinates" who decided to use the PAC as a platform, he declared.

There are people in the force called "confidential recipients" who are there to listen to them. There are a number of avenues open to these people who want to highlight the action of the few who would tarnish the excellent reputation of the hard-working and courageous many. Why didn't they follow the process, he wondered.

"They did! They did!" hissed Daly and Wallace.

And what if they have no confidence in the process, for whatever reason, Ross wondered. It happens.

Clearly, this was something beyond the commissioner's contemplation. He had told the politicians their committee was not the place to be "discussing matters of such importance" as Garda misconduct.

Why not?

Because it should be discussed with him, as "accounting officer," said Martin Callinan.

"I think you should be the last person this is discussed with," came the reply.

They agreed to disagree.

At all stages, the senior Garda said he was primarily concerned with the protection of the force. His door was always open to people with issues to discuss.

When Mary Lou McDonald asked if he knew why a number of senior officers might have quashed penalties, the Commissioner said there are all sorts of reasons why they might "stand outside the process" but couldn't say, as he isn't a mind reader.

"I would consider that even outside your pay grade," agreed McDonald.

"Which isn't an awful lot, deputy," joked Callinan, which shows a salary of €188,000 doesn't debar one from having a sense of humour.

She understood his aim is to ensure that the good names of his officers are not sullied by untested allegations. But nor could the committee allow themselves to be used as a platform to "cast a black mark" against the good names of people willing to speak out.

Chairman John McGuinness said it was the committee's intention to hear what the whistleblowers have to say. There were specific questions to be asked.

The commissioner said he should be the one to answer them. He said there is no evidence to support the allegations and may have to take the court route if the whistleblowers are called.

The chairman's assurance that all names and private information would be redacted this cut no ice with Martin Callinan.

The Oireachtas versus An Garda Síochána in the High Court. A sensational prospect. Shane Ross said yesterday's meeting felt like "the dialogue of the deaf." We're all ears for round two.

January 24th, 2014

WALLACE CUTS THROUGH THE WAFFLE, FOR ALL THE GOOD IT WILL DO

Wallace cuts through the waffle, for all the good it will do

The country is driven mad with this bugging and whistleblower stuff. Day upon day upon day of it. Wild spinning. Claim and confusing counter-claim. Taped conversations and flying transcripts. Government Ministers tying themselves into knots trying to sell the latest twist. Judges and lawyers stacked in a holding pattern above Leinster House, waiting for their landing slot on the latest inquiry.

Statements handed down from the oracle at Garda headquarters and channelled through selected handmaidens. A supercilious Minister cherishing whistleblowers while aiming digs at them, making things worse by playing politics. Blowing his Taoiseach off course and into the Dáil to explain. An Opposition making hay.

Yet, at the heart of it all, there are important questions about how senior management in An Garda Síochána conduct their business. That's of interest to most people, even if they might be fed up listening to all the noise from the Dáil.

And into all of this steps Mick Wallace. A squeeze of lemon to cut through the lardy speechifying and point-scoring of the past few weeks. He won the day in the Dáil – for all the good it'll do him.

Yesterday, after the latest instalment in this saga, if the Taoiseach ran into a few of those random talkative citizens who confide in him on the street – and he never tires of telling the Dáil about them – chances are they will have sung the praises of Wallace. Chances are, they will have told Enda that the Independent TD summed up how they feel about how politics is conducted in Leinster House these days. Wallace was high up on the list of speakers on Shatterday – the Dáil sitting set aside to hear the Minister for Justice answer his critics. Alan Shatter, as had been widely leaked the night before, was going to come out fighting and lay to rest any outstanding questions about his role in the whole affair. He spoke for 35 minutes, giving a very detailed timeline of how the complaints of Garda misconduct were handled by the Garda and other authorities. He wasn't out to speak ill of anybody, but he managed to deliver several strong swipes at Fianna Fáil and damn the Garda whistleblower with faint praise.

Shatter was well prepared, mustering his rebuttal arguments well. The Government backbenchers relaxed. Then Fianna Fáil's Michael Martin blasted his "appalling" handling of the issue, accusing him of, at worst, "actively subverting the goal of dealing with allegations of improper behaviour".

He still had questions to answer over his relationship with the Garda Commissioner, his sacking of the confidential recipient and his claim that the whistleblower refused to co-operate with a Garda inquiry. The Sinn Féin leader followed suit. By then, three speakers in, the Government benches had all but cleared and a handful of deputies remained in the house.

Then it was Mick's turn. He began quietly, by outlining how he and others had been trying for 18 months to get the issue of Garda malpractice on to the political agenda. Attempts to suggest improvements to the oversight process had been ignored. "Your concern was with covering up, minimising and dismissing," said Wallace. "The Fine Gael party used to pride itself on being the party of law and order. How in God's name can it stand over that?"

Wallace became increasingly emotional as he spoke. Alan Shatter smiled across, looking like he was enjoying the spectacle. Then, not for the first time in his Dáil career, Wallace welled up as he instanced cases of people who feel they have been let down by the criminal justice system.

Struggling to maintain his composure, he quoted an email he received from the nephew of murdered priest, Fr Niall Molloy. "For almost 30 years people have hidden behind a wall of silence, deceit, corruption and cover-up; time for the light of justice to shine on them and reveal them to the people for what they are. Many, many people have gone to their graves overshadowed by this heartache."

You could see the anger building up in him, overtaking the emotion. His voice rose. "Minister, the people are right to be cynical about politics. They're right to be cynical about politicians. This place is a joke! We play games in here. Well, ye know what,

237

sometimes these games lead to the unfair distribution of justice or no justice being distributed. Sometimes these games lead to people losing their lives, they lead to murders, they lead to the families not getting any justice."

Alan Shatter's smile vanished. He put his hand to his face. "And what do we see so often, when bad things raise their head? We see our police force circle the wagons. We see our politicians circle the wagons. Do what it takes to cover up what we don't want to see. Do what it takes to hide the truth. Is there any appetite for doing things any different in this House?"

"Minister, you look up here at us and you'd say: how dare these people with their long hair and raggy jeans have the AUDACITY to challenge YOU! Well, I wanna tell you something: the people of Wexford who elected me to come here didn't elect me to come here and approve of your behaviour. They put me in here to challenge it. It is time for you to go Minister, and bring the commissioner with ya!"

That got them talking. He's a gas ticket, that Mick Wallace, going over the top like that. They'll have a good laugh over that in the bar. Sure you need lads like that for the bit of colour.

The statements continued on. Then it was time for questions. Alan Shatter was there to take them for the full half-hour allotted. It was a farce. A few questions. Fewer answers. And most telling of all, when asked if he agreed with the Garda Commissioner's assertion that whistleblowers are "disgusting", the most diligent Minister in Cabinet said he didn't read those highly publicised controversial remarks made by the commissioner to a Dáil committee. So he couldn't comment.

His parting short was to criticise whistleblower Maurice McCabe for taping a conversation with a senior officer. But if Sgt McCabe had not, he wouldn't have been able to disprove Shatter's statement that he disobeyed a direct Garda order to co-operate with an inquiry. And Alan Shatter wouldn't have had to obliquely blame the gardaí for leading him to "misunderstand" what actually happened.

Not that he apologised to McCabe for that misunderstanding. But he's out the gap for the moment, and that's all that matters.
February 27th, 2014

MINISTER FOR SELF-DEFENCE STAYED TRUE TO FORM TO THE END

Controversy upon controversy crashed into Alan Shatter but nothing, it seemed, could dislodge the Minister for Justice from his lofty perch at the Cabinet table.

And the irony is that when he finally resigned, it was over a controversy that hasn't even hit yet. Even so, with the report that was to be his undoing still under wraps, the outgoing minister for self-defence managed to issue a resignation letter that was long on self-justification and completely absent of contrition. True to form to the end.

In a heroic gesture, he says he decided to go to spare the Government the controversy that most likely will ensue from the Guerin report into the Garda whistleblowers' allegations. After all, that would only serve to "distract" from their important work and could hamper the Coalition's election campaign.

Why this controversy, when all the others were noisily ignored by Shatter's colleagues? Timing is everything. There were no angry voters complaining about the ongoing Garda saga during the other squalls. The difference is that, this time, the Government needed a head for the doorsteps. So be it. Shatter has gone.

But his parting shot makes it clear that he is not happy with the findings of this report and, typically, he leaves behind an argument with the Garda Síochána Ombudsman Commission and with Sean Guerin, the senior counsel who compiled it.

He indignantly points out that Guerin didn't even bother to interview him. Where did we hear that last? Ah yes, it was from the Garda whistleblowers. The ones the Garda top brass and Shatter didn't give a hearing to either.

Shatter, normally willing to spend hours defending himself against all-comers in the Dáil chamber, didn't stick around to fight his corner once his resignation had been accepted by Enda Kenny.

More than once – too many times – the Taoiseach, his Ministers and backbenchers praised Shatter to the rafters because of the hours he put in taking Opposition questions and appearing before committees. This was their "never mind the quality, feel the width" defence.

When Shatter was accused by frustrated Deputies of not answering questions, their stock response was to point to all the time he spent on his feet. Similarly, they brandished his work ethic: look at how early the man rises in the morning. "It's not the time you get out of bed that's important, it's what you do with that time," was Clare Daly's pithy response to that threadbare defence yesterday.

To say Leinster House was in shock at the sudden announcement of Shatter's unexpected withdrawal from his theatre of war is an understatement.

Right up to the last, in the face of yet another embarrassment over his breach of data protection law, senior members of the Government had been queueing up to back him. On Tuesday night, a spokesman for Kenny said the Taoiseach had confidence in Shatter. (Presumably, this was before he took delivery of the Guerin report, which set in train the chain of events that would lead to Shatter's shock departure yesterday afternoon.)

Yesterday morning Leo Varadkar was bullishly expressing his full support for the Minister for Justice, while as late as lunchtime the Tánaiste was hanging on in there behind the beleaguered Shatter. But by teatime Eamon Gilmore was regretfully opining that the minister's resignation had been "inevitable".

By coming into a sleepy Dáil chamber and stunning everyone with the news that he had accepted Shatter's resignation, the Taoiseach can say he acted decisively in dispatching a trusted ally from his Government. In reality, that act has been a long time coming.

Shatter's Doorstep Sacrifice was imparted to a sparsely populated Dáil by the Taoiseach just before Leaders' Questions. Business in Kildare Street is very much focused on the [local and European] elections, and proceedings in the House were trundling along as an aside yesterday afternoon.

In the morning, Shatter attended the annual Arbour Hill

ceremonies, looking like he hadn't a care in the world. Then, as scheduled, he took Department of Defence questions in the Dáil in the early afternoon. Nothing seemed amiss.

No one saw it coming when Kenny stood to make his announcement. There wasn't a whisper of a rumour in the corridors.

Three have now been downed by those whistleblowers the establishment tried its best to ignore. Oliver Connolly, the Garda confidential recipient appointed by Shatter, was first to fall on his sword. Then Garda commissioner Martin Callinan got the heave-ho in mysterious circumstances. Now, the kingpin.

One wonders what happened when Enda read the Guerin report and discussed it with his minister. Did Shatter go away to consider his fate? Did Enda send the secretary general of his department around to Alan to tell him of the Government's disquiet?

There hasn't been a word from Shatter. Maybe "Sources Close to Alan Shatter" can have a word with "Sources Close to Martin Callinan" and make a joint statement on the whole affair.

The minister who won universal praise from his colleagues for his work is out of a job. The Government will find somebody to fill the shoes they previously insisted were too big for a mere mortal to occupy.

Shatter may have been a great minister, but he had poor judgement and an uncompromising self-belief that was to be his downfall. Yesterday, he said the only way to avoid controversy for the Government was if he resigned. For someone so smart, it took him (and his colleagues who steadfastly defended him) a long time to work that one out. He should have been out the door as soon as he shot his mouth off about Mick Wallace on Prime Time. Now that would have been decisive.

May 8th, 2014

ANY OTHER BUSINESS

At the height of the economic boom the ever-popular Galway Races became as much a political event, around the famous Fianná Fail tent, as a horse-racing event, at least in the eyes of the media

Anything to avoid mixing with the little people

In the Champagne Bar, bottles were flying out faster than the helicopters across in the far field.

They arrived in black plastic ice-buckets resembling upturned top hats but with none of the style. And yet there was something touching about those men who returned from the bar, a bucket cradled in the crook of each arm, carefully carrying a new set of quads to the women at their table.

If you wanted to be anybody in that Champagne Bar at Galway Races yesterday, you had to have at least four bottles of bubbly in your brace of buckets.

Welcome to VulgarVille.

Take a helicopter across to Ballybrit racecourse from the hotel across the road - if you can stand the queue. A snip at just €350 return. Up and down in five minutes but apparently it's the only way to travel. That's what people keep saying here, as if 350 lids is nothing compared to saving an hour in a traffic jam.

Of course, once your helicopter lands in the field behind the stand, there's the rather undignified trek that has to be made up past the hawkers and three-card-trick merchants.

Unfortunately, you blend in with the Great Unwashed flooding with you towards the turnstiles. Who's to know you just arrived in a helicopter a few minutes earlier? Most unfair.

There should be special badges for people who arrive by air because there's only so much shouting a body can do to get the message across.

Of course, if you are a multi- millionaire telecommunications superstar like Denis O'Brien, you don't have to walk with the little people. A motorised buggy is laid on to convey you to the track.

Yesterday he pitched up at the main gates with PJ Mara perched on the seat behind, the pair of them like octogenarian golfers at Augusta determined to finish the old course despite their dodgy hips.

"I'm at the zillionaire's table," PJ said shamelessly in the Fianna Fáil "Tint". Speaking of shameless, Denis O'Brien wore a pink gingham shirt. You can do that sort of thing when you're stinking rich.

Nearly 30,000 punters paid through the turnstiles yesterday, a paltry 800 increase on last year's attendance. The popularity of the Galway Races is astounding. Witness the forlorn-looking ticket tout outside the track, urgently calling, "Anyone selling tickets?" The buying bit didn't come into it.

Officially, 520 guests paid into the famous Fianna Fáil Tint and it looked that amount again had piled in to see what all the fuss is about. Bertie Ahern was guest of honour, doing his usual walkabout in the crowd and then discreetly pressing the flesh back in the "tint".

One minute, he was deep in conversation with a princess from Bahrain.

Next he was shooting the breeze with a local grandee and after that, he had intense discussions with Kieren Fallon, the controversial champion jockey who has been banned from riding in England pending an investigation into alleged race-fixing.

Innocent until proven guilty is very much the attitude in Galway where Kieren is concerned - everywhere he went yesterday, the charismatic jockey was applauded. We thought Bertie was going to kiss him as he got up to leave his table.

No sign of the Taoiseach lashing over to Mick Bailey's table to give him a kiss, although builder Bailey has been a loyal supporter of Fianna Fáil over the years, particularly at Galway Races.

The larger-than-life Bovale boss enjoyed his afternoon in the company of Kerry footballing great Páidí Ó Sé.

SDLP leader Mark Durkan was spotted in the vicinity of the Tint, as was golfer Christy O'Connor jnr, publican Charlie Chawke, builder Seán Mulryan and MEP Marian Harkin.

Minister for Finance Brian Cowen managed a sneaky cigarette outside the Tint as TD GV Wright and MEP Eoin Ryan stood close to provide some camouflage.

His predecessor, commissioner Charlie McCreevy, stalked the parade ring after the big race, before departing in the company of Ted Walsh and JP McManus.

JP had a roller coaster day. In the second race, his horse Sporting Limerick was a faller, ending jockey Tony McCoy's Galway campaign.

Rory's Sister went on to win, leading to countless men declaring proudly, "I had Rory's Sister, " and nobody taking offence.

Things got better for JP in the next race, when Moratorium did the business, and then Far From Trouble made his week by landing the William Hill Galway Plate.

"I'm on top of the world," said JP, as journalists pressed him on Limerick's poor showing in the hurling championship. "Sure the hurling is the hurling and the racing is the racing," he declared. There's no arguing with that.

Minister for Sport John O'Donoghue presented him with the Galway Plate.

"It's the key race to win for me," said JP, who knows a thing or two about winning horse races. As for the Minister, he had backed the winner. "What politician wouldn't back Far from Trouble?" he pointed out, adding that he placed his bet with JP's brother, who happens to be a bookie.

Out of devilment, Bertie put a few bob on More Rainbows. He was delighted when he lost his money.

August 3rd, 2006

FROM THE ALTAR OF THE TEE
TO THE SHRINE OF THE GREEN

The fervent hordes progress with unshakeable faith from the altar of the tee to the shrine of the green. They dress the same. Talk the same. Think the same. Their eyes shine with the joy of the true believer.

Yea, though they walk through the valley of the squelching of muck, they feel no distress: for Tiger is with them. Their Pádraig and Sergio comfort them. Westwood, Monty and Woods - they will follow them for all the scores of their day, and then they will dwell in the clubhouse forever, boring for Ireland about the time they went to the Ryder Cup.

Golf. It's a cult. If you don't believe, you will never understand.

In terms of faith and adoration, unquestioning obedience, reverence for rules, outpourings of joy and crowd control, we are witnessing a golfing version of the Eucharistic Congress at the K Club this week. For the less zealous, it's more like an Electric Picnic for the sensible shoes generation.

From the crack of dawn yesterday, fans began streaming on to the course, laden down with the various accoutrements necessary to see them through two gruelling rounds of hero worship. That they willingly offered up their mobile phones to security men at the turnstiles bore true testament to their unswerving commitment to the game.

This is an overwhelmingly, but not exclusively, male celebration. From the grandstands to the four corners of the course, from the tented village to the vast media marquee, the sheer maleness of the occasion is impossible to escape. It brings with it a tedious fascination with the most minute details of the play, and a near-obsessive tendency for over-analysing everything from body language to wind direction to stance and swing.

Then there is the touching adulation that these grown men freely bestow on their idols, trailing them from hole to hole like lovesick puppies. Think teenage girls and Justin Timberlake, but with basso profundo yelling and without the vomiting. It is a happy occasion for these guys in their matching "weatherwear", who think nothing of rushing along with the herd, stopping at intervals to crane their necks so they might catch a glimpse of Phil Mickelson addressing the ball. Speaking of balls, Tiger's went into the Liffey twice and the home crowd nearly wept for joy. For some, just to see Tiger Woods is enough. But to actually witness him at close quarters hitting a drive is to sample heaven itself.

Periscopes, which look like customised bicycle pumps and come in a long leatherette pouch, are walking out of the shop in the tented village at €50 a throw. The men wear them dangling from their belts as an antidote to their girly patterned jumpers.

There are some things which all self-respecting spectators must have. First, there is the large identity tag around the neck, often used to house a pair of spectacles and a passport as well. Secondly, there is the Ryder Cup radio, which can also be worn around the neck, filling the fans in on what is happening when they are seeing very little from their crowded hillocks.

"This is really an event made for television, isn't it?" we overheard a gent whispering to his friend at the seventh tee. A rare moment of doubt.

Finally, no self-respecting golf disciple goes anywhere this weekend without a third item around their neck - the binoculars. All the better to see the big screen 100 metres away, showing them what they are unsuccessfully trying to witness through a tall lady's visor.

The radio provided live commentary and great entertainment. Reporters had to whisper, so as not to disturb the multi-millionaire golfers going about their business.

RTÉ's Des Cahill, stealthily creeping across the grass as he wheezed quietly into the microphone, sounded like an emphysemic David Attenborough trying to get close to a family of gorillas.

Is it too late to petition RTÉ to get Charlie Bird on the job? Following their chosen pairings around the full course is a little too demanding for much of the crowd. Men made the arduous journey to Straffan only to pitch up at the bar and watch the golf on television all day. Why? Because they are communing with their own. The equivalent of the wide boys at the back of the church.

A pint costs €5, while the various fast-food outlets are charging reasonable prices for the usual deep-fried offerings. A large "seafood and champagne" restaurant operates above the main food court. A bottle of champagne costs €120, the house wine is €26, and a Marquis de Riscal Gran Reserva - "cigar box notes, lovely maturity on the palate, fine balance with impressive length" - is €77. The half-lobster swims in at €42, a crab platter at €28, while a "roasted red pepper" costs an eyebrow-raising €22. Real golfers are not vegetarian.

The corporate suite brigade grinned down from their high-rise boxes on the edge of the 18th green. Guests included the usual suspects from the roll call of gala balls, political fundraisers and the Fianna Fáil tent at the Galway Races. "This event is more cultured and refined than the Galway Races, and all the worse for it," confided a zillionaire builder who begged not to be named because "I don't want to upset Michael (Smurfit) ; he's going around like a child in a sweetshop today."

Former US president George Bush watched from the clubhouse balcony and basketball legend Michael Jordan chewed on a large cigar as he trailed his friend Tiger Woods, while there were unconfirmed sightings of actors Leonardo de Caprio and Robert Redford. Former tánaiste Mary Harney, who escaped from the unfolding political drama back in Dublin, was thanking the God of Good Timing for her recent decision to give up the PD leadership.

As for the golfing faithful, they went home with joy in their hearts, even if it was a long day and they wished they had brought a chair. Just like the Pope's visit, in a way. They'll be talking about the Ryder Cup for just as long too.

September 23rd, 2006

Lola Cashman, a former stylist with U2, appealed against a Circuit Court order that she hand back certain items to the band, including a pair of trousers, a stetson hat and earrings. She lost the appeal

LESS A STETSON, MORE A STATE OF MIND

The Battle of Little Big Trousers rages on. It may have moved to a new theatre of war, but the terms of engagement haven't changed.

Bono's prodigal pants are still adrift in the wilderness. His iconic Stetson hat has yet to find a home. His knick-knacks remain a cause of legal contention.

This story mirrors the band's career, in a way. The boys have moved from playing intimate venues to staging stadium extravaganzas. Now, their garments and geegaws have moved from Dublin's Circuit Court to the dizzy peaks of the High Court. Throughout though, one, immutable, certainty: It's a crazy old rock and roll world, m'lud.

A quick run through the back catalogue. Her name is Lola, and yes, she was a showgirl, of sorts. She was engaged as U2's stylist during their American Joshua Tree tour in the early 1990s. After the tour, she parted company with the band, taking some items of memorabilia with her. U2 took her to court last year to get them back. Lola said she was "gifted" them. The band strenuously disagreed, and won.

This week, Lola Cashman began her appeal. Welcome to Stetsongate II - The Return of Bono's Pants. (But to whom? That is the problem.) Standing room only in court number five.

Bono finished up his stint in the witness box yesterday morning, looking impeccably styled. Black suit, charcoal silk shirt, skinny tie in a lighter shade of grey and dark sunglasses with that mud brown tint so beloved of loyalist paramilitary leaders. Crepe sole, teddy-boy style shoes.

Later in the day, when Lola Cashman was giving evidence, she struggled and failed to find the colloquial term for this type of footwear. In her time working for the band, she had persuaded drummer Larry Mullen to stop wearing them in favour of high-top runners.

We resisted a delicious urge to shout "Brothel-creepers, your honour."

During the tour, Ms Cashman asked Larry if she could keep a worn-out pair of his runners. The drummer consented. Bono sighed, he realised her request for the old boots "should have been an early warning sign".

And so to Nana Mouskouri. The White Rose of Athens was introduced by senior counsel for Ms Cashman, John Rogers, who is to the Irish courtroom what Bono is to Madison Square Garden.

On home ground, the talented Mr Rogers has been going down a storm.Would it be true, he asked U2's lead singer, that Lola was a straight talker? Indeed, did she not say at one point that Bono looked like Nana Mouskouri? Not so, she replied bravely: "It was me, I said I looked like Nana Mouskouri".

Whereupon the two fell to musing whether this is true. "I entirely agree that you don't look like Nana Mouskouri" concluded Mr Rogers. A badly styled titter ran around the court.

But Lola remembered differently. She recalls meeting Bono at his LA villa when the stylist's job was on offer. Back then, he was wearing a look which was very black, "all tucked in", with his trousers in his boots, topped off by long black hair. As she saw it, the image didn't really work on stage.

"It gave him this Max Wall/Nana Mouskouri look, and I told him." Max Wall, for the benefit of younger readers, was an English comedian with a very funny walk. He wore a little black jacket and tight trousers tucked into bootees. He would prance around, hunched up, with his bottom sticking out and his little legs flapping up and down. Picture it. Bono: Max from the neck down and Nana from the neck up. No. Best to move on.

The court had earlier heard that Ms Cashman was in the habit of wearing clothes from Bono's stage wardrobe. This issue was ventilated when Fintan Fitzpatrick, who was Lola's assistant at the time, said the singer is a size 42.

Mr Rogers couldn't imagine the stylist "would easily fit into" these clothes. Perhaps not, said Fintan, but she could wear his hats. "His hat size is completely different to hers. His head is much bigger," exclaimed the lawyer.

Both men agreed Bono had a much bigger head. The titter did another lap of the room. However, Mr Fitzpatrick was adamant that it "would be completely unbelievable" for Bono to give away his hat. "Stetsons are a state of mind," film-maker Barry Devlin later observed during his evidence.

The job of a stylist is very complicated, explained Lola. It was not just about clothes, but developing an image. When she first met Bono "he was wearing hats. When I went there, he was wearing trousers." Oh, thank God.

October 19th, 2006

GETTING TO THE BOTTOM OF LOLA'S PLONK WITH A FEROCIOUS THIRST

Lola opened the plonk in court on Wednesday, and it was allowed to breathe for a full 24 hours before Bono's lawyer could contain himself no longer. Paul Sreenan attacked it like a man with a ferocious thirst, determined to get to the bottom of Lola's plonk before the afternoon was out.

Let's call this cheeky little number Chapeau Bono, because its arrival heralded a dramatic development in the hat department yesterday.

U2 say their former stylist, Lola Cashman, took items of band memorabilia following their tour of America in the late 1980s. These included Bono's famous Stetson hat, an unremarkable looking piece of headgear which is apparently more revered in the world than the Turin Shroud.

It was "gifted" to her, says Lola.

Grabbed, more like, say U2. They want to know exactly how she came by it.

In legal correspondence, Ms Cashman was vague on details. At one point, she said she was given a "back-up" hat, as opposed to the actual one worn on stage. (That's right, Bono has a back-up hat in the wings in case of a millinery emergency.)

However, during last year's Circuit Court case, she said the singer gave her the Stetson when he was running around backstage after a concert. Oh, and he was in his underpants at the time.

Paul Sreenan was agog. He thought people would be interested in her tale of Bono in his undies.

Lola, however, chose not to mention this unsettling gobbet of information in the book she wrote about her experiences with the band.

But here's the twist. On Wednesday when she was giving evidence, Lola recalled fondly how, when she asked Bono for his Stetson, "he plonked it" on her head. Not put, or placed, or positioned, but "plonked".

"When was the first time it was ever said that Bono plonked this hat on your head?" he inquired.

Lola paused, twiddled her spectacles in her hands and finally ventured a tentative "Yesterday?" The soft-spoken lawyer paused so this reply could sink in. In the silence, people fell to thinking: if Bono had been a plonker, why didn't she say so earlier?

Back to the sacred Stetson. Lola Cashman thinks it is more than iconic. For her it is "symbolic". Why? "It validated what I achieved on that tour." It can only be a matter of time before Bono's hat is responsible for miracles.

Besides a few old clothes and some souvenir tat, Lola also got a book out of the tour. The court was treated to extracts. Remaining commendably deadpan, Paul Sreenan quoted from the dust-jacket: "Once in a while, a rock biography comes along that redefines the genre." Going on what court number 5 heard yesterday, Lola's isn't it.

Written in breathless schoolgirl prose, the book is a compendium of U2 tittle-tattle and appalling trivia, delivered in an unrelenting tone of awestricken excitement.

But then, Lola had to spice up her story of minding U2's wardrobes if it was to sell. In the face of a charge that she betrayed the band's trust, she murmured that she hadn't written about "who was sleeping with whom". Cue the creak of chequebooks opening across the water. Lola may have to sign up again with publicist Max Clifford, something she did briefly last year.

"I feel I'm just trying to defend myself against allegations that I have an Aladdin's Cave of goods to help myself to," she said yesterday.

If the best examples of the treasure to be found therein are Bono's little breeches and his iconic, symbolic, miraculous hat, then Ms Cashman might just have to write another book.

October 20th, 2006

Spiritual search turns into a stampede as impatient lose faith in double visionaries

The double Visionaries were in no doubt. Joe and Keith didn't need to give an ETA - estimated time of apparition, because they could confidently announce a DHA - definite hour of arrival.

It was apparition by appointment on Saturday.

Our Lady relayed the time and co-ordinates to the two men when they spoke a few weeks ago: 3pm on October 31st, inside Knock Basilica. She would make an appearance and give a message to Joe Coleman and Keith Henderson, who say they are spiritual healers and "Visionaries of Our Blessed Mother".

Despite Joe's prediction that 50,000 people would turn up, the real figure was about 10,000. Most were Travellers. The young women moved in giggly groups, hundreds of them, wearing astonishingly skimpy outfits, impossibly high heels and lashings of spray-on tan. On a very strange day, in the most incongruous of surroundings, they stood out as the most compelling vision of all.

Joe and Keith arrived at midday driven by a supporter - a PR company owner from Dublin who said she was there in a personal capacity. Joe, who lives in Ballyfermot, says Our Lady has been appearing to him since he was a child.

When he saw and spoke to Our Lady in Knock on October 11th, she told him she is very angry with the Church. "They have insulted the Blessed Virgin Mary . . . She wants respect from the church."

Joe is angry too. He claimed the Knock authorities refused to bring a statue of Mary into the Basilica (as she had requested) and that they had intended to lock the doors, but that the bishop bowed to pressure. Pat Lavelle, manager of the shrine, was at pains to point out that the Basilica is open all year round. Joe, accompanied by "secondary visionary" Keith and two women holding large crucifixes, loudly vented their anger at Lavelle.

But Lavelle pointed out that the Basilica is always open. "It's only because yis came under pressure. Why don't you tell the truth. The lies that comes out of you. You should be ashamed of your life."

Lavelle countered that, in the face of the indisputable facts, Joe was the "liar".

"You should be ashamed of your life. Don't you dare call me a liar. I am a visionary for our Blessed Mother. How dare you."

"Are you a clairvoyant?" - the conversation continued. "I am what I am. What are you?" - "I'm the manager of the shrine." "You're a liar . . . I invited people to see our Blessed Lady - what I done last time . . . Do you not understand the truth? Why are you denying the people, the Christian people of Ireland from all over the world?" He was shaking with rage.

Keith was more relaxed. The 33-year-old became a visionary in April, after a visit "out of curiosity" to Medjugorje. "Our Blessed Mother appeared to me on Apparition Hill." He's seen her four times (including the imminent 3pm arrival). What happens? "I go into total awe with her and I see her pure essence."

Anxious women approached them in the car park for details. Keith pointed to the Basilica. "In that church today, she's appearing at three o'clock. You would want to get in early to get a seat." People came up to touch them, whispering requests. "No, I'm not doing any healing today," declared Keith.

Maura Martin, "a friend", wafted ahead with a serene expression, holding a large crucifix and rosary beads. People approached her, one with a child in a wheelchair. She laid her hands on them and kissed them, although nobody seemed to know who she was. Not that it seemed to matter . . . I asked her why she was blessing people. She said the crucifix she was holding was over 100 years old. But does she have a special power? Why was she kissing people? She didn't reply, just kissed me on the cheek, flashed that serene smile and glided on past.

"We need to be in the Basilica for 2. We normally pray for an hour before Our Lady comes," said Joe. People approached reporters for information. "What time is Our Lady appearing?" We all said she was due at 3pm, like we were describing the next bus to Claremorris.

The church was packed. There wasn't a priest in sight, even though there must have been a fair few lost sheep among the 7,000-strong congregation.

Joe and Keith were the centre of attention. A woman in a pink fun fur went on to the altar and started to sing a hymn. The church was noisy. Suddenly, she flicked her rosary beads aloft and let out an unmerciful shout.

"The tabernacle is here! Stop talking!" The tabernacle may have been there, but she mustn't have known that the Blessed Host had been removed.

The prayers started. Joe and Keith were in position at a table near the altar. Forty minutes to go. Time passed slowly. Keith checked his watch every so often. He had a strange smile on his face, his eyes rolling. Both men prayed, hands pressed together.

Ten minutes. Joe checked his watch. Five minutes. The girls behind us were getting slightly hysterical. One of them was wearing a leopard print trilby. "What time is it? Are you sure Our Lady is coming here?" Four minutes. More watch checking. Our Lady must be very punctual. There were children screaming. People praying aloud. People eating crisps and sweets. Camera phones flashing. All eyes on the two men. They sipped water, an oasis of calm. Joe caressed the crucifix on the table. The rosary finished to applause.

Three. Two. One minute. "Oh, my God!" shrieked one of the girls. It was time. We held our breath. Where is she? Joe, smiling, held out his hands, palms facing outward. Keith still had that strange smile, only it was bigger, and his eyes seemed to have disappeared into the back of his head. Nothing for 15 minutes, just Joe nodding his head and mouthing an occasional "Yes". He lifted up the crucifix. A few tears ran down his cheek.

People were drifting away. The rosary was in full swing again and the girls weren't giving up. They prayed even louder. Joe opened a fresh bottle of water.

At 3.20, there was a kerfuffle at the upper end, opposite the choir stalls. A rush of relieved people galloped for the doors. "She's outside. F*** ya! We shudda stayed outside!" squealed one of the girls, and they took off for the swelling stampede.

It was frightening. Chairs flew over in the rush. The place emptied, but the Double Visionaries stayed put, with a faithful few still around them.

They gazed rapturously ahead. Keith got to his feet and started to laugh. And then Joe spoke the only words we heard from him.

"Thank You, Mother" he said. A woman started to sob and another began to sing Ave Maria.

We headed for the action. On the way to the doors, two buggies in the aisle blocked the way. "Is this your baby?" demanded an angry-looking man. A newborn gurgled up from under a blanket. It wasn't ours. "It's disgraceful," said his wife. "They've abandoned their babies and everything."

The huge crowd was staring at the sun. It was a typical winter sun. Very bright. The comments were, to put it mildly, daft.

"I can see the sun! I can see it! . . . It's coming out from behind a cloud! Look, look! It's pink now. Oooh. That must be the rays." Two couples in their 60s or so - the Traveller/settled ratio had evened up a bit outside - marvelled at the sky, soon to settle into a fabulous winter sunset.

"It's a disc. Yes. A disc. It's like . . . it's like the Host." A young woman watched, shuddering with excitement. "It is. It's dancing!" It's just the sun, we said to the lad next to us. "Do you not see the colours?" he pleaded. "Sure people took pictures of it the last time, and they saw a lady in it." I looked up, for sure, but not for too long, because it hurt. Half blind, I headed indoors and tripped over a child in the gloom.

Jason and Crystal Delaney from Salthill in Galway didn't go outside. They had seen an apparition of Our Lady on the wall above the choir stalls.

"A minute ago it was beaming, changing from Our Lady to Our Lord," insisted Jason. And if you looked hard enough, you could indeed discern a face in the play of light and shadows. When I squinted a certain way, I thought I could make out Bruce Forsyth.

Let's not forget the thunder. There was none in Knock on Saturday, but Jason heard it. People said afterwards that it sparked the stampede. (Not the woman who hurried out carrying a crucifix or the teenage boys who ran out, making a lot of noise and knocking over chairs.)

Brenda Wilson, the woman in the pink fur jacket who led the rosary "to keep the spiritual atmosphere going", felt the Earth move.

"I did hear an amazing rumble, though. I felt it here," she said, thumping her chest. "I felt it in my soul, like a mini-earthquake." She flew in from London, and said it was marvellous to witness such a display of devotion on October 31st, All Souls' Day. "I work with exorcist priests, and I know about devil worship."

Amid the hubbub, the Double Visionaries were spirited out and whisked away in a van. Joe said he had received a message from Our Lady, but she didn't want him to reveal it yet. Maybe later. He seemed a little deflated.

In Claremorris, in the comfort of the McWilliam Hotel, the receptionist told us a guest came in and said she heard that a little boy had been cured of blindness.

Then everyone went to the Halloween dance.

It's all change in Ireland. A few years ago, the country was busy lauding and worshipping "visionaries" like Seán FitzPatrick of Anglo Irish Bank.

Now we have Joe and Keith.

November 2nd, 2009

The international rugby match against England played in Croke Park in February 2007 was a highly emotional affair, fraught with history

HAIR-RAISING CRY OF ANTHEMS FILLS CROKER WITH PRIDE AND JOY

The music swelled in Croke Park, and somehow, we swallowed the lump in our throat. We sang. Misty-eyed, we sang our hearts out.

The message, not the words, mattered: Here we are. All of us. Happy. Proud. This is Ireland. We are Ireland. Live with it.

Before this rugby game, there was too much talk of sell-outs and patriots spinning in their republican plots. The good humoured maturity of the Irish fans settled that question before an English boot touched the ball.

On this significant Saturday, with the Cross of St George flying alongside the Ulster flag and Irish Tricolour, England came to Croke Park to play a non-Gaelic game. There was tension in the air.

This journey to the crucible of the GAA had been a long one. Fourteen people shot dead by British forces during a match in 1920. The Hogan stand, named in memory of the young Tipperary footballer killed in that massacre. Hill 16, built on the rubble taken from O'Connell Street after the Easter Rising.

And now, here we were, minutes away from a rendition of God Save the Queen. Oh, passions were high alright. But only about the game.

Outside, the riot police, on standby, stood by. A few streets away, the pursed lip brigade of stubborn old men rehashed their desiccated rhetoric for the media. Then they lodged a protest letter with the GAA.

Back inside the stadium, back in step with time, the English sportsmen got a generous welcome. But when Brian O'Driscoll led out his Irish squad, the noise was deafening.

The players lined up to meet President Mary McAleese. It seemed like an age before she returned to her seat, heightening the sense of anticipation before the national anthems.

The teams waited. The crowd hushed. Finally, but not before

she was grabbed and kissed twice by Bertie Ahern, the President sat down. The Garda Band and the Army Number One Band struck up. The English were in good voice. They made themselves heard.

At last, our turn. The Irish may need two anthems, but those who wear the green share a singular passion. Amhrán na bhFiann and Ireland's Call were belted out with such hair-raising intensity that men and women were crying as they sang. No dishonour in that. On the field, the players battled with their emotions too. Hooker Jerry Flannery, in floods. John Hayes, a scary looking prop forward with a shaven head and greased up cauliflower ears, blubbered.

How could England have touched these men, imbued with such an unshakeable sense of destiny on this historic day? They couldn't. In their play, O'Driscoll's men reflected the maturity, confidence, spirit and passion of the fans who cheered them. Marvellous. Ireland 43 - England 13. Cry God for Croker, Ireland and the oval ball!

February 26th, 2007

DAY OF OPTIMISM AND CELEBRATION FOR NEW CITIZENS JOLTS HEARTS OF NATIVE CYNICS

"A rare day you will remember and you will cherish." Taoiseach Enda Kenny was addressing people who were about to become citizens of Ireland, but his words resonated beyond his target audience.

For them, yesterday was a day of hope and optimism and celebration. It was the happiest of events; the end of a long and difficult process when they would finally swear their fidelity to the Irish nation and their loyalty to the State.

They had prepared for this moment. But it delivered a major jolt to the heart of the native cynic.

In these times of unrelenting gloom and pessimism, those 25 minutes in a drab hall in Dublin stirred emotions that surprised us.

And when the colour party presented arms and the Army band struck up the national anthem, you could see the Government officials and the army men and the journalists blinking back tears.

The declaration had been sworn, aloud and proud. Now, the new citizens stood as one and faced their flag. One man placed his hand across his heart. It was a solemn, powerful few minutes.

This was the fourth of eight citizenship ceremonies that took place yesterday in Cathal Brugha Barracks, and seven more are scheduled for today. In all, more than 2,000 people will join the ranks of Irish passport holders.

Before last June, people who applied successfully for citizenship had to make their declaration before the District Court. They would turn up on the appointed date and swear loyalty from the witness box, waiting their turn in the queue. If there was time, a judge might congratulate them and call for a round of applause.

More often than not, there wasn't.

When he came into office Minister for Justice Alan Shatter set up a system of citizenship ceremonies to properly recognise the significance of the event.

Retired judge Bryan McMahon, who presided magnificently over yesterday's events, congratulated Mr Shatter "for endowing this ceremony with a sense of pomp and a sense of occasion".

He told the gathering to "bring with you your stories, your music, your dancers - the dances of your own native land. Enrich our lives with what you have to offer."

He hoped that, in the future, one of their children or grandchildren would be leading out a team on All-Ireland final day.

The Taoiseach posed for photographs with his citizens. The new voters fell quickly into the Irish trait of thrusting babies into a Taoiseach's arms, as he remarked on the "moving, meaningful and very touching" ceremony.

There was a huge sense of happiness and achievement among the participants. Many were planning a party to celebrate.

They wore their tricolour lapel pins with pride.

As we left, heading back to Leinster House and the latest row, another batch of applicants was coming through the gates.

And we thought of Eamon Dunphy on the Late Late Show the other week, drawing applause from some of the audience when he called Ireland "a kip" and "a dump". He was wrong. Yesterday, together, we felt proud to call ourselves Irish.

February 3rd, 2012

THE MOOING DIVAS
OF THE FARMING WORLD

The gates were closed and locked for the judging. Outside the shed, anxious exhibitors peered through wire fencing as three women got to work, poking spoons into jars of lemon curd and slicing small slivers off the Victoria sponges.

They worked their way methodically through tables laden with apple tarts and brown bread, fruit cakes and tea scones. There was intense discussion over an Oxford lunch.

It was just as intense among the spectators outside, particularly when one of the judges appeared to be measuring the size of Maureen's third radish. "Why are they doing that? Nothing wrong with them, I can tell you." (The small and perfectly formed radishes were part of her domestic arts entry, which also included a crocheted blanket, three pods of peas and a pot of jam.)

But it's always the cattle that get the glory at the agricultural shows - those mooing divas of the farming world. It was no different at the annual Mullingar Show yesterday. The animals get their pictures in the papers and the lion's share of the attention. Sometimes it rankles a little with the home-crafts people.

Eamon from Roscommon - roses, mixed bunch, Sweet William and rhubarb jam - knows the effort that goes into raising flowers and potting preserves. "There's more creativity to our stuff - anybody can wash a cow," he sniffed.

It was like New Year's Eve in Peter Mark over at the cattle, what with the amount of turbo-charged blow-drying and frantic backcombing going on.

The Mullingar Show has been in existence for 175 years, save for a couple of lapses during two World Wars. It's the second biggest show of its kind in the Midlands, and has been luckier than its Offaly counterpart with the weather in recent years.

David Wall (14) was busy applying soap to a Simmental's coat. "It's like hair gel for cattle," he explained, as he expertly fluffed up the end of its tail. We didn't expect to see a Dub in the middle of the action. Wall, a student at Newbridge College in Kildare, explained that he comes from a farming family in Newcastle, Co Dublin and he's a veteran of the shows.

Hooray! A rosette for David, a victory for the Dubs in Croker, and one in the eye for rezoning.

There was, of course, a "Beef to the heel Mullingar heifer championship". Sadly, the competition was confined to four-legged females, cruelly dashing our hopes of a Dublin raider bagging the title.

Back at the indoor classes, there was an anxious moment when one of the judges appeared to choke on a morsel of coffee cake. "Must be very dry," mused the women outside the wire, watching the plates to see where those red first-prize tickets were going. The onions were so shiny they had to be anointed with Mr Sheen, but no, they weren't. The beets were cut in half to reveal perfect ruby rings , while the eggs came in the sort of hues that don't seem to figure on the supermarket colour charts.

Tracy and Derek Pullein could have explained their provenance, had they been on the scene. But they were down the way at the poultry show, where the judging also took place behind closed doors so they could concentrate.

How do you judge a bird? Tracy held up a hardback book: British Poultry Standards (sixth edition). "That's the bible," she said. "It sets the standard, like when you're not sure of a duck- bill colour."

Trevor Chadwick was overseeing the competition. The raucous crowing of the cocks was nearly as bad as leaders' questions in the Dáil.

A clutch of fluffy grey duckling were a hit with the children. "They're too young for a class yet, so they're just an exhibit. There's the mother," he said, pointing to another cage.

"But that's a big hen."

"She's the brood mother."

The Golden Bramah looked stunning, with its shiny henna feathers. "Great birds to be broody," Chadwick remarked. Great for sitting on duck and geese eggs, apparently, because they have a big wide bottom.

You knew you were near the horses when the accents became more RDS and men and women strolled about, rears encased in jodhpurs that would put the Golden Bramahs to shame and cover a fair few duck eggs. "Dahling? Have they done the hunter showring yet? Where are the beagles?"

The sun shone and Sen Labhrás Ó Murchú performed the official opening, making a long speech from the back of a trailer to an empty field. The judges were still deliberating at the domestic end.

As we left, head muzzy with the smell of cowpat and hay, Supermac burger, pullet feather, porter cake and sweet pea, Richie Kavanagh was tuning up his guitar on the back of a trailer and chef Frank Moynihan was demonstrating how to make parsnip and pear soup. A woman was handing out No to Lisbon leaflets at the gate as a small girl passed, dressed as a shepherd, leading a rotund little black dog with a bolster of white cotton wool on his back. Her sheep for the dog fancy dress.

What's not to love about an Irish country summer?

July 13th, 2007

Stories flow thick and fast as Kerry bids farewell to noble warrior Páidí Ó Sé

They carried him down and laid him to rest at the foot of Mount Eagle, on the edge of his home village beside the Atlantic sea.

Back on the outside again, near the corner, in the green and gold. Number five, of course. Páidí Ó Sé, forever now on the wing.

"May the Ventry sod rest lightly on this noble warrior."

After a day of many words - never scarce in the west Kerry Gaeltacht - those final ones lingered in the little graveyard. The Ó Sé family, heartbroken, stood together for their final public farewell to Páidí. The crowd held back to give them their space.

Pádraig Óg Ó Sé approached the mound beside the open grave, a shovel in his hand. Slowly, he began to dig and lift, the sandy soil hitting his father's coffin and the Kerry jersey draped carefully over it.

Then the footballing men moved in. Some wore the red and white armband of An Ghaeltacht - Páidí's club, and some wore the green and gold armband of the county team.

They took it in turns to heft the shovels, silently going about their work until the jersey vanished from view and the hole was filled. It didn't take them long.

As the light began to fade, they returned along the road to Ventry, leaving the silence behind them. A huge crowd piled into Páidí's pub at the Ard a Bhóthair crossroads. Pints were poured and big pots of tea produced and the talk started again, taking up where the two-day wake left off.

There were hot dinners and sandwiches for the mourners, but there was nothing very mournful about the scene as the stories started to flow - one yarn about Páidí more outrageous than the other.

That's because there was a lot more to Páidí than football.

Speaker after speaker at his funeral Mass tried to explain the essence of this impish dynamo.

"He was a hero . . . a leader . . . an adviser and a friend to many people in his life," said chief concelebrant Fr Kieran O'Brien, trying to capture a sense of one of Ireland's most loved sportsmen.

On and off the field, from "his riveting talks to his funny stories, he lived a life full of energy. He didn't just belong to Ventry, he belonged to the country. He had time for everyone, and was passionate and understanding."

And never let it be said in this GAA bastion: "He was the last wall of defence from those who wanted to steal Sam from the Kingdom."

This time last week, the eight-times All-Ireland medal winner had been busy planning his annual football tournament for next year. He had big ideas for it and was going to make it one of west Kerry's major contributions to the Gathering. His revamped website went live to publicise it. A few days later, aged 57, he was dead.

At his funeral, there was still a sense of disbelief in the air.

Fr O'Brien - an old handball friend - spoke of the shock felt all over the country when news of Páidí's sudden death was announced. "Like a stone thrown in a pond, the sorrow spread."

Páidí's wife, Máire, and children Neasa, Siún and Pádraig Óg sat in the front row with his brother Tom, along with nephews Darragh, Marc, Tomás, the latest generation of football stars from Ard a Bhóthair .

"This crossroads has 23 senior All-Ireland medals to its name," marvelled Danny Lynch, former public relations officer of the GAA and a neighbour's child.

Lynch was among the large gathering outside the Séipéal Chaitlín. It was a bitterly cold winter's day, but the footballing men stood stolidly for almost two hours, trying to catch some of the broadcast fitfully relayed out to the car park.

Many of the younger players waited outside without overcoats or gloves, seemingly impervious to the chill in the incense-heavy air.

On the steps of the altar in the small stone church, beside the Christmas crib, was a copy of Páidí's autobiography and a CD of traditional Irish music, his beloved Kerry jersey, a pint glass and a pack of cards.

Perfectly packed for his trip.

Uilleann piper Seán Óg Potts and fiddler Paddy Glackin performed Seán Ó Riada's Mass with the Cór Chúil Aodha and, later, Luke Kelly's brother Jimmy performed a haunting rendition of Raglan Road. There were tears and applause for him, and for Sláine Ní Chathalláin, who sang The Boys of Barr na Sráide.

It was a very male gathering. Sportsmen, sports fans, politicians and quiet big men with beautiful Irish.

There was much talk of Páidí's friendship with Charlie Haughey. Haughey's sons Ciarán and Conor came down on Monday night, along with their sister Eimear Mulhearn, and they were among the first to arrive at the church for the midday Mass.

There was no sign of Bertie Ahern, who got an honourable mention from the altar, but there was a warm welcome for Brian Cowen. Of all the taoisigh Páidí befriended, it seems Cowen was his favourite.

Cowen was always going to come to Ventry this Christmas - the two had planned to meet over the festive season. But it happened, tragically, sooner than he expected.

Afterwards, he joined builder Tom Bailey and Seán Quinn jnr in a snug for a drink.

Micheál Martin, the current Fianna Fáil leader, paid his respects, while Minister for Communications Pat Rabbitte skipped the Cabinet meeting to attend his old friend's funeral.

And the stories came and came. The kids in the local club "would stand on their heads in the snow for Páidí".

And the "Greats". They were all there. Ogie Moran, Pat Spillane, Jack O'Shea, Jimmy Deenihan and the rest. Old Dublin foes, among them Anton O'Toole, Paddy Cullen, Gay O'Driscoll and Robbie Kelleher. Watching it all was Mick O'Dwyer, looking heavy of heart and weary.

Tom Ó Sé, the brother, brought some laughs. "He liked the craic, he was a rogue. Páidí was a great character and we'll remember the yarns."

The blackthorn was cut back along the road to the cemetery. The cortege made its way slowly past the pub and the general grocery. Then it passed over the mountain stream to the gates, where Páidí's nephews shouldered the coffin to his final resting place. Under a watery sun, with the waves breaking on Ventry strand, Kerry buried its larger-than-life son.

The Christmas decorations remained up in the pub. The singing started at nightfall. It was the beginning of a long goodbye to the man who was known to one and all as "Páidí".

December 19th, 2012

Farewell to the Man Who Gave Dublin Football That Star Quality

We grew up in the grey shadow of Croke Park, but never really knew it.

It was the place where country people went on a Sunday. They would park their cars on our street and cut through Ballybough and up the Clonliffe Road.

Going to "the match."

It rankled, even though we didn't have a car.

The younger boys collected English football cards, untroubled by the swelling roars from Croker as they sat out on the path swapping them.

Heighway, Bremner, Best, Giles, Osgood. These men were their sporting stars, but distant ones they could only see in a magazine.

Micheál O'Hehir provided the soundtrack for those teenage Sundays. There was always Gaelic on the radio, but it was background noise, no more.

Until Heffo came along.

And with him, these gorgeous young men with flowing hair and attitude and slacks that flared from the hip. Real football stars, not photographs from a packet of chewing gum.

They were exciting, they were sportsmen, they were winners and they were ours.

This was Gaelic football, this was showbiz and this was DUBLIN!

Summers would never be the same.

Kevin Heffernan, the manager, gave a lot to the GAA. But he gave a lot more to his city.

He gave us pride and a sense of belonging and he gave us some of the best times ever.

The team and the hysteria, came from nowhere. It was 1974 and suddenly, Dublin were in an All-Ireland final.

We went mad.

Those things that everyone takes for granted now - the hype, the hoopla, the chants, the songs, the dressing up and the painting over - it didn't really happen back then. Heffo's Army changed that forever.

We swarmed up the grassy slopes behind Hill 16, packed on to the terrace and swooned.

When it rained, the dye from our paper hats ran down our faces. When it rained, the grassy slopes turned into a swamp and you risked life and limb sliding down.

It always seemed to be raining, but it didn't matter. Croke Park meant something now.

The Corpo made Kevin Heffernan a Freeman of Dublin in 2005. All they did was put an official stamp on what happened 30 years ago.

Now, the man who shaped our seventies summers is gone.

Oh the Jacks are back, the Jacks are back, let the Railway end go barmy, 'cos Hill 16 has never seen the like of Heffo's Army. That's what we sang. Thanks, Heffo.

January 26th, 2013

OH, WHAT A TWISTED WEB WE WEAVE . . .

And then the chairman clicked his heels and we all woke up in Kansas – except this wasn't somewhere over the rainbow, even if it felt like it at times.

We were in the real world, where rainbows do exist and, for the lucky ones in the loop, there really is a crock of gold at the end of that rainbow. But what the Public Accounts Committee found was a steaming crock of something else.

It was the astounding story of the cosseted CRC officer class that commanded most attention yesterday. On its own, it stands out as a stunning example of that certain breed of senior executives in Ireland who move through the world swaddled in the sense of their undoubted entitlement.

That's bad enough.

But what is worse – after two days of hearings involving a procession of management bigwigs from a number of organisations – is the depressing feeling that the carry-on at the CRC is not an aberration in the top echelons.

Through the thick pall of management jargon that has settled upon the committee rooms since Wednesday, we have seen a cohort of people who have a great welcome for themselves. They talk like men who have learned their patter from the Top Gear school of macho management guff.

High performance utility models . . . key motivators driving the core engine . . . bonus payment models . . . absolutely outstanding performers . . . delivering on service . . . importing synergies.

And our runaway favourite, from Prof Noel Whelan of St Vincent's hospital yesterday: "We are going to swing around into compliance."

That got a laugh.

But back to the CRC, where former chief executive Brian Conlan – only in the job for four months before he stepped down, but eight years on the board – rapidly overheated and suffered an engine blow-up within minutes of being questioned by TDs about the organisation's "dodgy" accounting practices.

He was up on blocks for the rest of his time before the committee – a rather pathetic sight. His evidence was mortifyingly awful as he tried and spectacularly failed to give a credible account of his time with the organisation.

At least that was the overwhelming opinion of the committee.

The members gutted him.

He is a former chief executive of the Mater hospital. One can only hope he was more clued-in during that particular tour of duty, because he confessed to not having a notion of what was going on under his nose at the CRC in Clontarf.

Why? Because, like Bo Peep, Brian had lost his feet and didn't know where to find them. This was his explanation for not noticing that the organisation had a €700,000 "donation" on its draft account which was nothing of the sort.

"Lots of things were happening. I was finding my feet."

Somebody should have told him they're just below his knees, attached to his ankles.

That money, half of all the charitable donations for the cash-strapped services that the CRC provides to children and adults with physical disabilities, was used to give an enormous goodbye payment to chief executive Paul Kiely when he retired.

Oh, and the same Paul Kiely misremembered the full amount of the good fortune visited upon him thanks to the volunteers who sold Santa Bears and stood out in the cold rattling collection boxes. He only let on about half the amount of money he received.

Unfortunately, Conlan knew nothing about it. "I'm as surprised as anybody here today," he declared yesterday.

Meanwhile, there was the question of how he actually got the chief executive's job.

Conlan was on the subcommittee to find a replacement for Kiely. At that time, he said he had no interest in the job and had attended a meeting with recruitment agency MERC with a view to recruiting someone. (As it turned out, the company was not involved in the actual selection process).

According to MERC's website, it is "Ireland's leading executive resourcing firm specialising in the recruitment, assessment and development of senior business leaders".

Anyway, as it turned out, the CRC had a "senior business leader" among its ranks. Brian Conlan threw his hat in the ring only when he saw the "job specification".

Conlan was at the meeting which led to his appointment but he sat back in his chair and said nothing.

At this point, the celebrated incident of Michael Wall came to mind. He was at a function in Liverpool when Bertie Ahern was surprised with a gift of a large envelope stuffed with cash, but Bertie didn't deem Michael to have been present because "he didn't eat the dinner".

Rather like Brian Conlan at the meeting to seal his appointment. "I was physically there, but I didn't partake."

He probably spent the time trying to find his feet. Honest to God, you'd wonder if some of these senior business leaders could be trusted to hit their backsides with a tennis racket.

Conlan, when asked if he should apologise for what went on at the CRC, replied weakly: "If I have done anything wrong, I certainly will apologise."

But in his view, "I did my level best to spread myself as much as I could."

The committee's verdict on the day?

"Pure dynamite," exhaled Kieran O'Donnell.

"Gobsmacked," squeaked Shane Ross.

"Deception," thundered John Deasy, speaking of a "twisted web".

Is there anything to be said for another tribunal?

I'll get me coat.

January 17th, 2014

The long awaited Anglo trial concluded when its former chief Seán
FitzPatrick was found not guilty of making illegal loans, but his two former
colleagues, Pat Whelan and Willie McAteer, were convicted and later
sentenced to 240 hours of community service each

Anglo verdicts greeted in silence
as two never flinched

As Judge Martin Nolan awaited yesterday's verdicts, one very
interested party kept tabs from a discreet distance. Around the
corner from the Dublin Criminal Courts of Justice, parked up in
a side street called Montpelier Hill, Seán FitzPatrick sat in his car.

The jury in the case of Pat Whelan and Willie McAteer had
retired again following lunch. It was a familiar scenario to
FitzPatrick, who shared that same dock the day before with his
two former colleagues, only to be cleared of all charges before
the afternoon was out. He was a very happy man when he left the
building, giving a little speech worthy of an Oscar winner as he
thanked his family and his lawyers and his two "special friends".

Given all that had gone before, one might have expected Seánie
to give the area around the courts complex a wide berth.

Instead, he returned to the scene and waited for the results
from the Anglo jury to come in. At one point, he left the vehicle
and smoked a cigarette, nervously pacing up and down. He was
dressed casually in navy chinos and a lilac sweater, his courtroom
suit no longer required.

As it happened, the seven women and five men took less than
an hour to return a decision. When word came through that they
were ready, the PR man who has accompanied FitzPatrick for much
of his time at the trial was there.

Brian Harmon, who is also a lawyer and specialises in strategic
communications, was a familiar face to some of the business
journalists covering the case. He has acted as spokesman for Denis
O'Brien, among others, over the years. Soon after the verdict was
read out, he made his way to FitzPatrick's car and they left.

Minutes earlier, Pat Whelan had left the court, refusing to

comment as he walked swiftly past the photographers and up past the turn for Montpelier Hill. The group abandoned him and returned to the steps to catch Willie McAteer as he left.

The verdicts, when they came, were greeted in silence. When the jury indicated its return, it precipitated a mad scramble back to the courtroom by the defendants and their legal teams. Word spreads fast in the courthouse. There was standing room only by the time the forewoman spoke.

The two defendants sat and gazed straight ahead. Did they notice how the jurors, positioned in the box directly opposite them, pointedly avoided looked them in the eye?

"Please answer: Yes or No, have you reached a verdict on any of the remaining counts?"

"Yes."

There were 16 charges in all. The first concerned a loan to one of the Quinn family. Had an illegal loan been advanced? "Not guilty." For an instant, there was a discernible flicker of hope from the defendants. But the next 10 counts concerned loans to the so-called Maple 10 "Guilty . . . Guilty . . . Guilty . . . "

They never flinched, looking numbed, staring into the distance. The list was book-ended with more "not guilty" verdicts on the remaining Quinn family loans, but it scarcely mattered.

Judge Nolan thanked the jurors for their "great service to the community and the country". The defendants, one-time big players in the finance game, stood before the court and were told they would be sentenced on April 28th. The court rose.

For a few seconds, the men stayed stock still. Then McAteer pitched forward slightly, both hands clutching the steel rail in front of him. They quickly left the courtroom with their lawyers.

It was Whelan's 52nd birthday yesterday. He'll have had better. They could face up to five years in jail and/or a €3,000 fine.

There would be no smiling statements from them on the steps of the court. No "special friends" to thank, whoever they might be.

Passersby stopped to ask if they were the "Anglo lads". Others wanted to know what was happening. Not one of the interested bystanders had a good word to say for any of them, although the only name they knew was Seánie FitzPatrick's. "One law for the rich, another for the poor eejits like us," said one man, shaking his head in disgust as he wheeled his bicycle on towards the Phoenix Park.

And yet, the jurors had done their duty. Those who had followed the case closely praised their diligence and the subtlety of their verdict.

In the court of public opinion, that will probably count for very little, as will the torrent of evidence heard over the 10 weeks of the trial. It was difficult to follow, but as the days passed, it revealed the nature of big business here and the unsettlingly close relationships between forces that should be independent of each other.

It would have been what we learned from this trial, if we didn't already know.

Forget the racing and the old school rugby, the helicopter jaunts to Formula One, the overseas soccer skites and those Croker pilgrimages to cheer on the county. Above all, there is one sport which the people with money, influence and power in this country absolutely revere. They don't just follow it – they play it.

Business kings, blue-chip legal and banking consultants, regulatory authorities and ruling politicians excel in this exclusive code. The game is not about a final result. When they get the moves right, it should continue without limit. If it stops, the loser must face the music.

Sometimes – like in this trial – the Little People get a chance to observe these pinstriped wonders in action. Over the past six weeks, Dublin's Circuit Criminal Court has been treated to a fascinating top level exhibition match.

And that game? Pass the Parcel. Around and around, the "eminent" players advise each other on what decisions to make, dodging personal responsibility at every successful hand-off, feeding and gaining strength from each other in what becomes an unbreakable sequence of memory loss and corporate cahoots.

It wasn't me, it was him. They told me to do it. Not us, guv. Move along to the next big deal, nobody to blame here. When the sequence breaks down, we get what happened yesterday in court number 19. It is a very, very rare occurrence.
April 18th, 2014